Comparative Social Administration

Comparative Social Administration

Barbara N. Rodgers

John Greve **John S. Morgan**

Routledge
Taylor & Francis Group
LONDON AND NEW YORK

First published 1968 by Transaction Publishers

Published 2017 by Routledge
2 Park Square, Milton Park, Abingdon, Oxon OX14 4RN
711 Third Avenue, New York, NY 10017, USA

Routledge is an imprint of the Taylor & Francis Group, an informa business

Library of Congress Catalog Number: 2006051145

Library of Congress Cataloging-in-Publication Data

Rodgers, Barbara N.
Comparative social administration / Barbara N. Rodgers, John Greve, John S. Morgan.
p. cm.
Originally published: New York: Atherton Press, c 1968.
Includes bibliographica1 references.
ISBN 0-202-30938-X (a1k. paper)
1. Social policy. 2. Public we1fare—France. 3. Public we1fare—Norway. 4. Public we1fare—Canada. 1. Greve, John. II. Morgan, John S. (John Stewart), 1911- III. Title.

HV25.R63 2007
361.6—dc22 2006051145

ISBN 13: 978-0-202-30938-5 (pbk)

ACKNOWLEDGEMENTS

My first thanks are due to my collaborators and co-authors, Professor John Morgan and John Greve, who contributed two of the three national case studies, which constitute the first and major part of this essay in comparative social studies. I am grateful to them for joining this venture, for so successfully shaping their studies of the social services of Canada and Norway to fit the purposes of this book, and for their readiness to comment on the early versions of my comparative analysis in Part II. As neither of them was in this country for most of the time that the book was being written, this collaboration presented difficulties which they bore with fortitude. The comparative analysis is considerably better than it would have been without their constructive criticism. Any obscurities, any errors of fact or interpretation which remain are entirely my responsibility.

We should all like to acknowledge the debt we owe to the many people who helped us with the national studies. For my part I would wish to mention particularly M. Peyssard, late of The Ministry of Health and Population who kindly checked the first version of my French study, and Odette Derrick and the many people to whom she introduced me when I was making a field study of the social services of The Department of Indre-et-Loire.

Similarly John Greve would wish to acknowledge the debt he owes to the several persons at The Ministry of Social Affairs and the National Insurance Institution who contributed material, advice and comment so readily and generously.

John Morgan wishes to express his thanks to all of his colleagues in Canada who assisted him in compiling and correcting the information contained in the section on that country; and particularly the Director of the Research Division of the Department of National Health and Welfare and his staff who devoted an extraordinary amount of time to the review of the material contained in this chapter.

(Each of the authors of sections of this volume is of course responsible for any statements contained in that part of the book for which they are responsible and the good offices of those who have helped them must not be taken as implying responsibility either for factual statements or opinions expressed.)

I should like to thank my colleagues and one ex-colleague, Professor Peter Campbell, now of Reading University, who read various parts of the book and made valuable suggestions and criticisms. I am also much indebted to Vladimir Rys of the International Social Security Association, who directed me towards new sources of information and whose own writings on social security were particularly helpful.

The students who have attended my class in comparative social administration over the years have contributed, probably more than they realize, to this book. They were the reason for my embarking on it; they are largely responsible for the shape it has taken; I only hope that they and their successors will find it serves its purpose as a useful introduction to their comparative studies.

Special thanks are due to Muriel Cocker and Pam Smith, who found time to type successive versions of the manuscript among the many other demands on their time.

Last, but by no means least, I should thank my husband, who has contributed—and suffered—more than most husbands who have wives who write books.

BARBARA N. RODGERS
September 1967

CONTENTS

PART II: THE COMPARATIVE ANALYSIS

INTRODUCTION

Comparative studies present problems, but they can also be immensely stimulating to those who have studied in any depth some aspect of their own society. Pursued in conjunction with other academic studies they can encourage a more analytical approach to social phenomena, helping the student to see that simple description brings only a limited understanding. For no interesting and valid comparisons are to be found in the mere juxtaposition of parallel descriptions. Comparative studies increase the student's ability to distinguish the general from the specific, if only to identify what is 'generally true' for all countries and what is unique and 'specifically true' to any situation. They permit the cross-fertilization of ideas and encourage creative thinking about new solutions to old problems. Finally, comparative studies, assuming the student has really been able to enter into and work from within a new framework of reference, will often lead to new interpretations and fresh evaluations of social institutions with which he has long been familiar. 'Revaluation is the flower of comparison' wrote Mary Parker Follett.

It is a pity therefore that comparative studies in social administration have not as yet received much attention in British universities, and where a start has been made in the systematic teaching of the subject, teachers and students alike are handicapped by the lack of good studies of social administration in other countries. This is not surprising. Social Administration has only become established as a subject of academic study in the past two decades, and the *subject* (as a field of study and research) as distinct from the *practice* of social administration is still only recognized in a few countries.

The boundaries of this field of study may be somewhat ill-defined, but the core of it is well-understood: the development of collective action for social welfare—collective action on the part of government, employers, philanthropic bodies and consumers to meet human needs; in brief, the social services. Again there would be little dispute in this country[1] as to what constitutes the main body of the social services[2]: social security, health, and welfare services which make

[1] The terms 'social services' and 'welfare services' have often different connotations elsewhere.

[2] M. P. Hall, *The Social Services of Modern England,* London, which is generally regarded as the standard textbook for the subject.

special provisions for children and families, the aged, handicapped and other socially disadvantaged persons. How far certain aspects of a country's housing, education and employment services are regarded as social service varies. It depends not only on one's criteria but also on the way in which these more 'environmental' services have developed, the extent to which they make special provisions for minority groups and the closeness of their links with the more personal welfare services.

In studying the social services the student of social administration is concerned with their objectives (policies), their operation (administration) and their achievements (when attention is focused on consumer reactions or on what has been aptly termed 'the worm's eye view'). The emphasis given to one or other aspect of these social institutions may differ, but a serious study of social administration must comprehend all three approaches. Social policies are only interesting and worth studying if they are real policies (not mere paper plans), policies which are being actively pursued and which have already gone some way towards achieving their objectives. Thus, to quote David Donnison, 'Policy-making and administration are not separate activities. The "policies" of a social service are its functions—what it does—which may or may not coincide with its official aims. Its "administration" consists of the processes—going on at all levels, inside and outside the organization concerned—which determine those functions. Neither can be studied or understood in isolation from the other.'[1]

But it is not enough to understand the inter-relationships within the broad field of social administration—between policy and administration, or, a point made by Lord Beveridge in his famous Report, between the achievements in one field of social service and those in another. Modern social services are an integral part of modern society, influencing and influenced by all those economic, political and social factors which determine the particular society within which they have developed. The student of social administration must bring to his subject some understanding of these other disciplines—of economics, politics, and sociology—and be able to relate and apply them to his own field. 'To study the development of the social services in isolation from the history of their times is to tear a meaningless shred from the fabric of the past. To study the

[1] D. V. Donnison, 'The Development of Social Administration'. An Inaugural Lecture. p. 32.

contribution these services make to human welfare without thought of the contributions made to human welfare by full employment or political freedom leads too often to the conclusion that human happiness depends upon an arbitrarily defined set of public services, and the assumption that the current aims of these services constitute a definition of progress.'[1]

The student who has made his preliminary studies in the social sciences and has been taught to use them to broaden and deepen his understanding of social administration in Great Britain, will look for the same breadth and depth of approach in any comparative studies he may undertake. But comprehensive studies which give a clear picture (with sufficient but not too much detail) of a country's major social services, of its developing social policies and of its achievements, and which indicate at least the way in which all these things are related to the political, economic and social structure of the country in question, are hard to come by. For lack of such studies the student has to seek out his information from many different sources, not all in English, and the picture he gets may be distorted providing an inadequate basis for any valid comparative analysis.

Some aspects of social administration are better documented than others. For instance, there is much detailed information to be gleaned from the studies and bulletins[2] of the International Social Security Association (ISSA) and of the International Labour Office (ILO) about social security institutions and measures in countries all over the world. Similar comparative studies have been made of hospital administration and of other medical care programmes. Though useful, much of this information needs to be interpreted in the light of some rudimentary understanding at least of the 'ecology' of these social institutions and of the political, economic and social complexion of their country of origin; and that kind of understanding has usually to be sought elsewhere.[3]

In teaching comparative social administration it would be difficult enough to select material even if more systematic studies were available. How do we give the student an understanding of the similarities and differences of the social problems, for example, of an ageing population, and of the ways of dealing with them found in

[1] D. V. Donnison *op. cit.* p. 22. [2] Now the *Review*.

[3] Two notable exceptions are: R. Mendelsohn, *Social Security in the British Commonwealth*, London, 1954 and *Freedom and Welfare-Social Patterns in the Northern Countries of Europe*. Edited by George R. Nelson, 1953.

other countries? How evaluate their achievements in the context of *their* experience, not ours? How draw valid comparisons which will help the student to look more critically and analytically at social services in his own country, and to suggest new ways of tackling some of the problems which persist in most fields of social administration?

In this book, which claims to be no more than an introduction to comparative studies in social administration, a combination of approaches has been used.

In Part I, three case studies give an all-round picture of social policy and administration in *France*, *Norway* and *Canada*. Social needs, resources, and forms of social administration are related to the most significant social and demographic, economic and political factors of the country in question. Historical treatment is necessarily light, but sufficient to indicate how social policies have developed in the past, and what directions they are likely to take in the future. In sum, the case studies, like the book itself, are designed to serve as an introduction, as an exercise in the study of social administration in other countries. The student should be able to fill in, expand, and bring up-to-date the pictures presented, with the help of the bibliographies and references to official source material provided by the authors of each study. With some understanding of social policy and administration in three such different countries, as well as his own, he should be able to pick out the salient features and characteristic patterns of social administration in yet other countries, even if he has to seek out the information for himself from many different sources. He should have learnt to know what to look for, and what questions to ask.

On the assumption that the student is familiar with social administration in Britain, some comparisons of problems and ways of meeting them will be drawn in the course of each of the three case studies. The main purpose of these comparisons will be to help the student to understand *why* the response to broadly similar problems is different in the particular country under study. The student who wishes to draw valid comparisons in the field of social administration will inevitably have to master a good deal of straightforward information. This will be more interesting and more easily remembered if he is encouraged to think analytically and comparatively from the start. At the same time, it is only by studying the whole range of social services in one country at a time that he will come to appreciate their peculiar characteristics and that organic unity which stems from the interdependence and inter-relationships between a country's many institutions.

Despite this emphasis on the uniqueness of these national studies, France, Norway and Canada have been chosen as broadly representative of the Western European, Scandinavian and North American approaches to social policy and administration. They also represent three broadly different systems of government and administration. *France* still retains the general shape of the administrative structure given to it, and to so many other countries of continental Europe, by Napoleon. Its influence on the ways in which modern social services are administered today, whether by governmental or non-governmental bodies like the social security institutions, is seen most clearly in France. It is modifications of this structure, rather than of the Anglo-Scandinavian one, which are found in Italy, Belgium and many other European countries.

The *Nordic* group (Denmark, Finland, Iceland, Norway, Sweden) on the other hand, are known to have much in common.[1] They are all small countries in terms of population, with a well-established tradition of self-help, and local government, and for these and other reasons, have adopted a collectivist approach to the development of welfare services more easily than other Western countries. *Canada* provides us with an example not only of the North American approach to the development of social welfare, but also of a federal government. In Canada the inherent problems of federalism are increased in interest—and complexity—by differences in culture and outlook between those who live in the different provinces, notably in French Quebec. These differences are even greater than those existing in the United States of America.[2]

A more systematic comparative analysis of particular problems, and of the different forms of social administration designed to meet them is attempted in Part II. At this point examples are taken not only from this country and from France, Norway and Canada, but from other western countries with well-developed social service systems. By this time the student should be sufficiently aware of the dangers of studying a particular social service out of context to make for himself the necessary qualifications to any comparisons drawn.

To avoid superficiality only four areas of social administration will be subjected to this comparative analysis. But first, in order to

[1] See, *Freedom and Welfare, op. cit.*

[2] A. Birch, *Federalism, Finance and Social Legislation,* Oxford.

underline the interdependence of social policies in these different areas, and of social policy on economic policy, and vice versa, a short chapter will deal briefly with a broader theme: to what extent and in what manner have the four countries attempted any overall planning of social resources to meet social needs? For any kind of social planning is just such an attempt to find out as much as possible about potential needs and potential resources and to work with and not against these basic facts.

After this introductory chapter, the comparative analysis will be applied first to social security, since the financial and economic implications of the income-maintenance services so obviously places them within the context of economic and social development as a whole. We shall be concerned not so much with the broad aims of social security policies, for these are very much the same in all modern, industralized societies, but with the techniques, and with the particular combination of the different ways of effecting a redistribution of income (by insurance, assistance or universal benefits) to be found in different countries. Systems of co-ordination will be the subject of Chapter 3, co-ordination at both policy-making and field-work level. Here again emphasis is on administrative structures and techniques rather than on policies, for it is obvious that all countries with sophisticated social service systems have to tackle problems of co-ordination.

In Chapters 4 and 5, on the other hand, the comparative analysis will be applied to two major areas of social policy—policies for the aged and family policies. The social needs of old people and the welfare of families have been chosen because they constitute a recognized challenge to those concerned with social policy and administration in all highly developed industrialized countries today. But they are large as well as important areas of social action, and again to avoid superficiality, emphasis in these two chapters will be on the objectives and achievements, rather than on the operation of the relevant social services. Most of the services discussed in these two chapters will in any case have already been outlined in the national case studies in Part I, and the operation of some of them (e.g. the income-maintenance services) discussed in more detail in earlier chapters of Part II.

Finally, in a concluding Chapter, we will try to see how far we have been able to avoid the pitfalls and to reap the benefits of a comparative study of social administration anticipated in this introduction.

PART I

THE NATIONAL CASE STUDIES

FRANCE

CHAPTER 1

Introduction

In principle post-war France as much as Britain has accepted the rights and duties of a Welfare State. Indeed, in the French manner, they have been written into her constitution. 'Whoever, because of his age, his physical or mental state, the economic situation, finds himself unable to work, has the right to obtain from the community the proper means of existence.'[1] The interesting comparisons are not to be found in the objectives, or even in the extent of the social services available to her citizens, but in the differences of approach, crystallized in forms of social administration, which seem much more complicated than their British counterparts.

What lies behind this characteristic complexity? The short answer is French individualism, and the tensions and compromises set up in the attempt to promote the well-being of individuals through that 'collective action for social welfare' which constitutes the social services. The relationship between the individual and the state was thought out and fought out in France in the eighteenth and nineteenth centuries. The functions of government, and the governmental institutions necessary to maintain law and order and to provide certain basic public services were well established by the twentieth. It was, however, not clear what role the government should play in initiating and developing social services concerned with individual welfare. Collective action for social welfare must derive from some form of solidarity. The French tend to use their government to define, protect and enlarge the individual citizen's rights to social benefits, leaving the actual provision of services to financially autonomous, non-governmental bodies, representing particular groups of citizens.

[1] From the preamble to the 1946 and 1958 constitutions.

Direct provision of social services by the Government, central or local, is much more limited than in Britain, or for that matter, in most other European countries. In France solidarity more easily finds expression in voluntarism and mutual aid, with the Government there to hold the ring, to enforce the rights of individuals and to co-ordinate and control their representative organizations. Pierre Laroque has suggested that 'the creation of specialized organizations, closer to self-interest than regional or national administration, may contribute to recreating a feeling of solidarity, to creating the conditions of a democracy that is not only formal but social.[1] People feel closer to such organizations, which can be made more sensitive to their needs.

It is perhaps the same strong streak of individualism which adds another complication to French social administration—the attempt to shape services and benefits to meet the individual case. This is done not only by allowing for discretion in administration, but by providing highly differentiated social benefits, which individuals may claim according to their individual circumstances (their occupation, the number of children they have reared, whether their wife is working or breast-feeding her baby, etc.).

There are of course many other influences which have helped to shape French social policy. Before describing the actual operation of her social services we shall look at some of these demographic, economic and political factors. But in the last analysis the student should ask himself what makes for the essential unity of France's social services, what for all their complications, makes them one of a piece.

DEMOGRAPHIC FACTORS

Much emphasis has been given to demographic considerations, leading to anxieties about defence and *grandeur*, which are said to have shaped French social policy. They have been compared to the experience and fear of unemployment in Great Britain.[2] In the nineteen-thirties the demographic situation came to be regarded as a fundamental cause of France's decline and a conscious effort was

[1] Pierre Laroque, 'Service Social et Sécurité Sociale' *Revue Belge De Sécurité Sociale*, IV No. 2, 1962.

[2] Pierre Laroque, An argument used in an article in the *International Labour Review* (Vol. LVII, 1948) entitled 'From Social Insurance to Social Security: Evolution in France'.

made to reverse the trend of a hundred and fifty years. (Between 1800 and 1950 while the population of Great Britain rose from 10 to 47 millions, that of France rose only from 28 to 43 millions.) This family policy was vigorously pursued in the post-war years and fertility since the war is 20 per cent to 25 per cent higher than before (the number of births in 1938 was 636,000, in 1964 874,249). It is impossible to say how far the generous family allowances and other aspects of France's *Politique de la Famille* are responsible, but they must certainly have played some part.

The population of 45 million in 1960 rose to 49 million by 1966. Its composition over the period 1960 to 1975 is estimated as follows:–

In 1960	31·6% young	11·9% old	56% of working age (20–65)
In 1975	32·3% young	13·1% old	54·6% of working age

Up to 1966 the proportion of children continued to rise, but after 1966 the increase in the number of children born since 1946 began to swell the adult population. Because of the rising proportion of old people, however, the proportion of the inactive, or dependent, population to the active will only begin to decrease in the period 1975–80. The infant mortality rate was reduced from 72 per 1000 in 1936 to 50 per 1000 in 1951 and to 23 per 1000 in 1964.

An occupational analysis taken from the social security statistics[1] shows that in 1962 out of a total working population of some 19½ million, approximately 14½ million were employees and five million were self-employed. (In the UK only 1½ million out of 24½ million insured workers are self-employed.) This, together with the large[2] though diminishing proportion of workers engaged in agriculture, affects social security measures in particular by diminishing the risk of complete unemployment (France suffered much less than Germany and England in the nineteen thirties and still has no statutory unemployment insurance benefit), but also encourages strong sectional divisions. This is emphasized by the fact that the Ministry of Agriculture is still very much an all-purpose Ministry in France (like a Ministry of Colonies), and is responsible for social security

[1] *Statistiques de Sécurité Sociale* (Report for year 1962 published in July 1963). Practically the whole working population is covered for pensions by one or other of the social security schemes. The small numbers of students and war pensioners to whom cover is also extended have been excluded.

[2] Of 4·2 million agricultural workers, 1·1 millions are employees and 3·1 self-employed. Moreover, many agricultural employees have some land of their own (or a claim to benefit from family land).

services for agricultural workers as well as for many other aspects of rural life. The attempt in the immediate post-war period to extend schemes of social insurance devised for industrial workers to cover the different groups of self-employed met with fierce opposition from farmers, shopkeepers and professional workers, who objected to being 'proletarianized' by having their interests identified with those of industrial employees.

Since the Second World War France has welcomed immigrant workers to make good the shortages in its own labour force. From 1946 to 1962 ONI (*Office Nationale d'Immigration*) brought in 870,196 permanent (as opposed to seasonal) foreign workers and 240,879 persons under family immigration. It is difficult to know how many of this total of 1,111,075 foreign workers stayed. Between the census of 1946 and that of 1962 there was only a comparatively small increase in the number of foreigners but a substantial increase in the number of naturalized persons, suggesting that about 45 per cent of foreigners admitted settled.[1]

The need now is to expand and improve training facilities and employment opportunities to absorb the greatly increased number of young people who are coming up to working age. But manpower is only a part, though an important part, of France's economic and social planning.

ECONOMIC FACTORS

France's planning experience[2] goes back to 1946, when the government established the Commissariat General to deal with the post-war situation, when the immense task of rehabilitation had to be undertaken with limited resources. Through existing controls and nationalization of key sectors of the economy, the Government was in a strong position to direct the hard choices which had to be made

[1] To these foreign workers must be added the successive waves of refugees as a result of the struggle for independence in the French overseas possessions: 400,000 refugees from Tunisia, Morocco, North Africa and Vietnam, followed by 750,000 refugees from Algeria mainly of French descent. The refugees included some 300,000 active people who had to be found new jobs.

[2] See 'French Planning: Some Lessons for Britain,' *P.E.P.* Vol. XXCX, No. 475, 1963, for a closer analysis of French 'indicative' planning, and particularly for the attempt in the Fourth Plan to integrate regional with national planning and to cope with the disequilibria arising from foreign trade fluctuations. Up to 1958 French plans operated in an economy much less open to external influence than the British economy.

between priorities. France is at present engaged in the implementation of its Fifth Plan covering the years 1966–77. As with earlier plans the main objective is a steady, harmonious expansion of national production. Despite interruptions when 'stabilization plans' have had to be introduced to halt rising prices, curb inflation and build up gold reserves (the last occurred towards the end of the Fourth Plan) France has undoubtedly been remarkably successful in achieving a steady national economic growth; nevertheless certain sectors, such as agriculture, have not fared as well as others. French agriculture is changing slowly but is still mainly a system of small estates employing far too many workers whose standard of living is comparatively low.[1] Retail trade is another backward sector. Moreover, the new abundance is not always evenly distributed, and there are a number of less favoured groups, notably old people, holders of fixed incomes and a new category—refugees from Algeria. These inequalities and deficiencies cannot be regarded as a by-product of expansion, but result rather from a direct or indirect neglect of particular needs, which can and should be rectified by more careful social planning. Considerable increases in social investment and in social benefits were, in fact, allowed for in the Fourth and Fifth Plans. Similarly the gross regional imbalance between Paris and the provinces, between an expanding north-east and a declining south-west is being tackled by the part which new regional machinery is playing in the formulation and operation of the Plan. Each Plan has been a great methodological and technical advance upon the last.

Finally, to quote M. Luc de Nanteuil, writing recently on Economic Planning in France[2]:

> 'Of course planning has not been the only factor accounting for the remarkable development of the French economy and French prosperity. Some of the others are wellknown. In particular, France enjoys great natural resources, especially fuel and power resources. Agriculture has provided a reservoir of manpower to which incoming refugees from Algeria have recently been added.

[1] F.A.S.A.S.A. (*Fond d'Action Sociale et Aménagement de Structures Agricoles*) is attempting to do something constructive about this situation: training and resettling some in non-agricultural occupations, helping others to get sufficient capital to set themselves up on viable farms, etc.

[2] Luc de Nanteuil, 'Economic Planning in France,' *District Bank Review*, December, 1963.

Paradoxically, the war itself, with its political, economic and moral consequences, was a very important factor. Not only did the devastation necessitate a modernization of the economic machinery but with the decolonization of France's former overseas territories, economic expansion has to some extent been a substitute for past ambitions and this in some measure explains why successive and so different governments have stuck to the objective of a steady national economic growth.'

National planning has had to be related to international planning. Although in the Common Market countries the percentage of national income spent on social services is much the same—round about 15 per cent—the distribution of these social charges differs. The Treaty of Rome affects social planning mainly by its agreements about the free circulation of workers and the attempts made to harmonize social benefits and charges.[1]

The Commissariat General is part of the civil service but is attached to The Prime Minister's office and thus enjoys a relatively independent status within the administration. It endeavours to achieve the same sort of relationship with the various professional, economic and social groups. Largely immune to political changes and the vicissitudes of French governments it has been able to pursue fairly consistent policies in the social as in the economic fields.

POLITICAL FACTORS

While the Revolution provided the principle of national sovereignty (a Nation of citizens expressing itself through the State), it was Napoleon who established the administrative institutions, which gave it application. Since the end of the First Empire France has been notorious for the stability of its administration and the instability of its successive political regimes.

Since the start of the Third Republic sectional forces have, however, done much to promote and shape social policies. A new pluralism, developed under the Third Republic, can be seen in the strengthening of local democracy under the laws of 1871 and 1884, and in the legal sanction given to employers' associations and trade unions by the law of 1884. Employers, workers, consumers and

[1] 'Social Security in the European Economic Community' by Jacques Jean Ribas, Director for Social Security and Social Science in the EEC *I.S.S.A. Bulletin* XVI, No. 12, 1948.

beneficiaries of services, and local authorities have all achieved considerable political influence, operating as pressure groups, securing representation on numerous statutory councils and even fulfilling some of the state's executive functions.

In the 1930s the Popular Front, and in the post-Liberation period, the Socialists and Communists, who were predominant among the founders of the Fourth Republic, were responsible for much of the social legislation, which extended the traditional 'police' functions of the state, particularly of the local authorities, into a new role—that of a Welfare State. On the other hand, the Communist 'neutralization' of so much left-wing strength and the emphasis given by other political forces to the independence of the little man in French Society, complicated and weakened the effective implementation of many of these collectivist policies by subsequent governments. While it is still too early to assess the effect of the Fifth Republic on developments in social policy, the increased prerogative of the government which is characteristic of the constitution of 1958, has tended to strengthen the technical and administrative control by the executive. Nevertheless, the various sectional interests and pressure groups are by now so built into the administration of the social services, that any extensive rationalization or simplification of their basic structure would seem unlikely.

ADMINISTRATIVE FACTORS[1]

The Civil Service

France has almost twice as many national civil servants in proportion to its population as Britain, and they fill many of the posts which would be held by local government officers in Britain (e.g. in education, the police, civil engineering). Most of the Ministries[2] have extensive field services, so that almost every town of any importance is the centre of a prefecture or sub-prefecture and has its government

[1] The reader is referred to Ridley and Blondel: *Public Administration in France*, London, 1965, for an exhaustive and up-to-date account of French administration.

[2] The fourteen Ministries which have regularly survived the frequent regrouping of government services are: Justice, Foreign Affairs, Interior, Armed Forces, Finance & Economic Affairs, Education, Public Works and Transport, Industry, Agriculture, Labour, Health and Population, Construction, Ex-servicemen, Post and Telecommunication, *op. cit.*, Ch. III. In 1966 however the Ministry of Labour and the Ministry of Health and Population were combined into a Ministry of Social Affairs, but the old titles have been retained in this text.

offices, state road engineers are to be found in thousands of towns and villages, and school teachers in every parish. In France the advantages of a civil service career for the specialist as well as the administrator are obvious, and the service has always attracted good candidates. Competition is fierce and success in the entrance examinations and in the excellent post-entry training establishments, *les grandes écoles*, is a passport to a successful career not only in government service, but in the business world into which many pass after a certain number of years in the service. This interchange of top personnel with a common background of professional training and experience has important implications for national planning, which involves the private as well as the public sectors of the economy.

Originally recruitment and post-entry training was all done by the Ministries and even by separate departments within them. Some of the *corps*, created in this way, had such prestige as to become almost autonomous units within the different Ministries. In 1944–46 reforms based on British practice, established a Civil Service division under the Prime Minister, which attempted to break the entrenched powers of individual departments. The *École Nationale d'Administration* was established to achieve unity in the recruitment and training of non-technical, higher civil servants, along lines similar to what had been achieved by the famous *École Polytechnique*[1] for the technical branches of the service. Much of the three-year training at the *Ecole Nationale d'Administration*[2] is common, and involves a substantial period of field work in provincial administration and a shorter one in industry. Nevertheless, at the higher level, the corps with the greatest prestige (e.g. the corps of the *Conseil d'État*, the *Cour des comptes* and the *Inspection des Finances*) remain, and are able to recruit from the most successful students in the examination at the end of their second year. In their third year at the school, these students will receive their specialized training within the corps of their choice. The Social Service departments are still lowest in prestige.

This highly trained and professionalized civil service has an immense influence not only at national level, but through the prefectures on local policies and administration. To understand this

[1] Created by the Revolution in 1795, and used by Napoleon partly as a military school and partly as a technical school to train civil servants.

[2] See 'Twenty years of L'Ecole Nationale d'Administration'. Henry Parris. *Public Administration*, Vol. 43 Winter 1965.

some knowledge of French local government and of the ways in which it differs from the English system is essential. Here it is only possible to sketch in the main features.

Local Government

The Constituent Assembly of 1789 swept away the old confused, uncoordinated pattern of local autonomous bodies and substituted the commune and the *département* (subsequently referred to as department). The commune is the primary area for local government; it may be a small hamlet or a great town like Lille. There are some 38,000 communes in France, nearly two thirds of them with less than 500 inhabitants. Communes are grouped together into a department, a corporate body concerned with the interests which the communes are too small or parochial to look after. There are 95 departments classified according to their importance as *hors classe*, 'first', 'second', or 'third class'. There are two subdivisions of the department, the *arrondissement* and the *canton*. The *arrondissement* is of considerable importance in French local administration, but is a purely administrative subdivision of the department with no corporate personality and no elected council. The 95 departments are now grouped into 21 Regions with the prefect of the chief department acting as regional prefect.

The fundamental difference between the French and English local authorities, however, lies in the fact that both the commune and the department are areas for central government administration as well as for local government. Thus the Mayor is head of the administration of the commune, a prominent local political figure (elected by and from the *conseil municipal*), but in some respects a state official, although his contact with the Central Government is always indirect. He is bound by the decisions of the *conseil municipal* on matters of purely communal concern only.

The prefect is a vital element in French administration and combines a number of roles. He is the representative of the state and ceremonial head of the department (like the Lord-Lieutenant in an English county). He is the head of all government services in the department. Besides his own staff certain ministries have decentralized offices attached to the prefecture. Others are organized on a regional basis (not necessarily the standard regions mentioned later), but use the department as the principal subordinate area of administration. The head of each of these administrations is required by law to regard the prefect as the proper channel for communication with Paris and to keep him informed on all matters; thus the prefect is not just *primus inter pares*, like the English town clerk, he is their hierarchic superior. He is appointed directly by the Government by decree and is a member of the prefectoral corps of the Ministry of the Interior, the ministry responsible for the supervision of local authorities. Sub-prefects assist the prefects in the *arrondissements*. Finally, he is the chief executive officer of the department, but bound by the decisions of its elected body, the *conseil général* (with its executive committee, the *commission départementale*) only as regards matters of purely departmental concern. Unlike the communal staff, departmental staff are now all members of the national civil service. Like the prefect, they act in a dual capacity as agents of the central government and as agents of the department.

This parallel administration of central and local government functions, and a certain overlapping of permissive powers of the commune and the department often makes it difficult to see just where the initiative for the development of certain social services lies. However, in practically every case, approval for any such initiatives must be obtained from the appropriate ministry and the prefect. The political and financial tutelage of both communal and departmental affairs exercised by the Government through the prefect ensures this.

A new regional structure, which is being developed for planning purposes, was finally established by decree in March 1964. This 'functional' regionalism was 'born out of the dialogue taken up between *The Commissiariat Général du Plan* and *The Corps Préfectoral*.'[1] Regional prefects were appointed to the twenty-one planning regions, each supported by a regional administrative committee (of civil servants) and a regional economic development council (a consultative body of local authority, trade union, Chamber of Commerce representatives, and others, appointed by the Government). The regional prefect remains prefect of his own department at the administrative capital of the region, and his new functions are primarily concerned with economic planning, with carrying out the Government's policy for economic growth and regional development in his area. He has certain coordinating functions with respect to the public services in so far as they impinge on economic development.

[1] Jean-Lous Quermonne '*Vers un Régionalisme Functional*' quoted in an article by L. T. Sweatman on 'Prefects and Planning: France's New Regionalism' in *The Journal of Public Administration*, Spring 1965.

He has administrative control only over the work of all state services and public organizations working on a scale other than that of the nation or the department.

Semi-public Agencies

A further complexity is the entirely separate administration of social security services (except public assistance) by semi-public bodies, the *caisses* (Funds), managed by elected representatives of the beneficiaries. These Funds, whose organization at national, regional and local level will be described later, are institutions of private law charged with the administration of important public services; possessed of financial autonomy they are nevertheless subject to the control and supervision of the Ministry of Labour and Social Security, and of the Ministry of Finance.

The management boards of these social security Funds are composed primarily of representatives of employees, employers, and of the self-employed. In Britain it would not usually be necessary to hold special elections to achieve similarly composed boards; the workers' and employees' representatives would be put forward by the appropriate trade unions and employers' organizations. In France the unions and employers' organizations do in fact provide most of the candidates for these elections, but there are many employees, independent workers and employers who are not in any organizations. Moreover, the trade union movement itself is divided into three federations of different political complexion: the CGT (associated with the communists), the FO (associated with the socialists), and the CFTC (associated with the catholics). To these should be added a further group of non-political unions, CGC (representing senior staff or *cadres*).[1] No federation admits the accuracy of the membership figures of its rivals, and direct elections provide a means of deciding in what proportions the unions of the three federations are to be represented on each board. For the same reason direct elections are used to decide who shall represent the workers on statutory works councils.

Voluntary Organizations

Finally, there are the genuine voluntary organizations to be considered. What influence do they have as pressure groups, and what

[1] Much the same applies to the employers organizations where candidates are put forward by the National Employers' Federation, left wing groups and the poujadists.

part do they play in the initiation and administration of the social services? There are many national and local voluntary bodies running social services of all kinds: *colonies de vacances*, *crèches*, *clinics*, homes, social centres and cooperatives, etc. (and similar services are provided by public and private enterprises through their works councils). But there are proportionately fewer non-political, non-sectarian, non-patronal organizations than in Britain. The Roman Catholic church is directly responsible for many of these institutions, including, of course, schools, and gives its indirect support to others, such as the Family Associations, which, as will be seen later, play such an important part in France's family policy. Anti-clericalism is, however, still a significant force in France, and this together with the tendency for other sects, the political parties and employers to run services for the exclusive benefit of their own adherents or employees, makes for real difficulties in cooperation.

In order to introduce some sort of coordination and control into this situation the Government lays down stringent regulations for any voluntary social service 'recognized as of public utility' and as such, eligible for grants from public funds. One of these conditions is that any social worker employed must be a state registered *assistante sociale*. The common training and strong professional ethic of these workers is some guarantee that, at the consumer end of the service at least, the interests of the individual beneficiary will be paramount, whatever the motivation or interests of the sponsoring organization.

CHAPTER 2

Social Security (Income-maintenance Services)

THEIR DEVELOPMENT

The earliest social legislation in France as in Britain was concerned with the relief of the poor. *L'assistance publique* has nevertheless had a very different history from that of the English Poor Law. A departure from the idea of Christian charity in favour of the idea of social justice was proclaimed by the revolutionaries of 1789: '*L'assistance n'a été jusqu'ici regardée que comme un bien fait, elle est un devoir.*'[1] But it was not until the beginning of this century that the *assistances obligatoires* (statutory assistances) established this *right* to relief for certain categories of persons: free medical assistance in 1893, assistance to children in 1904, to the old, infirm and the incurable in 1905, to pregnant women and to large families in 1913. More were added later until practically every needy person fell into one category or another. This reformed public assistance service met the popular feeling that such common causes of distress as old age, sickness and large families should receive more generous treatment by granting these specially favoured groups assistance as of right. These rights were defined by statute but administered locally; relief of the residuary cases, which was left entirely to the commune, became a comparatively unimportant feature of the assistance service.

In Britain in the first half of the century the much hated Poor Law instead of being reformed was being slowly broken up, as special categories of persons were removed from its orbit altogether, to be relieved 'not by way of Poor Law'—old people by non-contributory pensions administered by Customs and Excise, the blind by special Blind Persons' Welfare Committees, the unemployed by a new central government body, the Unemployment Assistance Board. Finally, in 1948, the Poor Law was abolished altogether, its relief-giving functions being taken over by the National Assistance

[1] La Rochefoucauld Liancourt in a report to the Constituent Assembly, May 30, 1790.

Board, and its services in kind by various specialist departments of central or local government.

In France, as in Britain, assistance could be given in cash or in kind. One of the most important forms of statutory assistance—medical assistance—is today almost entirely an assistance in kind. Assistance for the aged may take the form of monetary assistance or of a place in a hospital or Home. Equally important was the movement away from the idea that the public assistance service was for the indigent only. Even in the nineteenth century many of the hospitals and Homes run by public assistance authorities, provided for paying as well as non-paying patients. Today the communes and departments use their permissive powers under the Social Aid legislation (the name was changed in 1953) to provide a wide and varied range of welfare services—clubs and restaurants for the aged and infirm, home helps and day nurseries for families in difficulty, etc.

The increasing coverage of the social insurance and family allowance schemes after 1930 gradually reduced the numbers of those in need of monetary assistance, but Social Aid has still an important role to play, particularly in the care of old people, and in the provision of medical care.

In 1935 all previous assistance legislation was consolidated, a common means test for all forms of statutory assistance introduced and the department made responsible for their administration. In the post-war period some new forms of statutory assistance were introduced: a Special Rent Allowance, to compensate those on low incomes who suffered from the decontrol of rents which started in 1948; a Constant Attendance Allowance for the severely handicapped or an allowance towards the cost of domestic help (*Aide Ménagère*) for other aged and infirm persons; and a Social Card (entitling its holder to certain benefits mainly in kind) for the *éconiquement faibles*, primarily old people on small fixed incomes badly hit by the rise in the cost of living.

In the 1950s the need was felt for a further codification and simplification of assistance law. The reforms of 1953–55 achieved something in the change of name referred to above, in a regrouping of the proliferation of statutory assistances (for the aged, the handicapped, the sick, families), and in clearly defining the role of the new *Bureaux d'Aide Sociale* as the focal point for receiving and investigating all requests for Social Aid, whether obligatory or permissive, and for developing new local welfare services in a more coordinated way.

Early in the century, while the government was transforming an old system of local relief-giving into a new public assistance service, guaranteeing assistance as of right to certain categories of unemployable persons, the workers were developing their own organs of mutual aid. A strong voluntary insurance movement developed, backed in some industries by employers' schemes and by the earliest pension Act of 1910—*Retraites Ouvriers et Paysans* (ROP). This whole movement was greatly strengthened by an Act of 1930, which introduced social insurance (for sickness, maternity, invalidity and old age pensions) for the lower paid industrial workers. This first scheme was administered by numerous Funds (*caisses*) run mainly by employers and workers, and by mutual aid societies which, like the British Approved Societies, came to dispense statutory benefits along with their friendly society activities. The state played very little part in all this. The scheme was financed wholly by contributions from employers and workers. The Funds tended to provide not only cash benefits, but services in kind, more particularly medical services in support of their sickness benefits.

An Industrial Accidents Compensation Scheme, based on the principle of employer's responsibility, was introduced in 1898.

Family allowances, yet another strand in the complicated pattern of modern social security schemes, have a longer history in France than in any other country, and were also initiated and financed entirely by employers. The first scheme was introduced by some employers in the heavy metallurgical industry around Paris in 1918. They were undoubtedly influenced by demographic considerations: the declining birth rate and the great loss of manpower in the 1914–18 war. The employers financed the scheme by paying part of their wages bill into equalization Funds (*caisses de compensation*) which paid out the allowances. Legislation was passed in 1932 to compel every employer in industry and commerce to pay family allowances and to belong to an equalization Fund. In 1939 the *Code de la Famille* extended family allowances to the whole population, introduced the maternity grant and single wage allowance and dealt with other aspects of maternity and child welfare, which have had some effect in reducing abortion and the infant mortality rate. Like the social insurance Funds, the family allowance Funds provided not only the statutory cash benefits but a variety of health and welfare services for their member families.

In the immediate post-war era these three schemes of social

insurance, industrial accidents compensation and family allowances, while retaining their identities and some financial and administrative autonomy, were brought together into a common pattern of social security administration. This major piece of reconstruction was carried out in three stages. In October 1945 the old social insurance Funds were abolished, a distributive system was substituted for the old funding system and the present network of national, regional and local social security agencies of the *Régime Générale* (the General Scheme) set up. These were also made responsible for the industrial accidents compensation Funds. In August 1946 an Act was passed reforming the family allowances scheme, reorganizing its Funds on a similar local area instead of an industrial basis, increasing benefits and adding a pre-natal allowance. In October 1946 an Act reformed the industrial accidents compensation scheme, turning it into a social insurance scheme (a similar transformation of an old workmen's compensation scheme was achieved by the British National Insurance (Industrial Injuries) Act, 1946), and associating with it certain preventive measures and rehabilitation services.

The administrative simplification and financial equalization between the different Funds, which it was hoped to achieve through the General Scheme, with its national, regional and local agencies, set up in 1945–56, has been only partially successful.

Certain special schemes (for workers in the mines, railways, gas and electricity and, most important, for agricultural workers) fought to retain their identity and were never brought into the General Scheme, while practically every extension of social insurance to cover the self-employed, has led to the setting up of yet more special Funds for the different professional and occupational groups. Nevertheless, by the 1960s universal coverage had been more or less achieved for family allowances and pensions; and health insurance which originally covered industrial employees only had been extended to agricultural workers. The basic social insurance scheme still provides no cover for unemployment.

However, as in every other developed country, the frontiers of social security are continually being pushed forward. Superimposed on the basic statutory social security minima is a growing marginal zone in which increasing numbers are getting supplementary cover for themselves: through voluntary mutual insurance schemes primarily for sickness, through occupational superannuation schemes originally introduced for salaried staff now extended to wage earners, and through employers' unemployment insurance funds.[1] In 1955 there were one million workers in industry and commerce contributing to superannuation schemes, by 1966 over seven million. An agreement between the Council of French Employers and the principal trade union organizations signed in December 1961 brought practically all wage earning employees of industrial and commercial undertakings between twenty-one and sixty-five into an approved supplementary retirement pension scheme. These superannuation schemes have since 1946 had to be registered with the Ministry of Labour and to submit to a certain amount of technical control. Most of the approved schemes are affiliated to a National Union of Workers Retirement Pensions Institutions, which in turn is affiliated to ARRCO,[2] which arranges for the pooling of financial risks and resources over a wide range of occupations. A similar agreement between employers and workers has led to the establishment of a national scheme of special unemployment allowances which covers most industrial and commercial workers.

THE SOCIAL SECURITY AGENCIES[3]

The Administrative Framework

In the organization of French social security, government departments with controlling and supervising duties work side by side with the Funds which execute the schemes. The Minister of Labour and Social Security is responsible to Parliament for general policy; supervision and control is exercised through the Directorate General of Social Security with its sixteen Regional Directorates. The Funds, managed by boards of elected members, are semi-public bodies with the legal status of private institutions and financial autonomy. They are subject to the same laws as Friendly Societies. With them lies the day-to-day administration of the Social Security Acts.

In the General Scheme[4] there are two parallel sets of Funds, the

[1] Covering, in 1965, some 7 million workers in industry and commerce.

[2] *Association des Régimes de Rétraites Complémentaires.*

[3] This description of the social security services does not take account of the De Gaullist reforms of late 1967. These measures were largely designed to cut costs and to increase contributions in view of the rising deficit in the social security budget. This deficit was 1500 million francs in 1966 and would have approached 300 million in 1968.

[4] In order not to make the whole picture too complicated only the General Scheme is described here. There are considerable differences in the organization, contributions and benefits of the special schemes, although their relation to the Ministry of Labour and Social Security is much the same.

Caisses de Sécurité Sociale for social insurance and industrial injuries and the *Caisses d'Allocations Familiales* for family allowances.

The Primary Social Security Funds are responsible for collecting social insurance and industrial injuries contributions, for paying sickness, maternity and death benefits and for medical treatment, for paying disablement benefits following industrial injury or occupational disease and for promoting local health and welfare services.

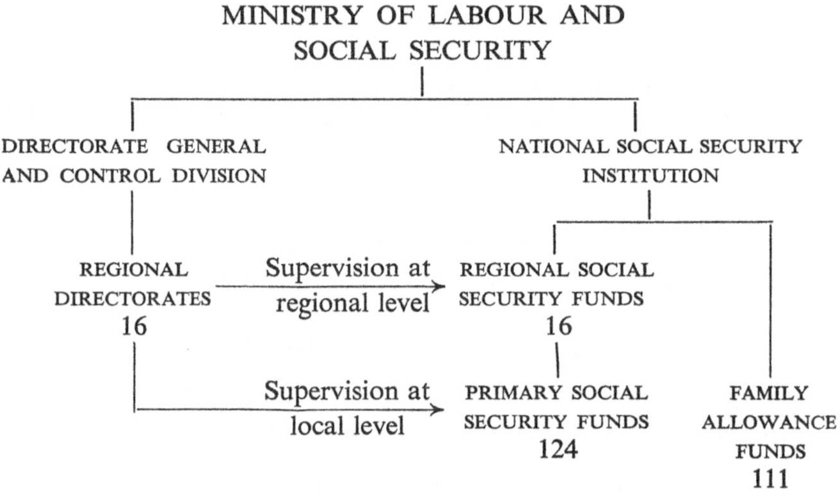

The Regional Social Security Funds pay all pensions, fix the contribution rates of different firms to the industrial injuries scheme, organize the medical control (of sickness benefits) and coordinate the health and welfare activities, including accident prevention, undertaken by the local offices. The Family Allowance Funds collect the family allowance contributions, pay benefits and promote family welfare through various social activities. Where their areas coincide with those of the local Social Security Funds, joint collecting services, *unions de recouvrement*, have been established to simplify the work of collecting contributions from employers and to reduce costs.

The Regional Funds and the National Social Security Institution receive a proportion of the contributions collected by the local Funds. Out of its allocation the National Social Security Institution operates a kind of re-insurance among the various social security offices on the one hand and the family allowance offices on the other. It also coordinates their health and welfare services at the national level.

Contributions and Qualifications for Benefits

For the employed workers in the General Scheme contributions are all calculated as a percentage of actual earnings up to a ceiling. The ceiling and the percentages are changed from time to time but in 1966 the ceiling was 12,960 fr., just under £1000[1] per annum, and the percentages:

	Employer	*Employee*
Social insurance	15%	6%
Industrial injuries	av. 3%	
Family allowances	14·25%	

Contributions payable by the self-employed and employers for their own account in respect of family allowances vary in accordance with earned incomes and are paid yearly.

Contribution qualifications for all the social insurance benefits are slightly easier than for most benefits under the British scheme, except for the old age pension, where they are much more severe. In the industrial injuries scheme there is no qualification beyond that of being a contributor; while in the family allowance scheme the right to benefit depends simply upon the following of some occupation or upon proof of inability to follow one. The unemployed and women living alone with two children, are deemed to come within this category. The State makes a grant towards the cost of benefits received by this non-active group, who of course pay no contribution.

Cash Benefits

In the social insurance and industrial injuries schemes benefits are related to actual wages (*up to the ceiling set for contributions*). Family allowances are related to a notional wage—the basic *monthly* wage to which zone reductions of from 0–5 per cent are applied according to the importance of the place of residence. (For employers and independent workers family allowances are calculated on a somewhat lower notional wage, as are also the single wage allowances.)

Under the Social Insurance Scheme:

1 Sickness benefit is paid from the fourth day normally for a maximum of six months, but may be extended for up to three or

[1] Throughout this study francs will be expressed in sterling at the rate of 13 francs to £1.

four years in the case of long illness. It is half the daily wage (up to the ceiling) and is increased to two-thirds from the thirty-first day of incapacity if the insured person has three dependent children.

2 Disablement benefit is awarded where working capacity is reduced by at least two-thirds and varies, according to the degree of incapacity, from 30 to 50 per cent of the average wage of the last ten working years. It may be increased by 40 per cent if there is need for constant attendance. At 60 is it replaced by an old age pension of at least equal amount.

3 Maternity benefit is paid only when the woman is insured in her own right and is for a period of six weeks before and eight weeks after confinement.

4 The Old Age pension depends in amount on the number of years of insurance (30 are required for a full pension), on the average wage over the past 10 years, and on the age of the pensioner at the time of the award. A full pension granted at the minimum age of 60 is equal to 20 per cent of the average wage, and there is an increase of 4 per cent for every year of insurance completed after 60. The pension is increased for a dependent wife or husband and if the pensioner has reared three children. Persons of at least 60 who prove they are unfit for work, or who have followed a specially laborious occupation can claim the 40 per cent pension awarded to other pensioners at 65. A proportionate pension is paid to those with only 15 to 30 years of insurance, life annuities to those with less than 15 years, and a refund is made to those with less than 5.

5 A Retired Workers' allowance was introduced in 1945 to fill the gap until the majority of workers had been in the insurance scheme long enough to be entitled to a substantial pension. Financed from the social insurance funds it is nevertheless essentially an assistance allowance for those whose total resources including the allowance fall below a certain sum. To be entitled to it one must be 65, or 60 if proved unfit for work, and had at least 25 years' employment. Since 1965 the allowance has entitled the beneficiary to medical benefits.

6 The Death grant is a lump sum equal to three months' wages.

7 The widow at the age of 65, or 60 if unfit for work, is entitled to a reversionary pension, related to the old age or disability pension her husband was drawing or would have been entitled to draw had he lived. She is only entitled to a widow's pension before 60 if permanently incapacitated. (The widowed mother with dependent children must depend on family allowances and social aid.)

Under the Industrial Injuries Scheme:

1 A daily allowance for cases of temporary incapacity is paid from the first day following cessation of work. It equals half the daily wage and is increased to two-thirds as from the twenty-ninth day.

2 Annuity for permanent incapacity is paid to those who are left permanently disabled and is related to their average wage in the twelve months prior to the accident and to the degree of their disablement (calculated on a rather more complicated formula than the British one).

3 Widows and widowers of the victim of a fatal accident receive an annuity of 25 per cent of the wage with a percentage increase for dependent children. Dependent parents may receive an annuity of 10 per cent. The whole of the annuity may not exceed 75 per cent of the wage.

Funeral expenses are paid within certain limits.

Under the Family Allowance Scheme:

1 Pre-natal allowances of 25 per cent of the basic wage[1] are paid for the first six months of pregnancy and of 12·5 per cent during the last three months. They are only paid if pregnancy has been notified and the mother undergoes three pre-natal examinations.

2 Maternity grants amount to twice the basic wage for a first birth and four-thirds for a second or subsequent birth. These grants are only paid if the birth falls within a prescribed period of marriage or of the birth of the last child. These very substantial grants are paid in two instalments, one on the birth of the child and one six months later if the child is still alive and dependent on its parents—or parent—because the grant is also made to unmarried mothers.

3 *Congés de naissance*—father is entitled to three days' holiday with pay on the occasion of each birth.

4 Family allowances proper are paid to families with at least two dependent[2] children:

22 per cent of the basic wage for the second dependent child

33 per cent of the basic wage for the third and each subsequent dependent child

[1] 314 francs (e. £23) a month in Paris (1967).

[2] Entitlement continues up to school leaving age, and is extended to 18 for the apprentice and to 20 for the student.

These allowances are increased by 9 per cent if the child is over ten and by 15 per cent if he is over 15. They are also increased by some 15 per cent by the *indemnité compensatrice*.[1]

5 Single wage allowances are paid to households dependent upon one source of income derived from employment—and are not therefore paid to employers and independent workers. They rise from 20 per cent[2] for a single child under five to 50 per cent for three or more dependent children of any age. A rather less generous allowance for the mother-at-home is made to the wife of the self-employed, if there is only one income coming to the family and if she is caring for three or more dependent children.

6 Housing allowances (and removal and improvement grants) depend on the claimant having at least two dependent children, spending a certain percentage of his income on rent, having a dwelling which fulfils certain standards of hygiene and is not under-occupied.

7 A special education allowance is payable on behalf of any child who is so seriously handicapped as to need special educational treatment. The allowance is to meet the costs of any education or training recommended by the departmental committee for disabled persons.

Medical Benefits

These are provided under the social insurance and industrial injuries schemes and take the form of refunds of medical expenses. While only the insured person is entitled to cash benefits, the whole family can claim medical benefits. Refunds can be claimed for:

(*a*) General and specialist medical expenses
(*b*) Hospital expenses
(*c*) Dental expenses
(*d*) Laboratory and pharmaceutical expenses
(*e*) Cost of medical appliances
(*f*) Travelling expenses

[1] The *indemnité compensatrice* now (1967) stands at 9·81 francs per month for the second child and 15·09 francs for the third and following children. This allowance was introduced in 1948. Prior to that date the wage earners paid a special income tax which, however, allowed for tax reduction in respect of family charges. After that date this income tax was replaced by a 5 per cent pay roll tax paid by the employer; this change removed the tax reduction in respect of family charges, and to compensate for it an *indemnité compensatrice* was introduced and added to the family allowance for wage earners.

[2] Based on a lower basic wage 194·5 francs in Paris (1967).

The sick person, who has a free choice of doctor, chemist, hospital or clinic, must normally pay for the treatment and claim a refund from his Social Security Fund. The refund is usually limited to 80 per cent of the approved cost which is calculated from a scale for each type of treatment agreed between the Funds and the professional associations and recognized institutions involved. Many private clinics and some doctors charge more than the conventional fee, in which case the patient gets a smaller percentage of the total cost refunded.

There is a full refund of the approved cost in the case of serious operations or of long term illness. In the case of industrial injury or occupational disease all treatment is free and paid for directly by the Social Security Fund without the insured having to advance the money as in the case of ordinary illness. For the insured woman or wife of the insured man all approved expenses of pregnancy and confinement are refunded in full, and bonuses are paid if the mother submits to pre- and post-natal examinations, if she attends a child welfare centre, and for breast feeding.

The Funds' Contribution to Accident Prevention and Health and Welfare Services

The social security organizations are not merely concerned with cash benefits and the refund of medical expenses, but are also making an important contribution to health and welfare services and to accident prevention, supplementing the work of local authorities, voluntary organizations and private enterprise. It is hard to give a clear picture as each Fund, subject to certain controls, provides or aids the provision of whatever health and welfare services it thinks most likely to benefit its members.

The percentage of the insurance and family allowance contributions to be devoted to these activities is fixed by the Minister and has altered little over the years. In 1965 the percentages and their distribution between the national, regional and primary Funds are shown in Table 1.

In addition, all fines on contributions paid in arrears (mostly by employers) are paid into this health and welfare fund. They are quite substantial, accounting for as much as a third of the total resources devoted to these activities.

In their provision of services the Funds must work within the general health and welfare policy laid down by the Minister of

Table 1

Percentage of Contributions for Health and Welfare Activities
(*Action Sanitaire et Sociale*)
1965—General Scheme Only

Percentage	Scheme	Percentage received by Nat.	Reg.	Prim. Fund
0·85	Social insurance		0·55 0·10[1]	0·3
3·0	Industrial injuries	1·0	1·0	1·0
	Family allowances:			
3·75	(*a*) employed persons	0·50		3·50
2·1	(*b*) employers and independent workers	0·1		2·0

[1] An additional percentage contribution paid into the recently instituted Regional Old People's Welfare Fund (*Caisse de Vieillesse*).

Health and Population, and, in the case of the industrial injuries scheme, by the Minister of Labour.

The Prevention of Industrial and Occupational Diseases

While the action of the Funds does not in any way reduce the force of government regulations or the activities of the Labour Inspectors and employers, it is an additional and powerful means of accident prevention and of associating employers and workpeople with the campaign against industrial injuries.

The Regional Fund fixes the rate of contribution to be paid by each firm for its industrial risks. Both the National Social Security Institution and the Regional Funds try to identify the sectors of industry in which an effort to prevent accidents is specially called for, undertake technical research and spread the information obtained. They can require industries or particular firms to adopt preventive measures; they have an expert staff of consulting engineers and of safety officers and finally some very effective financial inducements. Besides being able to modify contributions to correspond with risks in each firm they can impose supplementary contributions or allow rebates to meet either serious shortcomings or special achievements. Moreover, they can through subsidies or loans give help to firms to adopt better safety devices. All these efforts are guided and coordinated at regional and national level by technical committees set up in each industry, on which employers and work-people are equally represented.

In theory at least the French industrial injuries scheme is making the maximum use of financial sanctions and incentives to prevent accidents. What would seem to be less satisfactory is the present division of functions between the Labour Inspectorate and the Social Security Funds. The Labour Inspectors have the right and duty, as have the British factory inspectors, to investigate every accident immediately after it has occurred. The technical knowledge thus gained should be at the disposal of those primarily concerned with accident prevention, but the Labour Inspectorate have to spread their staff too thinly (owing to the tight budgetary control of the French civil service) to do the kind of advisory and follow up work done by British factory inspectors. The Social Security Funds are not so limited in their employment of good technical staff, who are free to do intensive work, but there is a tendency to concentrate their efforts on the larger industrial concerns, and to miss many opportunities of accident prevention because they are not in a position to follow up every accident.

Health and Welfare Services

By agreement the social insurance Funds concentrate on health services, while the family allowance Funds support services which are primarily social and concerned with the welfare of the family. The machinery set up to ensure that this is done and to sketch out a national health and welfare policy for the social security organizations is the *Comité Technique D'Action Sanitaire et Sociale*, composed of representatives of the Ministries of Labour, Health and Population, and Education, of the social security organizations (including representatives of the special schemes), of the medical profession and of the Family Associations. These are largely Catholic bodies representing the families themselves; they have regional and national as well as local organizations. The Committee is divided into three sections: health, welfare and medical supervision. It defines the types of institution or service which the various Funds might consider establishing or supporting, suggests the way in which they might distribute their efforts and lays down the conditions on which the support of the Funds should be given to outside agencies.

At regional level there are commissions similarly composed to the Technical Committee, with two sub-committees for health and welfare, which may co-opt other interested persons. The regional commissions play an important part in local planning and co-ordination, and are also responsible for the supervision of agreed schemes. Both the regional and primary Funds must get the agreement of the regional commissions for any new ventures; in addition any health services require the approval of the Ministry of Health's regional medical officer, and the construction or acquiring of new buildings or the granting of exceptional cash benefits the approval of the Ministry of Labour and Social Security.

Where a Fund wishes to finance an establishment or service provided by a voluntary organization or local authority, it may do so by a grant or loan for building or equipment, or by paying for services rendered to its members—services such as the provision of convalescence or a home help, which are not among the statutory medical benefits for which the 80 per cent or 100 per cent refund can be claimed. The advantage of paying for services rendered is that only those who have contributed to the Fund benefit. On the other hand, a more direct contribution can be made to the extension or improvement of existing services by grants for capital expenditure, more particularly since these are only made on three conditions:

(*a*) That the outside agency has not sufficient resources to carry through the extension or improvement itself.
(*b*) That where, as is usually the case, the Fund is only granting a proportion of the money needed, the remainder is available from other sources.
(*c*) That the Fund is given representation on the controlling body of the outside agency commensurate with the financial help it is giving.

Frequent reference will be made to the contribution of the social security organizations to France's health and welfare services in later sections. Here it is only necessary to indicate the extent and nature of the involvement of the different Funds of the General Scheme in the provision of these social services, remembering that most of the special schemes are engaged in a similar *action sanitaire et sociale*.

Table 2

Social Insurance Funds

Distribution of Expenditure on Health and Welfare Services in 1964

LOCAL FUNDS	*Percentage*	REGIONAL FUNDS	*Percentage*
Cash benefits	60	Schools for nurses and workers	2
Social workers	5	General hospitals and dispensaries	45
Hospitals, dispensaries, etc., of all kinds	25	Psychiatric services	23
		T.B.	5
		Other specialized services	14
Maternity and child welfare	7	Maternity and child welfare and services for handicapped children	6
Health education	1	Health education	2
All else	2	All else	3
	100		100

Table 3

Family Allowance Funds

Distribution of Expenditure on Welfare Services

	Percentages in			
	1947	1950	1960	1964
Cash benefits	14	15	10	10
Housing grants	—	18	30	20
Holidays	50	26	21	20
Home helps	3	6	14	12
Foster homes and homes	—	9	7	11
Social workers	11	10	7	12
Social centres	—	1	3	4
Other	22	15	8	11
	100	100	100	100

As can be seen from these tables the primary Funds still devote a substantial proportion of their free moneys to granting their members additional cash benefits. These usually take the form of discretionary, supplementary allowances, or of grants to meet some emergency or exceptional need. The regional Funds naturally invest most of their resources in specialized regional institutions, the primary Funds in more local enterprises and in services to the individual. Table 3 shows up the trends in the family allowance Funds' spending in social welfare in the post-war years: a much greater investment in housing (housing grants usually take the form of subsidies to housing associations of one kind or another), more spending on such community care services as home helps and social centres and less on extra cash benefits and children's holidays, which become less necessary as personal incomes increase. Finally, taking account of the fact that the family allowance Funds have considerably more to spend than the regional and local social insurance Funds put together, the total expenditure of the three Funds on health and welfare services was distributed as follows:

Table 4

Distribution of Expenditure on Health and Welfare Services by all Funds in 1963[1]

	Percentage
Housing	19·10
Holidays	14·50
Medical equipment	18·44
Cash benefits	13·89
Home helps	8·39
Social workers	8·83
Foster homes and Homes	5·57
Maternity and child welfare and handicapped children	1·61
Social centres	2·17
Other	7·50
	100·0

[1] A total of 795,252,000 Francs (representing about £60 million). From *Notes Statistiques: Sécurité Sociale*, January 1966.

SOCIAL AID

Despite the substantial contribution which the social security organizations are making to the health and welfare services, their prime concern is income maintenance—a redistribution of incomes through cash benefits in favour of the family and of those who for various reasons are unable to work. Social Aid, on the other hand, although originally the only source of statutory assistance for those in need, is today mainly concerned with the provision of services, medical and welfare services of all kinds, which are more readily described under the appropriate headings in later sections.

Assistance in cash is indeed still available to all the old categories of persons likely to be in need, and as was shown more categories were added in the post-war period. But because of the nature of the means test (the old family means test has been very little modified), and of the extremely low level of the obligatory assistance allowances which are well below subsistence, this form of assistance, administered and financed by the department with some contribution from commune and State, has become of marginal importance. Its inflexibility and dependence on local resources prevented it from fulfilling the role of the British National Assistance Board,[1] which fills in the gaps and supplements national insurance and is the ultimate guarantor of a national minimum to all, insured and non-insured alike.

In the case of the aged, who because of their numbers present the most serious problem, the French post-war social security scheme had its own built-in assistance, the Retired Workers' Allowance, given on a means test to all who at the time of retirement were insured but not yet entitled to an adequate pension. This Retired Workers' Allowance, financed out of employers' contributions, first featured in the General Scheme, but as separate pension schemes were set up for various professional and occupational groups they too provided an assistance allowance for those not entitled to a contributory pension. A special allowance (*l'Allocation Spéciale*) was available, after 1952, for the few who when they retired were still unattached to any pension Fund. It was financed from state moneys. These retirement allowances were regarded as temporary measures until all would be entitled to a full pension. But there have been too many of them, they have had to go on for too long and they have become increasingly inadequate even if measured in terms

[1] Now, the Supplementary Benefits Commission of the Ministry of Social Security.

of bare subsistence. In 1956 the Government finally recognized that additional resources would have to be made available to social security and to local public assistance agencies alike, if the poorest old people were to receive even a minimum subsistence income. A National Solidarity Fund (largely financed from a special tax on motor cars) was set up to pay supplementary grants to all old and disabled persons who in spite of any pension or assistance allowances to which they were entitled had resources below a certain ceiling. In 1963 nearly 2½ million persons were receiving this supplementary grant—half of all those in receipt of a pension or allowance from the social insurance Funds.

The assistance to which those who can prove need are still entitled under the Social Aid legislation are set out below in the three broad categories into which they are now grouped. Medical aid is not described here as cash allowances are only exceptionally given under this heading. *Statutory* benefits in kind to the aged and handicapped have been added, but not those which are only given on a *discretionary* basis.

A. Social Aid to the Aged[1]

(*a*) Basic allowance—all in receipt of this will also be entitled to the special and supplementary allowances mentioned above. (55,000)[2]

(*b*) Rent allowance—75 per cent of the rent if no underoccupation. (115,500)

(*c*) Home Help (up to a maximum of 30 hours a month) or an allowance of 60 per cent of cost of home help services. (3500)

(*d*) Social Card—entitling the holder to certain benefits in kind: medical assistance, free legal aid, the reduction of one return railway journey a year granted to all those entitled to holidays with pay, etc. (609,000)

(*e*) Placement in a private home, in a hostel, Home or Hospital—pocket money is paid in these cases. (148,000)

B. Social Aid to the Handicapped

In this category a distinction is made between those with a handicap of anything less than 80 per cent, and the *grands infirmes* with

[1] Those over 65, or 60 if unfit to work.

[2] The figures in parentheses show the approximate numbers of old people in the metropolitan area of Paris entitled to these benefits in 1961. See, *politique de la Vieillesse* published in 1962 by the *Documentation Française*.

over 80 per cent handicap, which includes the blind. All are referred in the first instance to the departmental committee for vocational guidance for the disabled, which has an adult and junior section. The cost of any rehabilitation or re-education services recommended will be met by Social Aid if not covered by social security benefits.

In addition *all adult handicapped* are entitled to:

(*a*) Basic allowance—to which the supplementary allowance will be added.

(*b–e*) Rent allowance, home help, social card and placement in Home or Hospital (as for the aged).

The *severely handicapped* may also be entitled to:

(*f*) Unemployability allowance, or, if his earning power is severely reduced, a supplement to his wage.

(*g*) Constant attendance allowance.

(*h*) *Carte d'invalidité*—entitling him to special seats on public transport.

For *severely handicapped children* there is a special cash allowance for the parents or guardians, or the cost of a placement will be met by Social Aid. It is compulsory to notify such children to the *Mairie*.

C. Social Aid to the Family

(*a*) Basic allowance.

(*b*) Increased for children—not cumulative with family allowances.

(*c*) Increased for dependent relatives—not cumulative with any social security or social aid benefits to which the dependent may be entitled.

(Outside servicemen's families, and some widows and single women with dependent children who are unable to work, there is little call on this form of social aid today.)

CHAPTER 3

Housing

In modern societies, and for all sorts of reasons more particularly since World War II, the relevance of a country's housing policy to that collective action for social welfare which broadly defines our area of study, is being recognized. It has relevance where priority is given to it as a form of social investment, and where social security measures are taken to ensure that individuals and families with low incomes can afford to pay for decent accommodation. The distinctive characteristics of French housing policy[1] can be best summarized under these two headings.

SOCIAL INVESTMENT

The French government has skilfully combined purposefulness and eclecticism in its drive to raise housing production after a slow post-war start in the 1950s. An unusually wide range of agencies have been employed—private, public, French and foreign—but despite a rate of output higher than that in Britain for every year except one from 1958 to 1963 (inclusive) there is a steady public demand for increased effort. A recent survey made by the National Association of Family Allowance Funds and the Centre for Research and Information on Consumption (1967) showed that more than 27 per cent of the families of town-dwelling French wage-earners were living in overcrowded and comfortless dwellings. The state and its agencies have built or assisted (usually through finance) 90 per cent of all dwellings built in France since 1945.

Construction and Management

Municipal housing on the British model is not found in France (or in most other countries) despite extensive state and municipal participation in the provision of housing. Housing may be built and managed by private individuals, companies, or various kinds of

[1] For brief comparative description see: 'Housing in Britain, France and Western Germany', *Planning*, Vol. XXXI, No. 490, August 1965, P.E.P.

public or semi-public bodies. Local authorities channel their activities through HLM (*Habitations à Loyer Modéré*—low-rent dwellings) organizations. These bodies may be set up by decree at the request of a municipal council, a syndicate of parishes, or a departmental council (*Conseil Général*), and local authorities can nominate a third of the members of their governing boards. It is possible for private individuals to establish HLM organizations which are subject to special regulations and supervision by the Minister of Construction. These organizations may build and manage rented housing, or function as co-operative of tenants or owners.

Some of the large construction and management societies, particularly in and around Paris and big towns, combine private and public capital. Local authorities are not permitted to own more than 65 per cent of the capital of these societies, but the organizations are supervised by the prefect of the department.

There are three other common forms of construction and management organizations in France: property construction companies, building associations and building co-operatives. BATICOOP, which organizes a large number of housing co-operatives throughout France, is the largest and most widely spread organization in the field of housing co-operatives.

Housing Finance

Financial assistance by the state takes three forms:

(*a*) long term loans at reduced interest rates to organizations building low-rent (HLM) housing;
(*b*) special subsidies (*Primes à la Construction*); and
(*c*) loans through two semi-public banks, the *Crédit Foncier* (a mortgage bank for existing dwellings) and the *Comptoir des Entrepreneurs* (for dwellings in course of erection).

The low-rent dwellings (*habitations à loyer modéré*) were first provided under an Act of 1894. The houses were originally known as 'cheap dwellings' (*habitations à bon marché*) and intended for poorer wage-earners, but the income limits were gradually raised, the character of housing provided changed, and by the 1960s about 90 per cent of the population would have qualified for an HLM dwelling. New regulations were introduced in 1963 to lower the upper income limits required for qualification for HLM. Simultaneously greater funds were made available for HLM construction.

SOCIAL SECURITY

The terms on which families with children can obtain housing allowances from the family allowance Funds, and the aged and handicapped rent allowances from Social Aid, were described in the previous section. It must be noted that families are only entitled to housing allowances if their dwelling is of a certain standard. Many of the poorest and largest families are unable to benefit from the allowances because there is no suitable accommodation available for them.

In protecting tenants from having to pay the market price, rent control represents an indirect form of subsidy, albeit at the expense of the landlord and related to the type of accommodation rather than to the means of the tenant. As in Britain, rents were controlled —and tenancies protected—during the First World War and the controls remained in force during the inter-war period. New controls were introduced in 1941—to include houses built since 1914—and reformed in 1948. Regulations which formulated principles (or criteria) for the determination of rents were laid down at the same time.

CHAPTER 4

Health Services

The early development of public health, and later of personal health services, followed much the same pattern in France as in Britain. Today, the differences, more particularly in the methods of financing a full range of modern medical care services, are quite striking.

The National Institute of Statistics and Economic Studies (INSEE) and the Centre for Research and Information on Consumption (CREDOC) estimated that in 1958 the total expenditure on medical care was 1.100 thousand million old francs (roughly £845 million). This figure covered:

doctors' fees and their collaborators	280 thousand millions
expenditure on drugs	284 thousand millions
hospital expenses	360 thousand millions
dental costs	160 thousand millions
expenditure on orthopaedics and spectacles, etc.	16 thousand millions
	1100

How were these medical expenses met? The various social security schemes provided 455 milliards, Social Aid 100 milliards, the State (for war victims) 10 milliards, while 535 milliards were borne by the patients. Although collective bodies were financing a growing proportion of medical expenses, half of these were still met out of the family budget. This is explained by the fact that certain fees may be charged in excess of the scales of reimbursement laid down by the social security agencies and that patients still pay the full or part cost of many of the drugs.

The percentages benefiting from the refunds of medical expenses under social insurance schemes, supplemented by many mutual insurance societies, and from the free medical assistance provided under the departmental Social Aid service were as follows:

75[1] per cent of the population covered by various social insurance schemes
8 per cent covered by private insurance only
2·8 per cent inscribed on free medical aid lists

leaving 13·7 per cent of the population only without any cover.

The proportion of 'protected' persons (not only the insured himself but those who are dependent on him) varies between occupational groups and with age. Eighty per cent of the population under 35 years is now covered by social insurance, but of the over eighties only 51 per cent of the men and 29 per cent of the women have any insurance cover. More than a third of the population receives some benefits from a mutual insurance society, but in most cases this supplements their social insurance benefits. Some 1,360,000 persons receive free medical aid, and a further 28,000 sufferers from tuberculosis and 110,000 mentally ill are receiving free treatment under the Social Aid legislation.

How far, and in what way, people are protected against the risk of heavy medical expenses is, however, primarily an issue of social security. The arrangements which any country makes to cover this risk for the majority of its citizens profoundly affects but does not wholly determine the quantity, quality and distribution of its total resources of medical equipment and services. To make any assessment of a country's social policy in this field it is necessary to take a look at who initially provided, who presently administers and which particular organizations are responsible for developing the various services in response to new needs and to advances in medical, and medical-social, knowledge and techniques.

Overall medical consumption is steadily increasing in France as in most other countries. It represented according to INSEE and CREDOC's estimate:

4·16 per cent of general consumption in 1950 and
8 per cent of general consumption in 1960.

The Fourth and Fifth Plans for the next decade are likely to increase it still further. How have all these developments affected the different elements which together constitute the French health services, because there is no National Health Service in France?

[1] The extension of medical benefits to those in receipt of the retired workers allowance and to more of the agricultural population has raised this percentage to 87·6.

THE DOCTORS

There are 52,866 doctors of all kinds in France (1966). About three-quarters are in private practice, the remainder are employed in industry (France has a well-developed industrial medical service), in the social security agencies (to advise and control the administration of medical benefits), in psychiatric and TB hospitals, and, to a limited extent, in departmental and municipal public and community health services. Although the overall proportion of 10·8 doctors to every 10,000 inhabitants is high compared with many other countries,[1] the geographical distribution is very unequal, and there is little incentive in the present system for doctors in private practice in particular to move into the under-doctored areas.

The French medical profession remains firmly attached to the principles of liberal medicine, and there has been no public demand for the nationalization of medical services. Those who are entitled to free medical aid may choose their doctor from a list of approved doctors, who are paid directly by the department. An insured person can call any doctor on the Social Security register (doctors who have signed the convention on fees). He can change doctors during the course of illness or even consult several doctors at the same time. Special increased repayment is available if he wishes to consult a specialist, or a doctor on the highly qualified list who may charge more than the conventional fee. If, on the other hand, he is treated by a doctor who has not signed the convention on fees, he gets a considerably reduced percentage of his bill refunded.

Since 1960 departmental conventions have replaced the tariffs agreed between the doctors and the social security agencies, which were the subject of continual discussion and revision between 1945 and 1960. By 1966, 78 out of all the 95 departments had departmental conventions to which all the doctors subscribed. In the others an inter-ministerial commission fixes the conventional fee to which doctors may subscribe individually. In Paris, where the doctors have always declined to accept the conventional agreement, half the doctors have signed as individuals.

[1] Much the same as in England and Wales, higher than in Sweden, lower than in Germany and Italy.

THE HOSPITALS

Hospitals are usually the first subject of public provision. Those founded under the *ancien Régime* were all charitable foundations.[1] After the Revolution, and more especially after the public assistance authorities had to provide statutory assistance (in the form of hospital care if needed) for lunatics (1838), for the sick (1893) and for the aged, infirm and incurable (1907), the commune and the department became the major providers of hospitals, either directly or by paying for those chargeable to them if placed in voluntary ones. Although most hospitals are communal, inter-communal, or departmental by origin, legislation from the Act of 1851 (the first hospital charter) onwards has gradually brought them into a common pattern of administration. Each hospital is endowed with a corporate personality and financial autonomy but is administered by a specially constituted committee, on which the various interests—the commune, the prefect, the medical personnel and the social security agencies, etc.—are represented. The director of the hospital, whose qualifications are administrative rather than medical, is appointed by the Minister of Health. The medical staff in the University Hospital Centres is nominated by the Ministers of Health and Education; in other Hospitals by the Prefect, except full-time practitioners who are nominated by the Minister of Health. In the post-war reorganization hospitals were designated as Regional Hospital Centres,[2] Hospital Centres, Hospitals, Rural Hospitals, *Hospices* (caring for chronics and incurables), and the *Commission Nationale de l'Organisation Hospitalière* at the Ministry of Health was set up as a central planning body. Since 1958 private[3] hospitals and clinics, which mainly confine themselves to medical, general surgery or maternity wards have come under much closer supervision by the Ministry of Health. Projects for setting up private institutions have now to be submitted to the Ministry, which is responsible for co-ordinating the siting of public and private establishments nationally.

The enormously increased costs of running and equipping a

[1] In Paris *l'Hopital Général*, founded in 1656 by Louis XIV, was in fact made up of several establishments: *La Pitié, la Salpetriére, Biceter* and *Scipion. L'Hôtel Dieu* goes back to the seventh century.

[2] All except one are University Centres.

[3] There are as many as 200,000 beds in this private sector as against rather more than 400,000 beds in the public sector.

modern hospital is reflected in the cost per day charged to each patient, whether he is accommodated in a first or second class bed. These day payments constitute the hospital's main income and today are more often paid on behalf of patients by the social security agencies or public assistance authorities than by patients themselves. Endowments are negligible and the capital grants so urgently needed to build new hospitals and modernize old ones have in the past had to come from the same sources—commune and department, and regional and national social security agencies. With the high costs of modern equipment and the larger planning areas, these sources are now inadequate and unsatisfactory. Most of the very substantial grants made by the social security funds come from the General Scheme, that is from the insurance contributions of employers and employees of only a section of the working population. Central government control and supervision is extensive, but up to the 1950s its grants-in-aid for capital developments were negligible. Since then they have increased considerably (but do not normally exceed 40 per cent) and will have to continue to do so if more initiative is to be given to the central government where the responsibility for planning and developing what is virtually a national service now lies. The role of the hospital is changing and its influence is steadily growing. Functional rehabilitation of the physically handicapped is now regarded as a basic task of the hospital service but in 1960 only eighteen hospital centres had a rehabilitation department. In addition to hospital out-patient departments 'town clinics' or polyclinics, grouping the various tests and examination services which any medical practitioner will be able to call upon, are to be developed. Experiments in hospitalization 'at home' may lead to the development of a badly needed home care service based on the hospital rather than the departmental health service.

THE ATTACK ON SPECIAL DISEASES

Towards the end of the nineteenth century and in the first half of the twentieth, the State developed new concerns: to promote the health of mothers and children, and to combat certain diseases, known in France as *les fleaux sociaux* (the social scourges). These movements, paralleled in other European countries, developed naturally out of the earlier nineteenth century preoccupations with the control of disease and removal of insanitary conditions through environmental health services[1] and with the provision of hospitals for the sick poor. In France, the diseases singled out for special attack because of their social and economic implications have been mental illness, TB, venereal disease and cancer,[2] to which some would now add alcoholism.

For obvious reason, the *mentally ill* are always the first subject for special legislation and for some kind of public provision. An Act of 1838 required every department to provide, or join in the provision of, a mental hospital, and *les aliénés* (lunatics) were from this time onwards the subject of a special statutory assistance. In this century, however, France has fallen behind in its mental health services. It was not until the late 1930s that preventive measures and more out-patient clinics were officially recommended, and even then little was achieved until departmental initiatives were stimulated by substantial central government grants from 1946 onwards. These grants were raised to 80 per cent in 1955 and have enabled the departments to develop their mental health clinics (there were 366 of them in 1955) as the focus for work with mentally handicapped children (ascertainment, recommending for special residential treatment and community care) as well as for the care and after-care services of the mentally ill. Mental hospitals, on the other hand, have been and still are very over-crowded, and their comparative neglect in the first half of this century, means that the quite considerable capital investment in new psychiatric hospitals and the modernization of many old institutions started in 1955 will have to be continued for many years to come. The Government's Development Plan (1962) proposed that each department should provide clinics (staffed by a psychiatrist, or assistant psychiatrist, a psychologist and one to two social workers) for preventive and after-care work for each 70,000 of its population, and that each clinic should have the use of 200 beds in the departmental psychiatric hospital. If this plan is not yet being implemented in many departments, it is because the government has failed to come forward with its share of the capital needed to provide an adequate number of psychiatric beds to support the preventive work of the clinical teams.

[1] An Act of 1902 consolidated previous public health legislation, giving to all mayors certain police powers relating to sanitary control, subject to regulations made by the department. The departments and larger communes provide the necessary sanitary services through public health departments under a director of public health.

[2] France's public health services now include a small leper service, to deal with the disease among some of the refugees.

The anti-TB campaign and the progressive development of effective preventive, diagnostic treatment and rehabilitation services took place in the first half of this century. Two world wars as well as discoveries of new medical techniques for diagnosis and treatment have affected both the incidence and nature of this disease, and consequently and subsequently the statutory services devised to combat it. War pensions, a special public assistance, and later, social insurance benefits, ensured that those suffering from TB were able to benefit from such treatment as was available in sanatoria, in *préventorium* (for those with a primary infection), in the special units in hospitals and in the increasing number of dispensaries. The *Comité National de Défence contre la Tuberculose* campaigned indefatigably for public education, research and more treatment facilities.

The Second World War temporarily arrested progress but immediately after liberation, in 1945, a major piece of legislation strengthened and reorganized the various elements in the campaign, so that the best use could be made of modern techniques. The preventive work in home and dispensary (financed after 1956 entirely by the department of State) became an important section of the departmental health service, co-operating with the newly created departmental hospital centres for TB in the co-ordination of all work in this field, including the substantial contributions being made by the social security agencies, the maternity and child welfare and school health services. A national Tuberculosis Committee was set up at the Ministry of Health in 1948 to regulate and control all establishments treating TB patients and to organize the recruitment and training of all medical staff employed in them. This single corps of full-time medical specialists treating patients in sanatoria and administering the preventive medical social work of the dispensaries has been a strong unifying factor.

Mortality rates have fallen very considerably: from 120 per 100,000 in 1938 to 15·3 in 1964. Morbidity decreases more slowly and the number of chronic cases among the older generations still present a problem and, together with the higher incidence of TB among immigrants from North Africa, means that France is only just arriving at the position of having surplus accommodation to be turned to other uses.

While two world wars greatly increased the incidence of *venereal disease*, medical progress has opened up new and more effective methods of treatment. In the recent post-war period the compulsory school, pre-marital and ante-natal examinations have helped towards earlier detection. Public health measures, as in Britain, consist of a network of clinics providing free, confidential treatment—they were made a departmental responsibility in 1948, following the pattern of the TB legislation. The use of compulsory powers is, however, rather different. Compulsory notification was introduced in 1942 and made effective in 1948, but the names are only given of those who refuse treatment; hospitalization can be administratively enforced. Since 1946 the medical and social record of prostitution is kept by the sanitary instead of by the police authority.

With most of the *fléaux sociaux* of earlier days (malnutrition, infant mortality, infectious diseases) largely suppressed, or, like TB and VD, more or less under control, cancer has become in the popular mind the prime enemy. And indeed as people are living longer more are dying from this disease. In France in 1936 there were 137 deaths from cancer per 100,000, in 1962 192. In the present state of medical knowledge, research, early diagnosis and treatment all present particular difficulties, not least because all involve such a wide range of specialized knowledge, skills and equipment. The three essential elements in the French anti-cancer campaign are the register of those treated, the special anti-cancer centres (for treatment and research) and extension clinics (for early detection and follow up). The two former were built up over a quarter of a century but were given statutory recognition by an ordinance of 1948. There are at present some twenty centres, where patients can receive highly specialized treatment and be followed up through out-patient departments. The register of these patients and of their response to treatment provides the essential material for research, both at these regional centres and nationally, at the *Institut National de la Santé de Récherce Médicale*, where a national register is kept.

The extension clinics (*les consultations avancé*), administered and staffed by the regional centres, are not yet fully developed. Until they are, early detection, closer cooperation with general practitioners and with the many other hospitals treating cancer patients, and a more comprehensive register of information about all cancer patients will not be achieved. The medical-social problems presented by the incurable and chronic patients must be also solved locally. The palliative treatment and constant nursing care, which they need, cannot be appropriately given in the anti-cancer centres, nor would it seem wise to develop special institutions for them. More facilities for home nursing would be the happiest answer in many cases. The cost of this to the individual can be largely met by long-term sickness benefit or by free medical assistance (there is no special categorical assistance for cancer patients as there is for the mentally ill or tubercular), but no responsibility for *developing* such a home care service (involving home nurses, home helps, invalid requisites, etc.) has been specifically laid on the departmental health and welfare service. Paris Public Assistance has used its permissive powers to try out a form of hospitalization 'at home' for all kinds of patients whose conditions calls for close medical supervision without requiring hospital admission. But *L'Assistance Publique de Paris* is a very special institution.[1] Administered under close ministerial control by a Director General and a Secretary General (appointed by the President of the Republic on the recommendation of the Minister of Health and Population), it is responsible not only for all domiciliary social aid both statutory and permissive, but also for all the hospitals and other institutions set up by the *Commune de Paris.* The national voluntary organization in this field, *le Ligue Française contre le Cancer*, still plays an important role in cancer education and in giving help in particularly distressing cases.

No one would deny that *alcoholism* is a serious social problem in France today, and it has been the subject of extensive studies in recent years by private and official bodies. Consumption of alcohol per head of the adult population in France is twice that in Italy, three times that in the USA and six times that in Denmark. Deaths from acute or chemical alcoholism increased from 1·2 per 100,000 of the population in 1946 to 11 in 1962, and those from cirrhosis of the liver from 6·9 to 31·2 in the same period. Nine per cent of the national income is spent on drink and from four to five million persons derive a living from its production and distribution.

All these facts and particularly the economic ones, make the attack on alcoholism a peculiary difficult one. Preventive measures are primarily social and economic, although treatment of the alcoholic is being increasingly seen in medical, or medical-social terms.

The main legislation is an Act of 1917, which attempted to repress public drunkenness by penal action and by some limited regulations

[1] *See Cent Ans d'Assistance Publique à Paris* 1848–1949 published by the *Administration Générale de l'Assistance Publique de Paris.*

related to the serving of alcohol; and a more extensive Act of 1954, which carried this control further by a system of licensing and taxation. It also allowed for the placement of the alcoholic, dangerous to himself or others, under the control of the Health authority, which can require him to attend special treatment or training centres. The social insurance and family allowance Funds have spent quite a lot of their free moneys on campaigns against alcoholism and the treatment of alcoholics. Since 1953 some measures have been taken to limit and control the production of alcohol, but in this area economic considerations naturally predominate, and there is more concern with over-production than with the implications of excessive consumption.

MATERNITY AND CHILD WELFARE

Towards the end of the nineteenth century, France was pioneering a number of maternity and child welfare services: Dr Budin's *consultations de nourrissons*, the first *goutte de lait* (milk depot) at Fécamp in 1894 and the large numbers of *crèches.* The first Child Welfare legislation was as early as 1874 (Loi Roussel). By the outbreak of the first world war children, large families and expectant mothers had all become the subject of a special statutory assistance, which provided health and welfare services to these vulnerable groups as well as assistance allowances. The infant mortality rate was reduced from 135 in 1906 to 100 in 1910. After the war the new employers' family allowance schemes took the lead, providing health and welfare services as well as cash allowances for the families of the employees of the increasing number of industrial concerns covered by the Funds.

Though much good work was done by the Funds, by many voluntary organizations, and public assistance departments, particularly in the large towns, co-ordination was lacking. In England the Maternity and Child Welfare Act of 1918, ensured a more uniform minimum service (notification of births followed up by health visitors, and the supervision of midwives), but one which was more limited and generally speaking, less imaginative in the scope and range of services provided for ordinary families. In France, this co-ordination was first achieved in Paris in 1930 by a voluntary organization, the *Office de la Protection de la Maternite et de l'Enfance de la Seine* (OPMES), which organized the notification of births and health visiting on a district basis, inducing the various statutory and voluntary bodies already in the field to make themselves responsible for following up all the births in certain districts so that there was complete coverage. In 1939 the *Code de la Famille* provided for the department to take over this responsibility, but the war threw everything into confusion and once again the infant mortality soared (1939: 64; 1940: 92; 1944: 77; 1945: 108). The reorganization envisaged in 1939 was finally effected by the legislation of 1945. Each department now has a PMI (*protection maternelle et infantile*) service. Its responsibility is to co-ordinate and fill in the gaps of a maternity and child welfare service which must make adequate provision for the following:

1. Compulsory pre-nuptial examinations[1]—normally carried out by GP's who call on the departmental service, however, for certain tests.[1]

2. The three ante-natal and one post-natal compulsory examinations. Again many of these are carried out by GP's or in the out-patient departments of maternity hospitals.

3. Child Welfare clinics—greatly extended since the war, the number of these clinics went up from 2000 before the war to 8250 by 1963. A number of the more rural departments have organized mobile clinics.

4. The issue of a *carnet de santé* (a personal health record card) for each child born.

5. The supervision of all establishments or persons caring for children under six, i.e. *pouponnieres* (residental nurseries), *crèches* (daytime care of the under three's), *garderie d'enfants* (nurseries for children from two or three to five) and *nourrices* and *gardiennes* (child-minders and foster-parents of babies and young children).

6. *Assistantes sociales*, the medical-social workers who combine the health education function of the British health visitors with social work.

The extent to which the departmental PMI service is co-ordinating others or making its own direct provisions, can be seen in the following analysis of all the *assistantes sociales* employed in the field of maternity and child welfare in 1963.

The total number went up from 2000 in 1946 to 5760 in 1963; 455 specialized in maternity and child welfare, 5305 were *assistants*

[1] Each *fiancé* is told only of the results of his own examination.

socials polyvalents (general social workers). They were employed as follows:

	Specialists in M. and C.W. work	*General social workers*
Department	373	2337
Municipalities	12	419
Social security agencies:		
General scheme	6	339
Special schemes	2	61
Agricultural scheme	—	669
Family allowance funds	—	675
Voluntary agencies	62	575
Other	1	230
	455	5305

CHAPTER 5

The Care and Protection of Children and Family Welfare

As part of the realignment and reconstruction of French social services after the last war important steps were taken at national and regional level to co-ordinate the various services which had grown up for the protection and treatment of *l'enfance inadaptée*, a term which, significantly enough, was being increasingly used to include all physically and mentally handicapped, deprived, neglected and delinquent children. Distinctions drawn earlier between the public assistance service for abandoned or 'deprived' (in the British sense) children, the special assistance for the severely handicapped and the mentally disordered, the preventive action of the maternity and child welfare and school health services, and the penal services for juvenile delinquents were seen to be largely unreal. At national level an inter-departmental committee of the ministries of Health and Population, of Education, and of Justice, was set up in 1945 to co-ordinate policies for *l'enfance inadaptée*. At regional level 16 regional *Associations pour la Sauvegarde de l'Enfance et de l'Adolescence* were established between 1943–47. These regional Associations set up under the auspices of (and largely financed by) the ministry of Health and Population, brought together all the interests concerned: not only the officials of these various statutory services, but representatives of the many voluntary organizations and persons with a specialist knowledge—medical, educational or social—working in this field.

In tracing the development of the various services to protect and treat these children, it is, however, easier to group them under the three broad headings of services for: (1) the physically and mentally handicapped, (2) the neglected and deprived, (3) the delinquent.

The Physically and Mentally Handicapped

The Ministry of National Education established a school and university health service, but in 1964 the service became the responsibility of the Ministry of Health and Population. It takes over the medical supervision of children from the departmental maternity and child welfare service with the first compulsory medical inspection preliminary to the child entering school at the age of six. The child's medical record (a *carnet de santé* is issued at birth) is kept up through subsequent medical examinations, carried out at regular intervals throughout his school and university career. Some 2000 *assistantes sociales* and nurses, between them, carry out the duties of school nurse and school welfare officer, follow up recommendations for any special medical, educational or social treatment and provide the liaison with the homes.

Facilities for treatment are largely provided by the departmental health services (particularly for those suffering from tuberculosis and mental handicaps), and by voluntary organizations, often grant aided by the department or the social security agencies. Most of the special educational treatment available is due to the initiative of voluntary organizations (France boasts such pioneers as Louis Braille for the blind, and l'abbé d'Epée for the deaf), now largely supported by public funds. Despite the efforts of many different voluntary organizations there is, however, a great shortage of special schools and training institutions for the physically handicapped. The Ministry of National Education has only recently started to provide special classes attached to ordinary schools and to organize a home teaching service (largely by correspondence) for suitable cases.

In France, parents are responsible for the boarding costs of their children placed in residential schools. A special family allowance was recently instituted to help parents meet the expenses of educating and training children with severe handicaps, and failing this, the statutory social aid for the blind and severely handicapped, introduced in 1945, is available on the usual proof of need. A further Act of 1949 lays a duty on any parent or guardian to notify the *mairie* of any severely (over 80 per cent) and permanently incapacitated child in their care.

The Deprived

Even before children became the subject of a special statutory assistance in 1904, attempts to improve the lot of abandoned children had gone hand in hand with attempts to forestall their abandonment. So today, this departmental child care service not only covers most of the work of the British Children's Departments (with the additional powers given them under the Children and Young Persons Act, 1963), but also includes various measures which have been taken to prevent the desertion of children, such as the *maisons maternelles* and *hôtels maternels* (maternity, and mother and baby homes mainly for the unmarried mother) and the monetary allowances made to such mothers, and to deserted wives or husbands. In most departments this has become a highly specialized branch of social aid, in which the prefect, advised by a *Conseil de famille* of six members of which at least one must be a woman, and the departmental director and inspectors of health and welfare play important parts. A team of social workers in the service of the department is usually responsible for the field work—for finding and supervising foster homes, for keeping in touch with the maternity and children's Homes and with the work of voluntary organizations in this field. A distinction is made between:

(*a*) Children protected by the service. These may be *enfants surveillés* (supervision cases), *enfants secourus* (cases in which parents or relatives are receiving financial aid to bring up the child), *enfants recueillis temporairement* (sometimes referred to as '*enfants en dépôt*' —children who come into care temporarily while mother is in hospital, etc.) or *enfants en garde* (neglect or delinquency cases under fourteen where the court has committed the children to the child care service, but where the parents have only been partially deprived of parental rights and there is the possibility of the children being returned).

(*b*) Wards of the State (known up to 1943 as *pupilles de l'assistance publique*). These are the orphans and abandoned children and the children of parents who have been deprived of all parental rights.

Where the ill treatment or neglect of children has led to court action, the children will not necessarily be removed from their homes. The parents may be put under the supervision (*l'assistance éducative*) of a social worker named by the court and/or, in appropriate cases, someone other than the parents may be authorized to receive the family allowances on their behalf and to see that they are spent in the interests of the children (*la tutelle aux allocations familiales*).

The Delinquent

Special institutions for the treatment of juvenile delinquents were developed in France, as in most countries, in the course of the nineteenth century: voluntary societies for the protection of children, training Homes and schools, and later such public institutions as the children's judges, juvenile courts and reformatories which were regarded as part of the penal system. New thinking and new policies found expression in the important reforms of 1945 and 1951, when the jurisdiction of the *juges des enfants*, presiding over the *tribunal pour enfants*, was extended to young people up to the age of eighteen, and the administration of the state reformatories (renamed *établissements d'éducation surveillée*), and of the new observation and remand centres was transferred to a newly constituted section of the ministry of Justice, *la direction de l'éducation surveillée*. This equivalent of the Children's Branch of the Home Office in Britain also controls and supervises the probation service and the many voluntary institutions receiving delinquents, conducts research into the causes and treatment of juvenile delinquency, and in recent years has carried out a vigorous programme of training for all the specialist personnel needed if these various services are to be effective.

Under the age of 13 there is no criminal responsibility; from 13 to 18 there is a limited responsibility, but the emphasis is still on education, training, and, increasingly, medical or psychiatric treatment, rather than on punishment. Only in exceptionally serious cases can those between the ages of 16 to 18 be referred to the *Cour d'Assizes des mineurs* (where the children's judge sits as an assessor) or be sent to prison. The children's judge is competent to deal with civil (care, protection or control) as well as criminal cases, and is helped in deciding on the most appropriate treatment for each individual case by the social histories provided by specialist social workers and by the observation centres—voluntary ones, many set up quite recently by the new regional associations, and three state observation centres primarily for delinquents.

The French system of probation, *la liberté surveillée*, uses only a small core of professional probation officers (*les délégués permanents*) who are directly responsible to the judge for all young people put on probation, but who recruit, train and organize voluntary workers (*les délégués bénévoles*) to do most of the work with the probationers. The functions and training of the professional probation officer were laid down by the Ordinance of 1945 and are quite distinct from those of the *assistantes sociales spécialisées* who at the request of the children's judge provide the home surroundings report. These social workers are not servants of the court but are employed by the departmental child care service, voluntary child protection societies, family allowance Funds and other specialist agencies involved in one way or another with *l'enfance inadaptée*. The regional observation centres will have difficult cases referred to them by these agencies as well as by the courts. In fact, one of the main purposes of the *Associations régionales de Sauvegarde de l'Enfance et de l'Adolescence* is to ensure that legal and administrative boundaries do not prevent the best use being made of all the specialist facilities available for the diagnosis and treatment of these children's problems.

Family Welfare

Although the focus of the services just described is the maladjusted, the deprived, or the delinquent child, they are all deeply involved in family welfare. Much of their work is concerned with supporting, rehabilitating or supervising families which have broken down or are seriously threatened by difficulties or handicaps of child, or parent, or both. France is fortunate, however, in having one major social service concerned with the needs of ordinary families—the family allowance Funds. No British statutory service has such a clear mandate to meet family needs as such, although The Children and Young Persons Act, 1963, gives local authorities powers, and indeed the duty, to go some way in this direction for 'families at risk.'

In France the family allowance Funds are continually experimenting in new kinds of family service: in the careful training of their home helps,[1] in the grants available for the improvement of household equipment, in the thought and imagination given to the teaching of home and child care, in the employment of family social workers, and in the provision of Homes, foster homes and holiday camps to rest or relieve one or other member of the family. The emphasis is not, as it is in England, on child neglect and problem families but on education and timely help for ordinary families—preventive action throughout. And all these things are of interest and concern not only to the administrators of the Funds and to the family social workers, but to the workers' and employers' representatives serving on the board of each local Fund, who decide how the money allocated for welfare services in their area is to be spent. Finally, there are the Family Associations to stimulate and educate their members in all matters concerning family welfare, to organize mutual aid and self-help schemes (in the rural areas they run many co-operative ventures), and to act as a pressure group if the interest of the State in the family allowance Funds should flag.

[1] A special one-year course trains young women to become what might more appropriately be called mother's helps.

CHAPTER 6

The Welfare of Old People

In the early 1960s there were approaching 5½ million men and women over 65 in France, with a ratio of 2 men to 3·3 women. As has been shown, the proportion of old people in the population is increasing (11·9 per cent over 65 in 1960, 13·1 per cent in 1965), but the social services more especially concerned with their welfare have only recently come in for critical examination. In 1960 the Prime Minister[1] set up a committee under the chairmanship of M. Pierre Laroque to study the problems of old age, and in 1961, *Le Comité National de la Vieillesse de France* was formed of representatives of the many bodies concerned with old people and their problems. It is indeed the multiplicity of agencies, statutory and voluntary, contributing to this broad field of old people's welfare, and, in France particularly, the fact that so much of what the statutory bodies provide is of a permissive nature, that makes any clear description or assessment of the overall position so difficult. Nevertheless, the Laroque Report has succeeded in summarizing existing (1961) provisions, service by service, showing who runs them, their quantity, quality, and distribution. Moreover, in its conclusions and recommendations, it has indicated the developments and trends which point the way to a more adequate provision of welfare services for old people in the future.

The services which are already universally available (if only on a means test basis) are primarily those concerned with income-maintenance: pensions and assistance payments, special allowances for rent and for those in need of constant attendance, medical benefit under the insurance scheme, or free medical assistance under Social Aid for the many needy old people with no insurance cover. The only other statutory service which must be universally provided under the social aid legislation is residential care for the aged, infirm and incurable who are unable to look after themselves but are not in need of treatment in hospital. The Laroque Report found that most of

[1] Or more specifically the *Haut Comité Consultatif de la population et de la Famille*. Its report, published in 1962, is entitled *Politique de la Vieillesse* and is published by the Documentation Française.

this residential care for old people was still provided in large institutions (*hospices*) usually attached to, or linked with hospitals, providing shelter for the infirm and incurables of all ages as well as for old people. These institutions were quite unable to provide the homely atmosphere desirable for the more active old people, and too inadequately staffed to provide the medical supervision and nursing care needed by the more infirm. Only since 1958 has the departmental social aid service been encouraged to provide the less institutionalized type of Home for old people only (*Maison de Retraite*), which voluntary organizations had been providing for many years. The cost of a placement in an approved voluntary Home can be met by Social Aid, only if there is no place available in a public institution. In 1960 there were about 270,000 beds for old people in 2000 public hospices, and 70,000 in 1100 voluntary Homes. Fifteen thousand of the old people in these voluntary Homes were supported by their departmental social aid service. For the future the emphasis is on a greatly extended provision of smaller old people's Homes, and on closing down the bigger institutions and re-equipping a number of the smaller *hospices* to care for the aged infirm. It is also hoped with more special housing accommodation and better domiciliary services to reduce proportionately, if not absolutely, the numbers of old people in need of residential care.

Up to 1960, however, as the Laroque report shows, few old people had benefited from the post-war housing drive. No more than 15,000 of the quarter million entitled to the rent allowance were living in new houses or flats, and there had been only a few isolated experiments in various kinds of special accommodation, offering old people the privacy of their own room or flatlet, combined with certain communal facilities, such as a restaurant, laundry or home help. The report suggests that one million special housing units should be built for old people between 1961 and 1976, one-third of which should provide welfare facilities of this kind. Since 1954 Social Aid could meet the costs of old people in this sort of intermediate accommodation (*logement foyer*) instead of in a Home, but with so little provision available few had benefited. In 1959 the national and regional social insurance agencies set up a special fund, *d'action sociale vieillesse*,[1] which has been used, first and foremostly,

[1] These funds, referred to on page 23, receive their money from the National Solidarity Fund (financed largely from a special tax on motor cars), from the 0·10 per cent levy on social insurance contributions, and from interest on certain investments of the Regional Funds.

to promote the building of flats and, secondly, *maisons de retraite*. A number of the mutual insurance and occupational superannuation schemes are similarly investing considerable sums in the construction of special accommodation for old people.

Communes and social aid bureaux, social security agencies and voluntary bodies have used their permissive powers to develop a variety of services to help old people who are living in their own homes. Outside the discretionary but fairly widespread relief given (the modern tendency is to give in cash rather than in kind) to the neediest old people, the services which reach a wider group include meals services, home helps and friendly visiting, social and recreational facilities and holidays.

Restaurant clubs are one of the most extensively provided services, but even so the coverage is still very inadequate and the distribution uneven. The Ministry of Health and Population reported to the Laroque Committee that there were 702 restaurant services, 172 serving snacks and providing club facilities, 530 distributing daily some 33,000 meals. Of these 224 were run by social aid bureaux, 125 by communes and 181 by voluntary bodies.

The Laroque Report recommended that the number of meals served should be doubled in the next five years. Old people holding the *carte sociale des éconiquement faibles* are entitled to free meals if a restaurant service is provided in their district; others will usually be charged a small sum.

Home help services for old people are even less well developed, and most of the existing services are due to the initiative of voluntary bodies, although social aid and social security agencies may be contributing to their running costs. The Laroque Report recommended that the social security agencies should use their old people's welfare funds to develop this service in a more systematic way. In 1960 it found that there were only 135 services:

54 (40 per cent) run by religious organizations
34 (25 per cent) run by Family Associations
27 (20 per cent) run by other secular voluntary bodies
9 (+38 grant-aided) by social aid bureaux
2 (+64 grant-aided) by social insurance funds

It was impossible to estimate the number of old people helped or the number of home help hours provided to them by these various services, as many were also providing home helps for families.

These were pioneered by the Family Associations, supported by family allowance Funds, and were well established long before the service was extended to old people. On the other hand, some of the agencies mentioned above are providing home helps as part of a wider service to old people, which includes laundering, friendly visiting or a more extensive home care service.

Experiments in an all round home care service which provides medical supervision, nursing and chiropody, as well as welfare services, have been made by a number of voluntary organizations such as the Red Cross and by the Paris Public Assistance. They are usually based on a dispensary or on a district social service centre. Their experience is extremely valuable as pointing the way to a more adequate and co-ordinated service for the more infirm old people, but in 1960 they were only to be found in 22 departments. Any development on these lines would need to be supported by many more geriatric and psychogeriatric departments in hospitals, by day hospitals, convalescent homes and other extensions of hospital care to link up with the community care service.

While advocating a very considerable expansion of all these different agencies serving old people, the Laroque Committee was concerned with problems of co-ordination both at the planning and consumer level. It recommended that departments and large towns, working through representative old people's welfare committees on the pattern of the national committee, should be made responsible for a more systematic development of appropriate services, that there should be more social workers specializing in the problems of old people and that in each *quartier* or group of small villages there should be one point of contact for old people which would lead them to all the social services they needed.

CHAPTER 7

Social Work and Its Co-ordination

Despite, or perhaps because of the complexities of their social services the French have a much clearer concept of the function of social work than we have in Britain. '*On s'attache une assistante sociale*' and thereby ensures that the beneficiaries of a service (which may be a Fund, a hospital or a school) will be dealt with individually and confidentially, that their health and welfare needs will be recognized, that they will be helped to establish their rights to the social benefits to which they are entitled, and to make good use of these and of any other services available. These social workers have all taken a common training in one of the fifty-four (mainly private) schools of social work, and received a State Diploma without which they cannot use the title of *assistante sociale*, or be on the register of persons qualified to take up social work appointments in the public or semi-public social services, or in the voluntary organizations in receipt of public funds. There was a long history of experimenting with different qualifications for nurses, health visitors and social workers, and much rivalry between the different groups before the professions of nurse (*infirmière*) and social worker-cum-health visitor (*assistante sociale*) were finally reorganized by an Act of 8 April, 1946. A virtual monopoly of social work was then given to the state registered social worker, who was at the same time to be qualified to perform health visiting functions. Today every registered social worker has had at least three years' strictly vocational training to make her as they say '*bonne à tout faire*' in the spheres of health education and social work.

The first year of training, which is the same as that for student nurses, is primarily medical, and approximately half of the student social workers complete the second year of the course leading to the nursing diploma before going on to the second and third years of their social training. Since 1960 the syllabus has been revised and includes more specific teaching in the basic social work skills of case work, group work and community work.

Once in the field, however, only a certain proportion remain general social workers (*assistantes sociales polyvalentes*), working usually on a district basis and doing an all-round social and medical-social work job for the families with whom they are in contact. Many confine themselves to one field, working only with TB or cancer patients or with children in need of care and protection, because the agency which employs them is only concerned with these matters, or because they are employed by an institution such as a school, hospital, prison or factory, which requires that they spend a lot of their time within the institution and only visit in connection with the special problems of the group with which they are concerned. Others, such as those attached to psychiatric clinics or the police, have become specialized because their work genuinely demands specialized knowledge and skills, which they learn from experience on the job, and in special courses organized as part of an inservice training. The only specialist qualification organized by a school of social work is that for social workers in industry. The *Diplôme de Surintendente* is obtained after an additional two-year (part-time), or one year (full-time) course taken at the *École de Surintendentes* at Paris.[1]

Two-thirds of the 18,000 *assistants socials*, who between them carry out practically all the social work and health visiting services in France, are employed in the public (State or local cummunities) or semi-public (social security agencies of all kinds) sectors, and one-third by voluntary organizations or industrial enterprises. Although the schools of social work turn out some 800 qualified workers a year, recruitment is getting more and more difficult and is far from corresponding to needs. Some important services are grossly under-staffed and there is the usual problem of getting enough workers to cover the rural areas.

Although a few men have in recent years entered schools of social work to prepare themselves for some of the more specialized jobs, they are never likely to be attracted in large numbers. The profession will continue to recruit mainly women and will have to compete with the numerous other openings offered to girls these days. The arduous and tiring nature of their work can hardly be avoided, but salaries are unattractive (compared with those for nurses and teachers) and

[1] It is possible to obtain a recognized qualification as a *conseilleur de travail* (roughly equivalent to a personnel manager) without training as an *assistante sociale* first. This specialized training is sponsored by the Ministry of Labour and provided by the *Institut de Science Sociale et de Travail*. Somewhat similarly a specialized training for *délégués permanents* (probation officers) is provided by *La Direction d'Education Surveillée*, at the ministry of Justice.

their status is low and certainly not commensurate with their responsibilities. A reassessment of their whole position, particularly in relation to the administrators of the social services, is urgently needed.

While the 1946 Act organized the profession, and in giving all social workers a common training and status made co-operation in the field much more likely, it did nothing to improve their distribution (both geographically and within the social services) and the use that was made of their all round training. The Co-ordination Act of August 1950 was an attempt to achieve a more rational distribution and employment of social workers, to take full advantage of their common training and to create a better relationship between the general and specialist social workers. An earlier attempt to get more uniformity into the social services approached the problem rather differently and did not go far enough. The *Ordonnance* of 2 November, 1945, laid on the departmental health service the duty of seeing that its whole area was covered for maternity and child welfare, either through its own services or by agreement with a voluntary body such as the Red Cross, or a semi-public body such as one of the Funds. The 1950 Act has a more comprehensive approach, bringing all social services into its ken, and a different approach, in that co-ordination is to be brought about by a committee on which the social agencies employing social workers and the social workers to be co-ordinated are represented.

In brief, the Co-ordination Act lays down the following procedure:

(*a*) A Liaison Committee (*Comité départemental de liaison et de co-ordination*) shall be set up, presided over by the prefect and to which the Divisional Inspector of the Population[1] (of the Ministry of Health and Population) acts as secretary. As this committee will be very large, most of its powers will be delegated to an executive committee of from ten to twenty persons. The executive committee, like the Liaison Committee, will be composed of *ex officio* members and representatives of the social services, of the consumers and of the social workers. (Social services are defined as those services organized by public, semi-public or voluntary organizations, which provide a service to families or groups through the intermediary of registered social workers.)

(*b*) A census of all the social services in the department must be made through the prefect and the Divisional Inspector of Population.

[1] Now the departmental Director of Health and Welfare.

Each social service must decide whether it wishes to be considered as offering a general or specialist service.

(*c*) The task of the Liaison Committee is to draw up and apply a scheme for co-ordinating the social services of the department. When drawn up this scheme must be approved by the Ministry of Health and Population and will then be made compulsory by a prefectoral order.

(*d*) Any organization refusing to fall in with the scheme may state its case before the executive committee and has a right of appeal to the Minister. The only power the committee has over voluntary organizations is to suggest to the public and semi-public bodies that they withdraw their approval and financial support. (Most voluntary organizations of any importance are receiving some public money. Presumably the prefect or Ministry could bring to heel any public or semi-public body which was refusing to co-operate.)

(*e*) The Liaison Committee should, if it sees fit, include in its scheme of co-ordination a secretariat, a mutual register and an information service.

(*f*) The co-ordinating service is to be financed by contributions from the services co-ordinated according to the number of social workers they employ and of their beneficiaries. The social security organizations will be assessed for the second contribution even if they do not employ any social workers.

The Act was passed in 1950, but the regulations for its application were not issued until 10 July, 1951. These regulations amplified the definition of general and specialist social services, laid down the way in which the various representatives to the Liaison Committee were to be elected[1] and established the principle that if a secretariat or mutual register is set up it must be under the direction of a social worker, to ensure that the confidence of clients is respected. The regulations also deal with the timing of the different stages in establishing a co-ordination service.[2]

It is not yet possible to make any general assessment of the results of this Act. Liaison and executive committees for co-ordination were duly set up, the 'census' made and schemes approved, although there

[1] Only social workers of at least five years' standing are eligible for membership but any registered social worker can vote for her representatives.

[2] The texts of the Act, the regulations and a circular elaborating the provisions of the Act still further for the benefit of the prefects and Divisional Inspectors of Health and Population, are to be found in *Informations Sociales* 1951, 'La Co-ordination des Services Sociaux'.

was considerable dragging of feet in some departments. How far the systems which finally came into operation were an improvement on such informal co-operation as existed before must vary enormously from department to department, as the pattern of services and the problems involved in their co-ordination will have varied. But the Act was liberally conceived, left much to local initiative and avoided giving any precise directions as to how co-ordination should be achieved.

A short description of one scheme, which came into force in 1955 in one department of France, Indre-et-Loire,[1] can only show one way of tackling the job.

In this department the Liaison Committee has 150 members, meets once a year to receive an annual report and to pass the budget for the next year. The Executive Committee has 20 members and meets four or five times a year as needed. There are 145 social workers to be co-ordinated:

33 general social workers *de secteur*, employed by the municipality of Tours or the department and working on a district basis.

58 general social workers *de catégorie*, employed by the Family Allowance Fund and the special schemes (in a predominantly rural department mainly the Agricultural Mutual Social Insurance Fund) and some voluntary agencies.

54 specialized social workers.

The town of Tours and the rural areas are each divided into districts, two general social workers being assigned to each *secteur*. In the town, one of these social workers is employed by the municipality and one by the Family Allowance Fund; in the rural areas, one by the department and one by the Agricultural Fund. Thus for the basic health visiting and general family social work the clients are left with some choice of social worker. Moreover, if they are beneficiaries of some other special Fund (e.g. those employed in the mines, the railways or the army), or of some local voluntary service, such as a dispensary or welfare centre run by the Red Cross or a religious body, they may prefer to be served by its general social worker *de catégorie*, rather than by either of those specifically assigned to their district.

[1] A pretty average department as regards size, density and structure of its population, etc.

Where a specialist social service, such as that of the courts or a mental health clinic, has some concern with the family, the specialist social worker must get in touch with the general social worker, who has what is called the *prise en charge* of that family, and work with or through her. A specialist social worker (such as a TB visitor or moral welfare worker), who is not tied by an institutional allegiance, may temporarily take over the whole family if it is more convenient that she should, while concerning herself primarily with the sufferer from TB or the child in moral danger, deal with any family problems which may arise. These might involve advice to a nursing mother or the investigation of an application to the Family Allowance Fund for a home help or a holiday for the children.

The mechanics of this system of co-ordination is a mutual register (*fichier*) kept by a permanent secretary and a part-time assistant, who deal with all enquiries and to whom the social workers must notify all their *prises en charge* or interventions, and any changes in the address of their clients, any transfer of responsibility or closing of a case. This involves only the recording of a few identifying facts about each family (name, address, occupation); any substantial co-operation, in the sense of sharing information or consultation, is left to the social workers concerned. This vital co-operation can be assisted or encouraged but not guaranteed by a mutual register. The *Déléguée Technique à la Co-ordination*, a senior social worker chosen for her tact and acceptability to all and sundry, can do more to foster the spirit of co-operation, and smooth out the difficulties which inevitably arise between social workers over particular cases.

In this department, the *déléguée* is appointed for six years and has a deputy who succeeds her. During her term of office she remains in her own job but is lent to the co-ordination service by her employer for a few hours each week. She has one regular weekly session at the office when any social workers worried about any lack of co-operation can come and see her, and short of personality problems most difficulties can usually be sorted out in this way. As well as keeping an eye on the register and dealing with inquiries from outside the department, she organizes an information service, a small library, regular meetings and conferences for social workers and their employers, and tries to increase opportunities for all social workers in the department to pursue advanced training or refresher courses. In this she is adding locally to the provisions made nationally or regionally by the *Association Nationale d'Assistantes Sociales* (ANAS).

The first two *déléguées* to be chosen were not employed by any of the major services—they were in fact both *surintendentes*, employed by industrial concerns. But now that the smaller services have more confidence in the scheme, the third *déléguée* is employed by the Family Allowance Fund, and her deputy by the Agricultural Fund. It is hoped to give each service a turn in supplying the *déléguée*.

Co-ordination in the thickly populated *Département de la Seine* (there are nearly 6 million inhabitants in the 80 suburban communes and the 20 *arrondissements* of Paris proper), with 4500 social workers to co-ordinate, is a different matter. The present system is the result of over 30 years' experience, beginning with the successful co-ordination of maternity and child welfare work by a voluntary organization in the 1930s.[1] Another voluntary organization, the *Groupement d'Action des Services Sociaux du Département de la Seine*, extended the co-operation achieved in the field of maternity and child welfare to other social services, and in 1948 this became a prefectorial service, *Le Service Départemental de la Co-ordination des Services Socieux de la Seine*. Today this service is well established, and has a large budget mainly subscribed by the local authorities and the social security organizations, although a small subscription is asked of every affiliated organization.

The department is divided into 100 areas (the 20 arrondissements and 80 communes) over each of which is a *déléguée à la co-ordination* elected by her fellows. Her secretariat is normally housed in the local town hall, where she has her mutual register, her information service and her regular office hours, during which she is available and provides a sort of Citizens Advice Bureau. She has her area divided into districts, the number of which varies from one in such small communes as Sceaux and Fresnes to thirty-five in the twentieth *arrondissement*. Each district is the responsibility of one of the general social workers (in some districts assisted by others), who does all the visiting of families in her area unless: (*a*) the client, whose free choice must be respected (though it is rarely exercised) expresses a wish to be visited by one of the other general social workers; (*b*) the family belongs to some special group, with its own general social workers covering its members in that area; (*c*) the intervention of a specialist social worker is necessary. Only a small proportion of the 1300 district general social workers are employed by the departmental Co-ordination Service, the rest are so to speak

[1] See p. 62.

lent to the service by other agencies—by the social insurance and family allowance Funds, by the voluntary organizations and municipalities.

The prefecture provides an information and advisory service for its 100 *déléguées*, who in their turn provide a similar service for the social workers of their *arrondissement* or commune. Moreover, a good *déléguée* holds a watching brief for her area and is continually looking out for new ways of cutting out overlapping and wasted effort and of filling gaps in the existing services—gaps which the system of co-ordination itself is continually revealing. Much therefore turns on her establishing good relationships, not only with her fellow social workers, but with the various officials at the local town hall. She has a Local Co-ordinating Committee, presided over by the mayor or his representative, which she must carry with her, for this is the body which is officially responsible to the prefectorial *Conseil de Surveillance* for carrying out its policies at local level.

While the Co-ordination Act of 1950 was obviously drawn up in the light of the system evolved for the department of the Seine, it has not been possible to follow quite the same pattern in Paris as in the rest of the country. The departmental Liaison Committee envisaged in the Act would mean a Committee of 900 persons in the Seine. So the *Conseil de Surveillance* has been retained, but a recent decree has increased its social workers' representatives from two to ten, corresponding to the ten new divisions into which the 100 areas have been organized. This (assuming they choose good people to represent them) should do something to strengthen the position and influence of social workers at the central planning level. It is after all *their* services which are being co-ordinated. But in the last analysis most depends on the quality of those chosen as *déléguées*, the local leaders, for it is only at local level that fruitful co-operation between those in direct contact with clients is achieved, and that the many different social services support and supplement rather than cut across each other.

SUGGESTIONS FOR FURTHER READING

Books such as Ridley and Blondel's *Public Administration in France*, and articles of particular interest in various journals, are fully referred to in the footnotes. The following, however, represent the *principal sources of on-going information and commentary* on social administration in France.

1. *Documentation Française* (14–16 rue Lord Byron, Paris 8°) publishes general descriptive works like *Les Institutions Sociales de la France*, 3 vols. (An English translation by Pierre Laroque is now available.) Or important reports like *Politique de la Vieillesse* (in French only). Some shorter straightforward descriptions of the French social security services are published from time to time in English.

2. *CEDIAS* (Musée Social, Paris 62.68) publishes up-to-date guides to the social services in considerable detail and in French only, e.g.:

Guides des Assurances Sociales
Guide d'Aide Sociale
Guide de la Famille
Guide du Logement
Guide du Travail

3. *The U.S. Dept. of Health Education and Welfare* Social Security Administration, Division of Research and Statistics (US Government Printing Office, Washington, DC) publishes reports on social security services in other countries from time to time. Of particular interest is Research Report No. 7 by Alvin Schorr, 'Social Security and Social Services in France', 1965.

4. Notes and articles providing up-to-date information and commentary on developments in the French social services also appear from time to time in the *following journals:*

Informations Sociales, published by the *Union Nationale des Caisses d'Allocations Familiales* (47, rue de la Chaussée d'Antin, Paris 9°)

and of course, though less frequently, in the *ISSA* (154, rue de Lausanne, Geneva) *Bulletin* and in the *ILO Review*.

NORWAY

CHAPTER 1

Introduction

Norway is a land of paradoxes. A third of the country lies north of the Arctic Circle, but the weather is often milder in the far north than in the south-east. There is much puritanism, but far less religious observance. People are strongly individualistic, but have developed a high degree of collectivism. Local authorities are self-assertive, but central control is firm, extensive, detailed—and increasing. The country is poor in natural resources, but living standards are among the highest in the world, and social and economic policies are ambitious. Climatic conditions, which might have discouraged attempts to aim for high standards of social provision seem, instead, to have spurred stubborn efforts—with impressive and sometimes remarkable results. The environment cannot be ignored in Norway, a mellow co-existence with nature is possible for only a few months of the year during the short and bountiful summer.

Norway is a mountainous sub-arctic country, 'gouged and weather-carved' as the national anthem says. It lies between 58° and 71°N—in roughly the same latitudes as Siberia or Alaska, but the worst effects of the Arctic climate which might otherwise turn much of the country into a desert of snow and frozen rock is held back by the relatively warm mass of the North Atlantic. The country is long and narrow, stretching some 1200 miles from north to south. About 70 per cent of its surface consists of mountainous rock, and there is a jagged and fragmented coastline strung with about a hundred thousand islands. The mountain masses are carved by deep valleys and fjords. Something like 20 per cent of the surface is covered by forest, and official estimates suggest that no more than 6 per cent of the land is cultivable. In fact, only 3 per cent is under cultivation and the rest is of marginal quality—usually being boulder-strewn, scrubby, and having a thin soil cover. About 85 per cent of bread grain, high proportions of most other foodstuffs, and half the animal fodder have to be imported.

Despite the moderating influence of the Atlantic, summers are short and become rapidly shorter as one moves north. Winters are long and icy—though less cold on the west and south-west coasts—and particularly cold in the central and eastern regions.

Norway covers an area of 124,000 square miles and is, therefore, larger than Great Britain (121,600 square miles), but has a population of only 3·7 million—about one-fourteenth of Britain's. A third of the population lives around the Oslo fjord in the south-east with almost half a million living in the capital itself. Apart from Oslo there are only three towns with 100,000 or more people—and two of them only exceed that figure by extending their boundaries widely to include surrounding districts with low residential densities. Bergen, second in status to Oslo and once a great Hanseatic port, has about 130,000 inhabitants. Trondheim now has a larger population than Bergen, but this has come about recently through the inclusion of some suburban districts. Outside a few urban centres the population is strung thinly in valleys or along coasts and islands—400,000 people or 11 per cent of the population live on islands—but industrialization and urbanization are increasing and many more people are moving to the towns.

Norway has very few mineral resources worth exploiting commercially. There is some iron and some copper-bearing ore in the north, and small deposits of pyrites, lead and sulphur. The mainland has no coal, but 300,000 tons a year are mined on Spitzbergen—this is, however, a relatively unimportant source of fuel. Coal and oil are imported but (apart from oils and petrol for road transport) their importance is declining as the output of hydro-electric power increases. Norway has the highest consumption of electricity per inhabitant in the world—by the early 1960s it was double that in the United States—and water-produced power is the country's greatest natural and industrial asset. Trees and fish are the other two, but their significance is diminishing as new light industries are developed. However, since some of the new industries are devoted to producing by-products of timber and fish, these old primary industries are unlikely to disappear.

The very large merchant marine—third biggest in the world, with about seven times as much tonnage per head of population as the United Kingdom—makes a major contribution to the Norwegian economy and to individual living standards. About 20 per cent of capital investment goes into shipping.

INTRODUCTION

Against the background of poor natural resources, a small and scattered population, the heavy dependence on the terms of foreign trade and on the world demand for freight shipping, social and economic policies in Norway might appear over-ambitious or even grandiose, but the achievements in each are convincing. Gross national product *per capita* is higher than in Britain, average earnings are about as high (but differentials between top and bottom groups are much narrower), and the social services are comparable in scope and levels of provision with those in Britain. In the mid-sixties about 38 per cent of public expenditure was for social purposes excluding housing, and over half of this was spent by the municipalities.

Economic and social planning are highly developed and closely integrated. Among the most important aims of economic and social policies are: full employment; a high degree of income redistribution through taxation and the social services; a comprehensive system of social insurance; extensive health and welfare services; and a high rate of house building. The insurance, health and welfare schemes form the structural framework of the Norwegian 'Welfare State' and they embrace the whole population. 'Comprehensiveness and universality' is one of the most important concepts of Norwegian social policy.

Within the wide framework of social provision particular attention is paid to the most vulnerable groups within the population—children, the aged, handicapped, widows and unmarried mothers, and alcoholics—and the expansion and improvement of services for these people have been given further priority in recent years.

Though countries may resemble each other broadly in their economic and social structures—and in economic and social policies—they can never be identical since each country has its unique combination of historical, geographical, cultural and other features. Each country produces its own pattern of social problems and the means selected for coping with them will tend to be influenced both by the society's needs and the resources available to it. Demographic, economic, political and administrative factors are particularly important in helping to generate needs on the one hand and social policies and administrative arrangements on the other.

DEMOGRAPHIC FACTORS

The most important facts about the Norwegian population are that it is small and scattered. The pattern of population growth since the beginning of the nineteenth century has been fairly characteristic of western Europe. The population almost doubled between 1800 and the middle of the century but then grew more slowly, increasing by a third between 1855 and 1900. This comparison is deceptive, however, as during that period well over half a million emigrated from Norway—and the home population rose by only 750,000. The outflow of population continued until about 1920, but at a reduced rate.

In the twentieth century, in common with other European countries, population has increased more slowly and the rate of growth was apparently influenced by the great economic depressions between the wars, which affected Norway particularly badly. Since the end of the depression in the mid-thirties the rate of increase has risen—apart from the war years—and Norway had a post-war 'bulge' in the birth-rate comparable to that in Britain and elsewhere. The Norwegian population is increasing almost twice as fast as in Britain—rising by an average of almost 1 per cent a year compared with about 0·5 per cent in the UK. The fertility rate in Norway is not much higher than in Britain—it is about 2·5 in urban areas and 3 in rural—but a higher proportion of the population (over 40 per cent) is rural, though the proportion is declining. The age at marriage has fallen steadily since the war and this has helped to increase the birth-rate.

The crude birth-rate was about 30 per thousand in 1900, 14 per thousand in the mid-thirties—before the depression ended—20 per thousand during the post-war bulge, and is now about 17 per thousand of the population. The mortality-rate has declined more rapidly than the birth-rates and this has contributed substantially to the rate of increase in population. At the beginning of the century the mortality-rate was 15 per thousand but by 1956–60 it had fallen to 9 per thousand and has been held constant at this level. The expectation of life in Norway is one of the highest in the world, being almost 72 years for men and over 75 for women.

The proportions of the population in the dependent groups are quite large, in 1965:

24·8 per cent were aged 0–14 years
7·6 per cent were aged 15–19 years
50·0 per cent were aged 20–60 years
18·5 per cent were aged 60 or over

8·0 per cent were aged 70 or over
49·5 per cent of population were men
50·5 per cent of population were women

Note. The figures are estimates derived from official statistics.

The productive group in the population—the age groups from which most of the labour force is drawn—is that between 20 and 70. With a quarter of the population aged 14 or under—and almost a third under 19—social policy has emphasized health and welfare services, income maintenance benefits, family allowances, education and housing for families and children. At the other end of the age scale particular attention has been paid to retirement pensions, medical care, welfare services and housing. In the economically 'productive' age groups, apart from social services universally available, developments have provided income during unemployment, occupational injuries, disability and other circumstances causing loss of income. In addition, there has been growing emphasis on rehabilitation and retraining.

ECONOMIC FACTORS

Central economic planning began in earnest in 1946 with the introduction of annual budgets as part of reconstruction planning after the war. These budgets were one-year economic plans and not confined to financial or fiscal matters. In 1949 the first 'long term programme' was launched and it covered the next four years. There has been a new programme for every four-year period since then and each plan embraces economic and social policies over a very wide front and in considerable detail. The annual budget is integrated with the four-year programmes, enabling them to remain flexible during their implementation. The long-term programmes are regarded as phases of a continuous process of 'rolling' planning.

The Norwegian economy was severely damaged by economic depression in the 1920s and the first half of the thirties, and was just recovering strongly when war came. By the time the war ended the economy had been partly devastated: industrial production in 1945 was 40 to 50 per cent lower than in 1938, machinery and equipment had been allowed to wear out, all buildings and services over a large area of northern Norway had been deliberately razed by the German army, much of the merchant fleet had been sunk, and part of the population had been compulsorily evacuated to areas of the country far from their homes. About a fifth of the national wealth had been destroyed. These facts are important, for they may help to account for the common agreement between political parties on what needed to be done and, very largely, on how reconstruction should be achieved. An unusually high degree of government planning was prescribed, implemented, and generally accepted—and collective measures were the main instruments in economic and social policies.

A remarkable reconstruction programme was concluded in the early fifties. The government then turned its full attention to a simultaneous expansion of the economy and the provision or improvement of a growing range of social services. The policies of the past decade or so have been directed to a fulfilment of the aspirations of the immediate post-war years. To attain these aims, taxation and investment were early raised to high levels and kept there. Norway has the highest rate of taxation on personal incomes in Europe and also invests a higher proportion of gross national product than any other country except Switzerland. Gross investment has remained fairly constant for years at about 28 per cent of GNP, compared with about 17 per cent in Britain. From the late fifties this stringent policy began to show striking results. By the first half of the sixties industrial production was rising by 6 or 7 per cent a year and the average increase in gross national product per head of population was 4 per cent a year. The current four-year plan expects this rate of increase to continue. The rapid improvement in living standards (a rise of about two-thirds in real terms in not much over a decade) has been widely spread among the population by means of adjustments in wage levels, steeply progressive taxation, food subsidies, housing grants and subsidized loans, improved benefits and pensions in social insurance, extensive building programmes in housing, education, industry and the infra-structure of regions (with special priority for the less developed areas), and the expansion of the social services generally.

These improvements are associated with far-reaching changes in the economy and in society itself. Industrialization and urbanization are rapid. The old basic industries of agriculture, fishing, whaling, sealing and forestry, which have declined rapidly as employers of labour since the thirties, now employ about 15 per cent of the work force. Manufacturing has not increased its share of the labour force very greatly since 1938—the proportion has risen from 30 per cent to 33 per cent—but the output has more than trebled in the intervening period. The most rapid expansion has taken place in service occupations, which now employ more labour than the other two industrial categories.

In 1945 less than half the population lived in towns or other relatively densely populated places; by 1960 this had risen to 57 per cent. The urban population has been growing by about 2 per cent a year since the second half of the 1950s—or roughly twice as fast as the national growth in population. It is predicted that by 1980 about 75 per cent of the population will live in urban areas.

A large share of the increase in urban population comes from internal migration (the net effect of international migration is negligible). The movement is from thinly populated rural and coastal areas to local, regional and national centres where economic growth is most vigorous. Of the 454 municipalities in Norway, half have fewer people now than five years ago and the flow continues.

Migration creates (or exacerbates) problems for social policy to solve both in the peripheral communities and the rapidly growing towns. Special economic and social measures have been used in efforts to reduce the difficulties of declining communities, including improvements in schools, housing, medical and welfare services, employment, and a number of other measures. In the towns which attract migrants, the problems which develop are mainly associated with rising demand for houses, schools, further education, medical and welfare services for mothers, children and young people, and the kinds of social insurance benefits which go to these age groups. 'Social care'—the co-ordinated provision of (or access to) a range of services through a single welfare office—is an important new development in social policy, particularly in urban areas.

POLITICAL AND ADMINISTRATIVE FACTORS

Reference has already been made to the apparent paradox of rigorous individualism and yet of highly developed collective effort on Norway. Geography, climate, history and religion have all contributed to these characteristics and helped to shape the political structures and attitudes. Until comparatively recently most Norwegians have been independent smallholders (scarcely farmers), fishermen, forestry workers or engaged in a combination of these occupations to make a modest living. They lived in scattered small settlements, individual smallholdings, or tiny fishing hamlets sometimes of no more than two or three families. Much of their lives was spent in small working groups, but a good deal of it might be solitary except for seeing other members of the family. Conditions were generally harsh and, spread over the year, the yields from agriculture and fishing were low. The three main occupations were particularly vulnerable to bad weather. Too much rain in the short growing season, prolonged stormy winds when the fish were due, or a winter of unusually heavy snow, could make all the difference between subsistence and starvation to hundreds of small communities. People were well aware of their dependence upon one another in the face of natural hazards and it is from such circumstances that collectivism has developed.

Government action to deal with poverty began in 1845—though there had been local efforts centuries earlier—and the Poor Law was soon followed by public health legislation. The importance of the local community and the tradition of local self-government have been recognized in social legislation since then, despite the increasing centralization of policy-making.

The Central Government has always been sensitive to the marked differences in conditions and opportunities in different parts of Norway, and social and economic policies have become steadily more specific in formulating measures to meet the needs of certain groups or districts. Regional policies are gradually being formulated to provide the framework and means for social and economic improvement at the local level, and co-ordination at regional level between central government and local authorities is taking shape.

Rising aspirations and standards in social provision (as part of steady improvements in material standards generally) have accelerated the processes of centralization. The small national population distributed in small groups—often widely separated—has meant that municipalities are usually not strong enough in resources to provide or even administer the growing variety of social services. These services are becoming more expensive; they depend increasingly upon larger numbers of trained personnel to perform and administer them; and they require larger populations and greater resources to make them viable.

The smallness and physical inadequacy of local authorities has influenced the administration of the social services in three different, but related, ways:

(*a*) a number of social services in every municipality are provided through the local offices of central government agencies (as in social insurance and services related to employment);
(*b*) there is extensive reliance upon collaboration with voluntary organizations;
(*c*) local government is being reformed.

To take the last point first; the political importance of the municipality (*kommune*) has declined and greater powers have been given to the county (*fylke*) in recent years. At the same time many of the least populated municipalities have been amalgamated (reducing the total from 732 in 1960 to 454 in 1967) as part of the process of making social and economic administration more effective.

MUNICIPALITIES

Despite centralization—a trend which will also be familiar to students of British local government—Norwegian municipalities retain considerable independence and perform a number of important functions. They are responsible for education, health and welfare services, and social assistance. And most people live in municipalities with their own old age pension schemes which are separate from, which supplement and are not intended to replace, national and occupational schemes. Municipalities also own and manage public utilities—such as water and electricity supplies—as well as having responsibilities for roads, refuse disposal, and fire protection. They are active in providing cultural services, and own art galleries, museums, public libraries, theatres, and 85 per cent of all cinemas, as well as other cultural amenities. Parks, recreation areas, athletics and football grounds and a wide range of other leisure facilities including skating rinks, swimming baths and skiing facilities are important items in municipal provision.

Municipalities are the primary tax authorities: they levy income and property taxes (though the latter are of comparatively little significance). They collect taxes for the state as well as themselves, and are not permitted to retain more than a certain proportion of tax revenues for their own purposes. Nevertheless, in 1964 63·5 per cent of tax revenues went to the municipalities. An increasing share of municipal revenue is passed on to the developing county administrations—a quarter of all municipal tax incomes is now passed on to the counties—which were of limited importance until recently but whose administrative and political powers are growing steadily.

Local authorities in Norway receive relatively less financial assistance from the state than those in Britain, and not much more than a fifth of municipal expenditure is covered by government grants. In contrast to Britain, again, more than a half of public spending on education is provided by the communes themselves, as is two-thirds of spending on health services, and a half of expenditure on employment services. They also take a major role in financing social work services. To some extent, however, comparisons between Norway and Britain in respect of the central government contribution to local government finance are not valid since, in Norway, the state has given local authorities power to tax incomes and wealth directly and to retain up to the equivalent of 19 per cent of total taxable income. This means that local authorities retain at source some revenue which in Britain passes directly to the state through the income tax system then to be used or redistributed by the government. Another important difference is that the municipal income tax system is much more sensitively adjusted to changes in the general levels of local economic activity and incomes than a property rating system which is the basis of local public finance in Britain. Municipalities may therefore benefit directly from the rapid general increase in incomes, but it also means that they are affected just as quickly by falling income levels. Redistribution at the local level to redress some of the imbalance in incomes and needs takes place, both through county administration and the provision of certain educational services, hospitals, hydro-electric schemes, roads, and in other expensive capital projects, and through an income equalization scheme operated by the state. This may be compared to the rates equalization arrangements in Britain, and its purpose is to try to ensure that municipalities with low tax incomes—usually in rural areas with small populations—can be brought up to around the average income level. More broadly, redistribution is carried out through central government social and economic policies of various kinds as in Britain and other countries.

COUNTIES

The word '*fylke*'—which comes from 'folk' or 'people'—is usually translated as 'county' in English, but this is likely to mislead both

British and North American readers. Compared in size with an English county, the average *fylke* is something between a county and a province—except for Oslo and Bergen, which are roughly equivalent to English county boroughs.

Norway is divided for administrative purposes into 20 *fylker*—or counties—each of which consists of from 15 to 40 municipalities (*kommuner*), except for Oslo and Bergen, which are single-unit county-municipalities. At the time of the 1960 census the *fylker* ranged in size from 37 (Bergen) to 48,641 (Finnmark) square kilometers, and in population from 74,589 (Finnmark) to 483,196 (Oslo).

The county is the second tier in the structure of government. Municipalities form the first tier (and primary units) and, strictly speaking, the county does not have a separate existence. In law the *fylke* consists of the municipalities in a given area—without them, therefore, it would not exist.

Counties are subjected to stricter control than communes by central government. The county budget must be approved by the Ministry of Local Government and Labour, which is also called upon to decide all questions receiving less than two-thirds of the votes in the annual meeting of the county council (*fylkesting*). The day-to-day administration of the county is carried on by a committee consisting of the county governor (*fylkesmann*) and four members who are elected by the county council—which is made up of the mayors of each commune together with the county governor (who has no vote at council meetings).

In general, the county undertakes tasks which the primary communes are too small to fulfil adequately, but its functions are becoming more comprehensive with the expansion of government policy measures. With the emergence of district and regional planning the importance of county administration increases and county governors have been given direct responsibility for physical planning. A recent building and planning measure (Building Act, 1965), broadly comparable to a fairly permissive town and country planning act, placed further emphasis on the county as an administrative and co-ordinating agency.

The county governor in Norway has no real equivalent in English local government. He is more akin to the departmental prefect in France, but has less power (up to now) and is less 'political'. Appointment of *fylkesmann* is made by the government and is a post of high status—Trygve Lie became a county governor after his term as Secretary-General of the United Nations. As head of the 'county commune'—consisting of the municipalities in his administrative area—the county governor is the government's representative at the semi-local level. One of his functions is also to interpret local conditions and problems to the central government. The importance of the governor's role is growing as the functions of the county increase, and he is one of the most influential agents of central administration at a time of expanding government activity. Thus, although centralization of policy-making is a strong trend in government, there is also growing activity at county level. This is an important feature of government efforts to rationalize the structure of local government. The municipalities are still vigorous and reorganization is intended to make them more effective, not to strip them of their powers.

REGIONS

There are no political or administrative regions in Norway comparable with Wales or Scotland in the United Kingdom though, as in Britain, various kinds of region are recognized for specific purposes and defined accordingly, with the result that 'trading regions' do not coincide with 'transport regions', for example. Five geographical regions are recognized, but this is of little practical significance in social or economic planning.

Administrative regions are not—so far at any rate—of administrative or political importance. Largely, one suspects, because the country is so vast in relation to population. Most people live on the coastal periphery, cross-country communications are poor or non-existent over large parts of the country, and much of inner Norway is of extremely limited economic value.

VOLUNTARY AGENCIES

Reliance on voluntary services may seem anachronistic in a society where economic and social planning by the state are so highly developed, but the voluntary agencies are themselves collectivist in inspiration, origin and operation. They are examples of popular self-help in a direct form.

The voluntary agencies are not isolated from state or municipality. They receive financial and other assistance from both, collaborate with official bodies, act within the framework of national policies and legislation and are, to varying degrees in different areas of their work, quasi-agents for the fulfilment of major social policies. But the voluntary organizations also have other roles: they raise funds, train social workers, provide clinics and hospitals, and many other social services. In some fields, particularly in health and welfare, they provide parallel institutions or services to those supplied by the state. Their work is especially important in sparsely populated areas.

As in other countries, the voluntary organizations in Norway were created and flourished in the absence of other forms of provision and in response to very pressing social needs—especially poverty and sickness. They have remained fairly responsive to needs, improving their methods and altering policies and services to meet new or changed needs, and have attracted substantial government support. Voluntary agencies are an integral part of the administrative structure of social services in Norway.

NORWAY AND SCANDINAVIA

The five Scandinavian countries (Norway, Sweden, Denmark, Finland and Iceland) have achieved a high degree of co-operation over a wide range of policies and activities. Apart from constant discussions between governments, ministries and other official agencies, there is a Scandinavian parliament—the Nordic Council—which meets once a year to discuss matters of common interest and make recommendations to member governments on the basis of the conclusions reached in the debates.

Co-operation has developed rapidly since the war and is becoming closer. Social policies in each country tend to have some repercussions in the others. This is partly because there are conscious efforts to reach the highest possible standards of provision—so that a major policy change in one country leads to self-scrutiny and, frequently, emulation in another—but it is also because nationals of the five countries are also virtually Scandinavian citizens. If they reside in one of the other countries, they enjoy the same social security and health service rights as the nationals of that country. There are normally no customs barriers and no immigration (passport) controls between the Scandinavian countries. In many respects the degree of freedom of movement, individual identification with the Scandinavian concept, and the benefits of membership, is higher here than ever it was in the Commonwealth.

CHAPTER 2

Development of Social Security

As in Britain and most other countries the care of the poor and helpless was for centuries the responsibility of kinsfolk and, beyond them, the local community. If, indeed, any care was given for it, it often amounted to no more than being allowed the freedom to beg. Impoverished communities lacked the resources needed to provide for even poorer individuals. Some forms of assistance sound familiar to students of the Poor Law in England. In Norway, up to the middle of the nineteenth century, orphans and paupers, young and old, were bound out to farmers or others who accepted responsibility for maintaining them in return for whatever work they could perform. Local authorities paid small sums to the employers of paupers. The churches continued their age-old tradition of collecting alms, but this was a harsh land and when the crops or the fish failed—as they frequently did—whole districts or regions were stricken by hunger and disease and there were few to dispense charity. In the long famine years people tried to exist on flour ground from tree bark.

The first national effort to organize and administer relief came with the *Poor Relief Acts* in 1845, and it is interesting to compare their provisions with the 1834 legislation in England. These Acts—one applied to towns and the other to rural districts—gave each municipality power to set up commissions for the poor. The commissions could collect and distribute funds to persons who were unable to support themselves—the old, sick, disabled, and orphans. The Acts represented the first tangible acceptance by the state of responsibility for those who needed assistance. Legislation relating to mental illness was introduced shortly after the Relief Acts and the first Public Health Act was passed in 1860. The statutes concerning poor relief, mental illness and public health created a foundation for the elaborate structure of social legislation which has been built up over the past century—just as the Poor Law and public health legislation in Britain evolved into the 'Welfare State'.

There was a long pause after the early activity in Norway. Meanwhile, dislocation and hardship, created by a rapid growth in population and the beginning of industrialization, increased the need for organized and more substantial relief. The second half of the nineteenth century in Norway was a time of suffering. There were waves of emigration to North America and elsewhere, unrest among the new urban workers, and growing pressure for more effective social action. Although poor relief was disliked generally, and long experience of it led to pressures for reform and the eventual separation of aid from conditional charity—there was not the same widespread hatred of poor relief as in England. But this was due more to differences in social structure than to anything else.

There have been four stages in the development of social insurance in Norway. The first stage covered fifty years from 1885 to the mid-1930s; but the second lasted barely a decade, spanning the period from the end of the great inter-war depression to the beginning of post-war reconstruction in 1946. The third stage was the one in which the foundations of the 'welfare state' were laid and the frame of the main structure built. This took about twelve years and by the end of the 1950s the fourth stage—of integration, co-ordination and expansion—was being planned. The last stage began to take shape in the 1960s and the National Insurance Scheme (described in the next chapter) is one of its central features.

First Stage

The first move in the development of social insurance and the protection of labour came with the setting up of a government commission in 1885 to investigate working conditions. The Commission's draft Bill of 1892 and the subsequent industrial legislation of the nineties were modelled partly on Bismarck's policies and statutes, and partly on the new industrial legislation in Britain. The Bill proposed accident insurance for industrial workers and also a health insurance scheme. The *Industrial Accident Insurance Act* was passed in 1894, but no action was taken over the proposals for health insurance. Accident insurance was extended much later to two other very important groups of workers in the basic industries—fishermen in 1908 and seamen in 1911. As in Britain and other countries, the first steps towards social insurance were taken in the industrial sector—for economic and political, as well as humanitarian reasons.

The first *Health Insurance Act* was passed in 1909 and implemented in 1911. It introduced compulsory health insurance for all wage-earners below a certain level of income. The income qualification was amended several times, extending the scheme's coverage and, finally, abolished altogether. Although the health insurance scheme was a national one, the manner of its operation was characteristic of much of the social legislation that followed. The scheme was organized on the basis of municipalities, with the aim of adapting the national policy and objectives to local conditions. The legislation specified the medical, surgical, preventive and remedial treatment to which insured members and their dependants were entitled.

The First World War, and the long depression which followed, prevented any significant development or expansion of social insurance for almost a quarter of a century, and helps to explain why old age pensions came so much later in Norway than in Britain, despite the early start made in other forms of social insurance.

Between 1918 and 1922 there was a great deal of discussion in the political field concerning old age pensions and disability pensions, and an *Old Age Pension Act* was passed in 1923, but the severe economic depression prevented its implementation. Developments in social insurance during the 1920s and the first half of the thirties were mainly restricted to changes in the scope of accident and health insurance schemes for industrial workers, seamen and fishermen.

Second Stage

A new phase in the expansion of social security was initiated in the mid-1930s, with health insurance legislation for fishermen (1935) and seamen in foreign trade (1936). But the most important piece of social security legislation was the long-awaited Old Age Pensions Act of 1936. Under this Act, as under the British Old Age Pension Act of 1908, old people were entitled to a pension on a broad test of means. It was different from the British non-contributory scheme in that it was not wholly financed from general revenues but from contributions from the State, municipalities and a flat rate levy (of 2·1 per cent) on personal incomes. After 1959 the income test was abolished (so that the pension became a universal benefit), and at the same time the financing of the scheme was changed in favour of something more akin to the British contributory scheme. Contributions to the pension fund were to be made by members and their employees as well as by the public authorities. One reason for the introduction of 'premiums' was the familiar argument that it was psychologically beneficial for people to feel that they were paying directly for what they were eventually to receive. An interesting feature of the 1936 scheme was that benefits were not uniform. They varied from one commune to another according to local costs of living. The aim was to provide equality of purchasing power for pensions all over the country, and it was up to the individual municipalities, who it will be remembered contributed to this scheme, to propose to the central department the level at which pensions should be paid above a certain national minimum.

There was vigorous activity in social policy during the mid-thirties, for besides the health and pensions legislation of 1935–36, acts were passed relating to the disabled and blind, and to the protection of labour. Several other pieces of social legislation were in various stages of completion when the country was invaded in 1940 and work on them was suspended until after 1945.

In the half-century or so of developments in social insurance up to 1945 much was achieved, but the schemes which had been introduced were designed separately to cope with a variety of specific needs, and they were usually restricted to certain social or occupational groups. So far, the history of social insurance had not been very different—in general trends and achievements—from that of England. By 1940, there was a loose patchwork of *ad hoc* social insurance, but it did not afford adequate cover for many social needs. Efforts to achieve greater integration and more comprehensive provision were delayed until after the war.

Municipal Schemes

Special mention should be made of the important contribution of municipalities to the development of social security, especially old age pensions. During the inter-war years local non-contributory old age pension schemes were introduced by many local authorities and, eventually, most of the population lived in municipalities which provided supplementary old age pensions. Apart from the general social assistance schemes for needy persons, many local authorities had categorical schemes under which allowances were paid to widows, the disabled, persons with tuberculosis, and for maternity. At present, more than half the population live in municipalities which provide what are now supplementary old age or disablement pensions. All but a few communes apply a means test, but those who do so have to follow regulations laid down by the central government in legislation (as the local authorities in Britain had to apply the National Assistance Board's means test in charging for residential accommodation under Part III of the National Assistance Act, 1948.)

For instance, pensioners are allowed to have an income equal to 150 per cent of the basic national pension before any deductions are made from the municipal supplementary pension. Thus the establishment of these municipal schemes is entirely voluntary, but once established they have to observe government legislation regulating matters such as conditions of entry and of payment.

Third Stage

In one of its earliest post-war declarations the government gave prominence to the need to co-ordinate existing schemes of social insurance and assistance into an expanded and more comprehensive social security system. In doing so, the government reiterated the views proclaimed in 1945 by the political parties in their joint programme for post-war reconstruction. This programme has provided a common basis of policy for the Norwegian political parties in later years and its main objectives were:

(*a*) integrated economic and social planning;
(*b*) a policy of full employment;
(*c*) a greater degree of equalization of personal incomes; and
(*d*) a comprehensive social security system to cover the whole population.

These goals were strikingly similar to those promoted by the organized Labour movement in Britain in 1944 and 1945, two years after the Beveridge Report. The report which led to such widespread discussion in Britain also helped to influence the policies formulated by the Norwegian government after the war. Several members of that government, as well as a number of other political and labour leaders and senior civil servants had spent up to five years of the war in England, and were well acquainted with the discussion and planning in British circles for social and economic policies to be put into effect after the war.

From 1946 there was a stream of new legislation in Norway covering many forms of social security and a growing range of social services besides. By the early fifties social security legislation had dealt with family allowances; insurance benefits for widows; wives and children; pensions for various occupational groups; industrial injuries; and disablement. In addition there were statutes putting into effect policies on child care, housing, education, employment and health. Not only was the pattern of new legislation strikingly similar to that passed in Britain at the same period, but cash benefits were close to, or identical with, British ones.

The momentum of social policy making—launching new legislation and improving old—was maintained and sometimes increased during the fifties and sixties. One major advance came in 1956, when the compulsory National Health Insurance Act extended its provision to the whole population. In 1957, the means test for old age pensioners was abolished and (since 1959) all Norwegian residents are entitled to the basic pension irrespective of other income. In 1960 a new, comprehensive system of industrial injuries insurance came into force, amalgamating the existing schemes and extending their provision to a much wider range of employees.

An official publication summarizes the aims of policy since the war thus: 'One of the central objectives of social insurance has been to secure for all members of society an adequate standard of living even at times when normal sources of income are not available.'[1]

By the late 1950s most of the ambitious programme drawn up in 1945 had been implemented. Meanwhile the economy had begun to expand rapidly after the early years of reconstruction, towns were growing, industrialization was increasing, social and economic standards had reached unprecedented levels and were still rising. Norway had become one of the richest countries in Europe with average *per capita* incomes almost equal to those in Britain. The term 'affluent society' was soon to be translated into Norwegian and pass into public vocabulary.

Fourth Stage

The last stage of the journey towards a comprehensive, integrated national pension system began formally in 1958 with the passage of an act for the co-ordination of pension and social insurance benefits. The legislation imposed uniform regulations regarding the calculation and payment of benefits on all social insurance and public pension schemes. The means test was abolished and the difficult work of co-ordination begun. Throughout the preceding sixty years or so a considerable number of insurance schemes had been introduced, developed, and amended, in efforts to meet the particular circumstances of various groups in the population. By the 1950s these schemes between them offered protection and assistance to

[1] *Sosiale fakta* Sosialdepartmentet, Oslo 1964 p. 13, ('Social Facts' Ministry of Social Affairs, Oslo).

large numbers of people, but, as in Britain, they constituted an agglomeration of a variety of arrangements, not a system. There was overlapping, there were gaps, and occasionally schemes conflicted in their aims. Some groups in society, notably women, were not adequately provided for since it was (and is) inherent in social insurance schemes that greatest attention is given to the chief income-earner, and benefits usually favour him even by comparison with his own wife and dependent children. While some people were left out of public insurance schemes—or inadequately helped when in—others, because of their occupation, were able to claim pensions or other benefits from more than one scheme, public or private.

The Co-ordination Act applied only to statutory schemes supported by public finance, such as the various social insurance and other public occupational pension schemes. Private pensions or insurance schemes did not come under the co-ordinating provisions, but they are required to supply information about participants to the authorities, especially for assessment of tax liability.

Co-ordination and integration was carried further by the new National Insurance scheme which came into operation on 1 January, 1967. It will take time for the new scheme to achieve its aim of equitability of treatment as between those who seek assistance from the many insurance schemes now integrated with the 'General Scheme', but it is hoped that difficulties giving rise to lack of uniformity, or of unequal treatment, will be resolved as experience of administering such a complex system grows.

Table 1 shows the relative distribution of benefits and allowances paid out in 1964, a typical year, under various schemes operating before the major reconstruction of social security began in 1967. It reveals that old age pensions and health service benefits dominated social insurance payments to individuals, accounting for very nearly 70 per cent of expenditure. If payments in respect of disablement, and rehabilitation, and industrial injuries are added—and these might also be classified as relating to health or fitness—the total moves towards 87 per cent. Unemployment, which is predominantly seasonal, is of little significance as a burden on social insurance funds, and the average level of unemployment has declined still further since 1964 to little over 1 per cent of the labour force—the seasonal rate of unemployment ranges from 0·5 per cent or less in the summer to over 2 per cent in the winter, but the winter rate is gradually being reduced. It is too early to say what changes in the relative distribution of payments may follow the implementation of the National Insurance scheme with its substantially increased benefits. In any case, any sharp relative growth in old age pensions and disablement benefits is likely to be modified as higher payments are introduced in other schemes—and these schemes are gradually incorporated in or assimilated with the new national insurance system.

Table 1

Social Security Benefits, etc. (1964)

Type of Benefit	*Kroner (millions)*	*Percentage of Expenditure*
Health	1107	35·5
Unemployment	100	3·2
Occupational injuries	125	4·0
Old age pension (basic)[1]	1071	34·3
Disability and rehabilitation	407	13·1
Survivors (orphans)	41	1·3
Family allowances	227	7·3
War pensions	40	1·3
Total	3118	100·0

(20 Kroner = £1)

[1] Excludes Kr. 65 million in supplementary pensions paid by municipalities under local schemes.

Discretionary social assistance in cash or kind—which is provided by municipalities—does not figure very largely in the social security picture. A variety of factors contribute to this, as far as the general population is concerned, and they include: full employment, social insurance, family allowances, tax reliefs, food subsidies, and relatively cheap housing made possible through government action. It is the retired who normally are most vulnerable to financial hardship in fully employed economics, and the numbers needing social assistance in Norway would undoubtedly be higher were it not for the fact that the majority of old people who cannot manage on the national pension are entitled to claim supplementary pensions provided by municipalities. In 1965, for instance, out of the 324,873 old people receiving the basic pensions, 87,721 were able to claim the supplementary municipal pensions. Table 2 shows how many heads of household of all ages received social assistance in 1964.

Table 2

Heads of Households Receiving Social Assistance (1964)

	All	*Receiving for first time*	*Expenditure (000 kroner)*
Rural municipalities	16,127	4,233	30,052
Urban municipalities	16,214	4,577	33,823
Total	32,314	8,810	63,875

(*Source: Statistical Yearbook of Norway*, 1966)

Note. In many cases recipients without domicile and those whose domicile was in another municipality were counted more than once.

The number of people receiving social assistance has remained fairly constant since the beginning of the 1960s. Social assistance was used by most recipients as a last resort—and it should be said that municipalities did not generally go out of their way to encourage applications—but a transition is taking place, and the provisions of the Social Care Act, 1964, are aimed at replacing the simpler, last resort, kinds of social assistance with a comprehensive battery of services to deal with individual problems in a wider setting.

CHAPTER 3

Social Insurance Today

THE NATIONAL INSURANCE SCHEME

In June 1966 the Norwegian parliament (*Storting*) passed the National Insurance Act, a major piece of legislation containing the blueprint for an extensive system of social insurance which, by stages, will replace existing public insurance schemes. This Act, together with the Social Care Act of 1964, formulated plans for rebuilding and expanding much of the Welfare State. But these were not the only plans for change in and around the social services, for the mid-sixties were a time of energetic activity in social policy, and important measures were being prepared or completed in connection with education, housing, physical planning, and other areas of social policy. Co-ordination and integration are two of the central objectives in Norwegian income-maintenance and welfare policies, and the Social Care and National Insurance Acts are the clearest expressions, to date, of these aims.

Scope

Membership of the new national insurance scheme is compulsory for all in paid work, whether employees or self-employed, and contracting out is not permitted. Residence, not citizenship, is the qualification for entry, and virtually the whole population is covered by the scheme. The few exceptions are employees of foreign governments.

The normal pensionable age is 70, but any person no longer in paid employment may claim a reduced pension at the age of 67. Alternatively, an insured person may elect to continue working until the age of 73 or more, thus qualifying for a higher pension. Certain occupations involving arduous physical work are specially provided for in the national insurance scheme of 1967. Under earlier legislation relating to occupational insurance schemes seamen, fishermen and forestry workers could retire on full pension at 60 (seamen) or 65 (fishermen and forestry workers) compared with the normal retirement age of 70. The National Insurance legislation provides for the retention of these conditions.

The special occupational pension schemes were not incorporated in or replaced by the new national insurance system, but integrated with it. Workers in specified arduous industries (named in the previous paragraph) may still retire before 70 without forfeiting their right to full national pensions on reaching that age. The gap between 60 or 65—depending on the industry—and 70 is bridged by special occupational pensions paid for jointly by employers and employees in the industries concerned. Persons not employed in seafaring, forestry or fishing and who are compelled by illness or injury to give up work are provided for under other branches of social insurance: health insurance, disability insurance, or occupational injuries insurance, for example.

It will be some years before the new insurance system is in full operation in accordance with the 1966 Act. This is due both to the gradual build-up of funds before maximum pensions can be paid, and to the policy of integrating a number of existing social insurance schemes by stages. On the day it came into force, the national insurance scheme replaced a variety of existing ones providing old age pensions, disability pensions, rehabilitation assistance, widows' and mothers' pensions, and orphans' pensions. Later the system will be extended to include the now separate social insurance schemes relating to health, industrial injuries, and unemployment. Various other publicly financed pensions arrangements will eventually be brought into the comprehensive national insurance system but, as yet, no details have been announced of how this is to be done. It is clear, however, that the complicated process of integration and co-ordination will go on for some years. The beginnings can be traced back to the 1958 Co-ordination Act, even further to the early post-war social insurance legislation and, beyond, to the wartime influence of the Beveridge Plan. It has taken time for these aims to find concrete expression in administrative action, but a retrospective view shows that though Norwegian social policy has proceeded empirically, step by step, the time-span of initiation, assessment, and adjustment has been shorter than in Britain.

Benefits

Until the introduction of the new national insurance scheme social insurance sought to provide 'basic benefits' to ensure at least a minimum standard of living and benefits were not related to the recipients' normal income. The 1967 scheme has a more radical objective: it aims to enable the pensioner to maintain something like the living standard he has built up during his working life—or, if his employment is cut short by disablement, for instance, to relate the benefit to the kind of income he might reasonably expect to have achieved in normal circumstances.

The new national insurance benefits—even the *basic* one without the addition of wage-related supplementary pension—are substantially greater in real terms than those paid before 1967. The aim is to provide a full pension (basic plus supplementary) normally equivalent to about two-thirds of pre-retirement income for the average income earner. In practice, however, the proportion of two-thirds is only a guide or norm, and the scheme provides higher than 'normal' pensions to lower income groups and relatively lower than 'normal' to higher income groups. Similarly, a married couple where only one has been working benefits relatively more than a single person though each insured had paid the same contributions on the basis of equal incomes. The married couple's pension will be about a third greater than that for a single person. If both husband and wife had worked they are treated as two single persons for pension purposes and receive a joint pension considerably higher than in the previous example. Additional benefits are paid to all pensioners for each dependent child.

As already indicated, the pension consists of two parts, a flat-rate basic pension (or other benefit) and a supplementary pension (or benefit) which is calculated according to income earned during employment and the number of years for which contributions have been paid. A points system incorporates both income and contribution-year components. Only the supplementary pension is wage-related.

In principle, an insured person is not entitled to a maximum possible supplementary old age pension until he has paid contributions for forty years, but it was recognized that such a ruling would penalize those who had already been paying social insurance contributions for years before the national pension scheme was established. The older the insured happened to be in 1967, the harsher the effects as far as he was concerned. Special arrangements were introduced to avoid this. They apply to persons who were over thirty years old in 1967 when the scheme began operating. Those insured who were aged over 50 in 1967 will be credited with double their actual years of employment ('earning time') and those from 30 to 50 at the time of the scheme's inception will be credited with sufficient earning time to give them the appropriate maximum pension.

The 'basic amount' is a central factor in the Norwegian national insurance system, and the major benefits (for old age, disablement, and widowhood) are calculated in relation to it. Thus the full *basic* pension for a single person is always equal to the basic amount—at present 5400 kroner or £270 a year, but to be raised from time to time as part of the adjustment to keep in line with general increases in incomes. The fixed supplement (not to be confused with the supplementary pension) for a wife (or where appropriate, husband) is normally 50 per cent of the basic amount, and the child supplement 25 per cent.

In calculating the supplementary pensions, only earned income up to a maximum of eight times the basic amount is taken into account—this is 'pensionable income'. The basic amount is also used for computing the annual total of 'pension points' earned towards the supplementary pension. A task which, incidentally, is to be performed by the income tax authorities. Since the basic amount is to be raised as incomes generally rise, pensions should also be related to prevailing income-levels at the time of payment.

The present income ceiling in respect of calculating supplementary pensions is 43,200 kroner a year (£2160) and equivalent to roughly twice an average male earner's income. Contributions are correspondingly limited by the ceiling on pensionable income. Due to the introduction of an income ceiling supplementary pension is only partially related to earnings and the levelling-off of pensions means that they fall progressively further below the two-thirds pension norm as pre-retirement incomes rise above the income ceiling.

As already noted, the national insurance scheme has been designed to relate pensions to increases in the levels of prices over time—to adjust to inflation and rising real incomes. It is hoped to achieve this flexibility through the pension points system. The supplementary pension is to be computed on the average of the 'best 20 years'—the years in which the insured gained the highest number of points. The scheme will take forty years (from 1967) to mature, and pensions or other time-and-income related benefits will not generally reach their maxima until 2007—unless in the meantime, there are substantial alterations to the system, and this seems likely in view of the great economic and social changes now taking place and expected over the next generation and beyond.

Disability Benefits

In principle, full disability benefits are equal in value to the old age pension which the insured would have received had he continued working up to normal retiring age. They too are made up of a basic and supplementary component, so that even housewives—who, if not employed outside the home, are not entitled to the wage-related supplement—can claim the basic pension as well as the various additional grants and allowances mentioned in the next paragraph. In practice, however, the benefit is also calculated according to the degree of disablement, so that someone whose earning capacity is assessed as being reduced by 50 per cent will be eligible for only half the full rate of pension while still of working age. On reaching normal retiring age he will be eligible for the old age pension.

A disability pension is intended to assist the disabled person to assist himself through his own efforts, and it will not normally be paid if rehabilitative treatment is a reasonable alternative. The 1966 National Insurance Act provides for various grants and allowances in connection with rehabilitation, and the aim is to make a disabled person as fit and self-dependent as possible. The allowances may be paid in the period before rehabilitation begins. Various other grants are available to disabled persons under the insurance scheme, covering transport to and from work, extra wear and tear on clothing, special expenses for food and housing, and for special attention or nursing in the home.

Widows, Mothers and Orphans

Widows do not automatically receive a full pension. The full pension for a widow is equivalent to two-thirds of the pension for a married couple which her husband would have earned (or, in fact, was already getting) on retirement. It is, therefore, related to the late husband's income. Two-thirds is the maximum pension, but widows' pensions vary according to their earnings without, however, falling below the equivalent of one-third of the appropriate full old age pension. The widow's pension is replaced by the old age pension when she reaches the age of seventy. Additional benefits are payable for children. The benefit for the first (or only) child is equivalent to 40 per cent of the basic national pension or benefit (i.e. excluding any supplementary benefits) and for other children the rate is 25 per cent.

Widows are encouraged to undertake training, retraining or rehabilitation courses where appropriate and are given full financial support ('educational grants') while doing so. Similar provisions are available under 'social care' legislation (see later section).

Children under eighteen who have lost either parent—but not both—are entitled to a flat-rate benefit as for the children of widows which is not affected by the income of the surviving parent. If both parents have died, the oldest child is treated as a 'widow' and paid the appropriate pension with further payments for the other children, if any.

Unmarried Mothers and 'Family Widows'

Unmarried mothers are provided for under the Widows' and Mothers' Insurance Act, 1964, which later became part of the new national insurance system. Benefits for children are fixed as already described, while the unmarried mother who is unable to work for some reason (including the need to care for her children) is paid a benefit equivalent to two-thirds of the normal income she could expect to receive in a job appropriate to her background, education and experience. Unmarried mothers are entitled to the usual maternity grants and benefits. They may also claim financial assistance—varying according to need—to meet the cost of employing someone to look after their child or children while they themselves are away from home at work, studying, undergoing training, or for some other legitimate reason.

'Family widows' are unmarried women who, through force of circumstances, have been at home for at least five years caring for their parents or other near relations and, as a consequence, have no income of their own. They come within the scope of the widows' and mothers' legislation and are entitled to comparable benefits. So are housewives whose marriages have been dissolved judicially owing to the disappearance or presumed death of the husband, and divorced women whose previous husband had been paying a maintenance allowance but has now died. But in the latter case the pension will not exceed the maintenance allowance which was being paid. The various kinds of benefit—for widows, unmarried mothers, 'family widows', and separated or divorced women—continue up to the age of seventy, when the recipient becomes eligible for the basic old age pension.

On the death of her husband a widow is entitled to a lump sum grant equivalent to one-third of the pension. In the event of pressing need an unmarried mother may be given a lump sum maternity grant equal to a third of her annual benefit.

Financing the National Insurance Scheme

The national insurance system is financed from four sources: contributions from insured members, from employers, and by municipalities and the state from tax revenues. Contributions were fixed so as to rise gradually over a transitional period covering the first ten years of the scheme's operation. At the end of ten years (that is by 1977) the proportions of contributions coming from various sources should be as in Table 3.

Table 3

National Pension Contributions as Percentage of Insured's Earned Income

Contributor	*Employed persons*	*Self-employed persons*
	%	%
Insured person	4·0	12·7
Employer	13·7	—
State	0·75	0·75
Municipality	0·75	0·75

Source: Social and Labour News from Norway No. 2, 1965. (Norwegian Joint Committee on International Social Policy)

A single combined premium covers old age pensions, disability benefits, war pensions and the other schemes now included in the national pension system. Just over 70 per cent of the premium is allocated to old age pensions, over 25 per cent to disability benefits, and the rest (nearly 5 per cent) shared among the smaller schemes.

The member's contribution is fixed as a percentage of pensionable income and, as mentioned earlier, there is a ceiling at 43,000 kroner (eight times the basic amount). Those with higher incomes do not pay a national insurance contribution for income lying above the limit. People whose pensionable income is less than 4000 kroner (£200) a year are exempt from paying contributions. Self-employed persons pay at a rate higher than wage or salary earners. (See Table 4.)

The heaviest contribution is paid by employers, and they will eventually be paying into the scheme three times as much as the insured employee. In 1967 the employers' contributions were expected to be equivalent to about 7 per cent of their total wages bill and were, therefore, well below the French level. The total contribution from all sources is substantial—for an employed person it is equivalent

Table 4

Contributions to General National Insurance Fund
As percentage of pensionable income from:

	Employment			
	Paid by:			*Self-employment*
	Member	*Employer*	*Total*	*Member*
	%	%	%	%
1967	4·0	7·0	11·0	5·4
1968	4·0	7·6	11·6	5·8
1969	4·0	8·2	12·2	6·2
1970	4·0	8·8	12·8	6·6

Source: The National Insurance Scheme (Ministry of Social Affairs, Oslo, 1967)

to just under a fifth of his income and for a self-employed person about one-seventh. The employee himself, however, pays less than a quarter of the contribution which is credited to him in the insurance fund.

The total contribution by central and local government will rise from 1·6 per cent of combined pensionable incomes in 1967 to 1·7 per cent in 1970 and go down to 1·5 per cent in 1977. The state and municipalities pay half each.

Table 5 shows the marked changes which were expected to take place from 1966 (the last year of the old arrangements) to 1967 (the first year of the new system). There was to be an increase of nearly 40 per cent in premium income and a redistribution of the burden so that, although all paid more, individual members, the state, and municipalities, paid slightly lower proportions (from 1 to $2\frac{1}{2}$ per cent) of the combined contributions, and the employers' share rose from 46 to 50 per cent. As the next paragraph points out, premium income in 1967 exceeded expectations, and the totals in the second column are too low.

It is intended that the national insurance scheme will accumulate a very large fund. Before the scheme came into operation it was predicted that by the year 2000 this fund would be three times as large as the scheme's annual budget and that in the first year, 1967, about 40 per cent of the increased premium income would go into

Table 5

Premium Income (estimated) in Millions of Kroner

		1966	1967
From:	Members	860	1170
	Employers	1065	1603
	Municipalities	215	221
	State	172	221
		2321	3215

Source: The National Insurance Scheme, op. cit.

the fund. By the middle of 1967, however, these predictions were seen to be wide of the mark as contributions flowed into the fund twice as fast as had been expected. This was due to an underestimation of levels and trends in income for the country as a whole. It is possible that the government will propose a reduction in the rate of increase in employers' contributions to slow down the flow of money into the fund. Similar action has earlier been taken in Sweden —and for the same reason.

A decline in individual savings is anticipated in view of the significant increase in members' contributions, but the financial planning of the scheme has taken this into account, and it is hoped that the fund accumulated will at least equal the probable fall in saving. At the end of the first three years, the national insurance scheme is expected to have a fund of 2400 million kroner (£120 million), and about ten times as much in 1980. Capital from the fund is made available for loans—mainly through various state banks—primarily for investment in housing, industry, agriculture and fisheries, with special attention being paid to the less developed regions.

The fund is administered by a special board on which the state, municipalities, government agencies, and other important organizations—such as the national bodies representing employers and employees—have places. Five regional committees have been set up to administer the use of funds in their regions which comprise the Oslo region, Southern, Western, Mid- and Northern Norway, respectively. The national board is a co-ordinating and advisory organ, it has nine members and each of the regional committees five. Funds will be made available in proportion to the population in each of the five regions. They will be in the form of bonds and bank deposits or loans, but not in the form of direct loans to the public or industry. The main purpose is to strengthen local credit institutions and increase the flow of local investment.

OTHER SOCIAL SECURITY SCHEMES

Many social insurance schemes are still outside the new National Insurance system, but they will be taken in gradually. They include schemes for unemployment, occupational injuries, health and the separate occupational schemes for seamen, fishermen and forestry workers.

(*a*) *Unemployment Insurance*

Voluntary unemployment insurance was introduced in 1906 for certain classes of wage earner and compulsory insurance came in 1939. There were several amendments and revisions afterwards and a comprehensive new Act was passed in 1959.

With some exceptions, unemployment insurance is now compulsory for all wage earners whose wage exceeds £100 a year. Others who are not obliged to join are persons employed in agriculture and in forestry connected with agriculture if they are closely related to the employer (or his spouse) and 'live in' with the employer as a member of the household. Also exempt from compulsory unemployment insurance are persons engaged in fishing, sealing and whaling; most public servants; domestic workers; representatives, salesmen, agents, etc., who are paid by results; and persons who are mainly or wholly self-employed. There is besides a special unemployment scheme for seamen. Since 1964 nationals of Denmark, Finland, Iceland and Sweden—whose permanent home is still in those countries or in Norway—employed on Norwegian ships engaged in deep sea trade have the same obligations and benefits in respect of the scheme as Norwegian seamen.

Altogether the exempt categories account for about one-fifth of the labour force, thus about four-fifths of all earners are insured against total loss of income during unemployment.

Benefits

The main purpose of the scheme is to compensate for loss of earnings during unemployment, but there is a wide and growing range of other services apart from income maintenance. The unemployed person may be granted financial assistance towards travelling and removal costs in a work placement; a grant to meet additional expenses involved in a change of employment and resettlement; and for vocational training. Educational and training activities among the unemployed and underemployed (a serious problem in the underdeveloped rural districts and coastal areas in many parts of Norway) have grown considerably in recent years.

To qualify for unemployment benefit, the insured must have paid contributions for a minimum of 45 premium weeks in the previous three benefit years (a benefit year runs from 1 October to 30 September) or for 30 premium weeks during the last benefit year. In other words, the insured must have been employed and contributing during these times. Benefits may be paid for a maximum of 20 weeks in any one benefit year—or 30 weeks for a person over 50 years old. Normally no allowance is paid for the first seven days of unemployment. The object of the last regulation is to avoid an excessive amount of paper work and administrative costs for very short-term unemployment. It is also considered that an insured should be able to last for seven days on his own resources without hardship. The limitation of benefits to 20 weeks in a year was imposed to prevent the fund from being exhausted during a period of mass unemployment. It is government policy to provide employment in public enterprises in the event of such a situation.

The rates of unemployment benefit are similar to those in the health insurance scheme and vary according to the insured's normal income. There are additional payments for dependants such as wife and children or, in certain circumstances, domestic help. Benefits are calculated on a daily basis.

The claimant must be willing and able to work—if unable to work owing to illness or other disability including old age he is not eligible for unemployment pay, but instead may claim from some other part of the social insurance system such as health, occupational injuries, rehabilitation, disability or old age pensions insurance. When able to work, the insured must register at the local municipal employment office and usually report twice a week in towns, and once a week in rural areas. He must be prepared to take suitable employment. The suitability of a job is judged according to the unemployed's practical and theoretical training, his aptitude and fitness, age and adaptability. The assessment is made by the local employment committee. Vocational guidance and training is stressed in this area of the social services.

A person need not be wholly unemployed in order to qualify for benefit. If he is able to find casual or part-time employment he may still qualify for partial benefit.

Finance

The unemployment insurance scheme is financed by employees, employers and the municipalities. Employers and employees pay an equal amount and the local authority adds an amount equivalent to 25 per cent of the assessed annual premium of each insured person. The contributions are paid into a local unemployment fund in each municipality. Local funds with capital in excess of a certain amount *per capita* of insured must pay 20 per cent of combined premiums and local authority contribution into a national reserve fund for unemployment. If, on the other hand, the local fund does not have sufficient resources to meet the demands on it during a fiscal year, the deficit is met out of the National Reserve Fund. The government reimburses the national fund to the extent of 60 per cent of its grants to local funds. If the National Reserve Fund should be exhausted, the government has guaranteed to take over its obligations.

(*b*) *Occupational Injuries Insurance*

In contrast to occupational injuries insurance schemes in most other countries the Norwegian one covers a very wide range of persons, occupations and contingencies. All employees (with the same very minor exceptions as in relation to health insurance) are compulsorily insured, and self-employed persons may join voluntarily. Included in the compulsory scheme—apart from the more usual classes of worker—are the armed forces (all ranks); conscripted civil workers; the police; personnel of the civil defence services; fire brigades; seamen, whalers and employed or self-employed fishermen; government employees working abroad; and employees of Norwegian civil airlines working at home or abroad. An unusual feature is the inclusion of all students and school pupils, so that, in all, about half the population is protected by the scheme.

Benefits

The scheme provides benefits to persons unable to work owing to 'occupational injury'—which means injury or illness suffered whilst following an occupation. Silicosis, lead poisoning, dermatitis, tropical or epidemic diseases to which seamen may be exposed, are some examples of occupational illnesses, but there are many more. Benefits are calculated according to the insured's normal income but there is an income limit beyond which additional earnings are disregarded. The limit is roughly equal to average male earnings.

While suffering from the injury or disease the insured receives free treatment including drugs, appliances, physiotherapy, hospital care, and accommodation and treatment at a rehabilitation centre. He is also entitled to cash benefits on the same terms as in the health insurance scheme for fifty-two weeks. On completion of treatment the insured may be eligible for a disability pension on the grounds of continued incapacity. Widows, children and other dependants are entitled to a survivors' pension if the insured should die as a result of his occupational injury or disease.

Finance

The occupational injuries scheme is financed entirely by premiums which are fixed so as to cover the cost of the scheme from year to year. The premiums vary from one occupation to another according to the assessed risk of injury or illness in different kinds of work. Employers bear the whole cost of the scheme and no contributions are paid by employees except in the fishing industry, where fishermen pay part of the total premium and the rest is met from public funds.

Students, school pupils, military personnel and conscripted civilians have their premiums paid by the State.

(*c*) *Occupational Insurance Schemes*

There are three important occupational insurance schemes in Norway which seek to meet the special needs of employees in some of the country's basic industries—namely, the merchant marine, fisheries, and forestry—each of which has its peculiar hazards. The schemes for seamen, fishermen and forestry workers are compulsory.

The benefits granted are broadly comparable to those in the other social insurance schemes: pensions for old age, widowhood, and dependant children (in the schemes for seamen and forestry workers); and disablement (in the seamen's scheme).

Subject to certain qualifications dealing with length of contributory service, seamen may retire at 60 on full pension (or 55 on reduced benefit), fishermen and forestry workers at 65—compared with the general retiring age of 70 in Norway.

(*d*) *Health Insurance*

This section deals mainly with the insurance aspects of medical care. Other aspects of the administration of the health services are described in a later section (see below, p. 128).

The health insurance scheme in Norway does not, at present, form an integral part of the national insurance system but is closely linked to it to provide complementary—but not competing or overlapping—assistance. It will eventually be incorporated into the national insurance scheme.

Health (sickness) insurance was introduced in 1911, but was obligatory only for lower paid wage-earners. Gradually, the scope was widened as more occupations and income classes were brought in. Admission to voluntary membership also became easier as time passed.

In 1956 a compulsory health insurance scheme was introduced for the whole population and residence, not citizenship, was the main qualification for entry. Foreigners living in Norway were included in the compulsory provisions. Temporary visitors (besides tourists) are exempted from the scheme unless they have paid employment in Norway. Employees of foreign governments or foreigners covered by health insurance in their own countries, need not join the Norwegian scheme. Certain Norwegians living or working abroad (in the diplomatic service, merchant marine, fishing fleets or for a Norwegian firm) must insure. Voluntary membership is open to temporary visitors (and nomadic Lapps) who stay in Norway for more than three months.

There are two major classes of membership: ordinary 'members' and 'family members'. 'Members' are the insured themselves—they are over eighteen years of age and pay premiums. The 'family members'—for whom no separate premium is paid—usually consist of the wife (or occasionally husband) and children under 18. But any person in the family who has an income above a certain modest level in his or her own right is obliged to become a premium-paying member of the scheme.

Ordinary 'members' are divided into five groups:

(*a*) employed;
(*b*) self-employed;
(*c*) fishermen, whalers and seal hunters;
(*d*) seamen in foreign trade and government officials serving abroad; and
(*e*) military personnel.

The first two groups pay similar premiums—but which vary with income—and receive commensurate benefits except that self-employed do not qualify automatically for 'sick pay' during illness but may apply for supplementary insurance which does provide sickness benefit. The last three groups all have special regulations accommodating their particular circumstances and they are generally eligible for higher benefits than the other employed and self-employed.

Scope of Benefits

The aim of the national health service is to provide the appropriate care (and after-care) for the treatment of illness, injury and deformity, and every resident in the country (subject to the minor qualifications already mentioned) is guaranteed treatment and other assistance under the scheme as long as it is required. There is no qualifying lower limit for the number of premiums to be paid before a member or his family may claim for treatment or related financial aid. People are treated whether they have paid their premiums or not, so that it is virtually a universal benefit rather than a social insurance scheme.

There is complete freedom of choice as regards doctors, and patients may consult whoever they select—they are not registered with one general practitioner as in Britain. Some kinds of dental care, notably extractions and the treatment of oral diseases, come within the insurance scheme, but conservative dental treatment does not.

In the great majority of medical and dental services (examinations, treatment, drugs) the patient has to pay a fee to meet part of the cost. There is a standard scale of charges agreed nationally between doctors (National Medical Society) and the government (National

Insurance Institution). Provided the individual doctor keeps to the scale, the patient will pay on average from a quarter to a third of the cost of minor treatment, but he is only required to pay for the first two visits to a doctor in respect of a particular illness. There is no charge for subsequent visits made in connection with the same course of treatment. There are two main reasons for charging fees and putting some of the costs (such as drugs and bandages) on the patient: charges help to finance the service and are also intended to act as some deterrent to unnecessary use of both scarce medical resources and the insurance funds.

A wide range of benefits is offered under the health insurance scheme apart from partial or full reimbursement of doctors' fees. The insured may receive free maintenance and treatment in a public hospital (for an unlimited time) or in a maternity home; midwifery services; a maternity grant and allowances; transport costs—where necessary—and this is an important item in a large, sparsely populated country where a journey to a doctor or a hospital may involve days of travelling by land and sea, or an airplane flight, and for subsistence while away from home; and a funeral grant. The scheme also meets a substantial (or total) share of the cost of dental treatment (but not conservative treatment); physiotherapy; treatment of speech and related defects; essential drugs and appliances, including hearing aids; domiciliary nursing; all examinations and treatment at recognized district health centres (family care offices); psychiatric outpatient clinics for children and young people, and investigations at hospitals' departments of social medicine.

Under certain conditions the health insurance scheme meets medical costs in full. This occurs when the illness or accident comes within the scope of the Occupational Injuries Act, and also when the insured belongs to one of the two special categories—seamen in foreign trade and public officials working abroad; and military personnel. In these circumstances all examinations and treatment are free, including medicines, appliances, and hospital treatment. Costs are met even when the insured is resident in another country and is treated there. Other groups of insured (ordinary employees and self-employed) can claim from the insurance scheme in respect of illness or injury when abroad, but are limited to the standard provisions of the scheme if they were in Norway at the time. There are exceptions, however, as Norway has reciprocal health service agreements with certain countries including Britain. In such cases a Norwegian visiting one of these countries is eligible for treatment on the same terms as a permanent resident of that country.

Cash Benefits

Benefits and premiums are broadly related to income. When unable to work owing to illness or accident the insured receives a benefit equivalent to between a quarter and a third of his normal earned income (depending on the income class he is in) and has additional small benefits in respect of any dependents. The benefits may be paid for up to 104 consecutive weeks during incapacity, after that the insured normally becomes eligible for some other form of assistance such as a rehabilitation allowance (see 'Rehabilitation Allowance' below). Whilst the insured is in hospital he receives only one-third of his basic cash benefit.

There are three other general qualifications in respect of sickness benefits:

(*a*) The insured must be fully incapacitated and unable to work before he becomes entitled to full benefit. If partially fit and working part-time his benefit is adjusted accordingly.

(*b*) An employee does not normally qualify for cash benefits relating to illness until he has been insured for two weeks or, for self-employed person, six weeks. But incapacity due to accident is not subject to this limitation.

(*c*) No benefit is payable for the first three days of illness.

None of the limitations mentioned applies to medical examination or treatment which are available immediately to any sick or injured person, as already pointed out.

An insured person is not necessarily dependent solely upon the comparatively modest cash benefit. The majority of employees also receive some payment (such as reduced salary) from their employers under a variety of arrangements. A large number of industrial workers are members of a voluntary scheme established in 1957 jointly by the trades unions and employers' organizations, but administered by the state social insurance offices, which gives them a supplementary sick benefit which might be two-thirds as great as their basic health insurance benefit. The combined total benefits from these two sources must not exceed 90 per cent of the employee's ordinary net wages after tax and compulsory social insurance deductions.

Financing the Schemes

Under the state health insurance scheme the insured pays a premium related to his income, but his contribution is more than doubled from other sources as follows: the employer pays a sum equal to 75 per cent of the employee's premium, the municipality adds the equivalent of 25 per cent, and the state 20 per cent. Thus, for example, if the insured himself pays 10 kroner a week, the other three contributors between them add kr. 7·5 + 2·5 + 2, making a total of 22 kroner a week to be credited to the insured in the scheme. The voluntary scheme for industrial workers is financed by weekly contributions from the insured and their employers with no additional support from the authorities.

Rehabilitation Allowance

There was an important change in the health insurance system in 1961 with the introduction of rehabilitation allowances. From that time the disability insurance scheme—now incorporated in the national insurance system—took over responsibility for long-term or permanently disabled people whose incapacity due to illness or accident lasts beyond the two years covered by health insurance. They are then transferred to the disability insurance scheme, but there are important differences in the terms under which the rehabilitation allowances are paid compared with sickness benefits:

1 They commence either when a patient begins rehabilitative—as distinct from curative—treatment or when incapacity has lasted more than two years.

2 The allowances are available to all members of the health insurance scheme whether or not they are entitled to the other cash benefits of that scheme. It applies to adults and to children aged under eighteen.

3 There is no time limit on rehabilitation allowances, they may go on for years, but only as long as treatment to improve capacity to work continues. If rehabilitation treatment is completed and the insured is still assessed as unable to work he becomes entitled to standard benefits under the disability insurance scheme.

4 An insured must have been paying into the health insurance scheme for at least five years (except for family members or dependents) before he can qualify for rehabilitation allowances.

(e) *Family Allowances: Scope and Benefits*

Family allowances were introduced in Norway in 1946. They are non-contributory and are financed out of tax revenues. As in Britain, they are more accurately described as 'child allowances' and any person supporting children under sixteen years of age is entitled to them regardless of income or wealth, or whether a child was born in or out of wedlock. As a general rule there is no allowance for the first child but each subsequent child is eligible for one. There have been exceptions to the rule about first children and allowances have been paid for only children where parents are divorced, where one or both parents have died, or to unmarried mothers to help them support a child. Family allowances (of 400 kroner a year) are also paid for all children in residential institutions such as orphanages, special schools or other children's 'homes'.

Benefits may be paid for a first child suffering from a long-term illness or other disability and who is not receiving a benefit from the disability insurance scheme. The examples given do not exhaust the possibilities, however, for there is a liberal regulation stating that a child allowance may otherwise be paid in respect of the first child where there are special circumstances which would make the payment of benefits reasonable—as when the family breadwinner is disabled over a long period.

Foreigners (except officials or employees of foreign governments) resident in Norway can usually claim family allowances after six months' continuous residence, but refugees qualify immediately on the same terms as Norwegian citizens. The allowances are paid on a rising scale, thus, at present, 400 kroner (£20) a year is paid on behalf of the second child in a family, 500 kroner (£25) for the third, 600 kroner (£30) for the fourth, and so on, the allowance rising by 100 kroner (£5) a year for each additional child.

ADMINISTRATION OF SOCIAL INSURANCE

The central administration of social insurance is in the hands of the National Insurance Institution which, in turn, is answerable to the Pension and Social Insurance Department of the Ministry of Social Affairs. The Ministry is responsible for the planning and implementation of social policy generally.

National Insurance Institution

The Institution is, nominally, an independent body comparable to a state board (like the late National Assistance Board) in Britain.

It administers or has ultimate control over all national and municipal social insurance schemes—including most of the special occupational ones—and has specific responsibilities for the fiscal and general supervision of local insurance funds. The National Insurance Institution is directed by a board of five members appointed by the Crown which also nominates one of the five as chairman. Members are appointed for four years at a time.

The national office ensures that all local offices and their funds are administered according to statute. It exercises supervision by means of audits and inspections (which may be unannounced) as well as through the usual administrative procedures. The Institution also arbitrates in disputes and appeals forwarded from local boards. On the financial side, it fixes the premiums for the numerous schemes under its control and aids local offices if their funds run into difficulties due to extraordinary circumstances.

There are over 450 municipalities and all but three or four of them —with tiny populations—have their own social insurance offices or 'funds'. Each local office has a five-member board of directors all of whom must live in the district and one member must be an employer. The board is elected by the municipal council and serves four years. The chairman may be paid but all other members have to serve without pay—membership (like jury service in Britain) being regarded as an obligation of citizenship. Members may claim travel allowances and compensation for loss of earnings. The manager of the local office is appointed by the National Insurance Institution from nominees proposed by the local board.

The local offices were originally established under the provisions of the Health Insurance Act in 1901 and were, therefore, primarily concerned with the administration of health insurance. Under that scheme they are legally independent entities and meant to be self-supporting—hence the local health insurance funds. Gradually, however, these local offices have accumulated a growing number of functions and responsibilities from the many other schemes of social insurance. With the increasing volume and scope of national social policies, particularly in social insurance, the independence of local offices has steadily diminished as they have come more and more under central control.

Although the administration of the social insurance schemes has reached a high degree of uniformity it is by no means complete, as the following summary shows:

ADMINISTRATION OF THE SCHEMES

1. *National Insurance System*

(*a*) *Old Age Pensions*

Administered centrally by the National Insurance Institution and locally by the insurance office.

(*b*) *Disability Pensions*

Administration by the National Insurance Institution and local offices. Each county has a County Board with responsibility for seeing that the terms of the Disability Insurance scheme are satisfied and otherwise to assist the National Insurance Institution in matters relating to the scheme.

(*c*) *Widows' and Orphans' Pensions*

Administration as in (*a*).

(*d*) *Rehabilitation Allowances*

Administration by National Insurance Institution and local offices. There is a County Board in each county which assesses applications for rehabilitation allowances before recommending payment. If the local insurance office disagrees with the board's recommendation the matter is referred to the NII.

2. *Unemployment Benefit*

Central administration by the Directorate of Labour, a department of the Ministry of Local Government and Labour. At lower levels the county Labour and Development Boards supervise and manage the unemployment insurance scheme, and in urban districts with unemployment exchanges the task is carried out by a board corresponding to the county one.

Payments of benefit are made through the local insurance offices which also collect premiums and municipal subsidies and keep accounts for the Unemployment Insurance Fund.

The board at the Directorate of Labour administers the National Reserve Fund (for unemployment) and is the highest organ of appeal or arbitration within the unemployment insurance scheme. In the counties and urban districts, the boards determine all matters relating to benefits but refer difficult cases to the national board.

The special unemployment insurance for seamen in foreign trade has its own central fund which is also administered by the Labour Directorate. In Norway, benefits are paid through the ordinary local insurance offices, and abroad through certain consulates.

3. *Occupational Injuries Pensions*

Administered by the NII and local insurance offices.

4. *Occupational Pensions for Seamen, Fishermen and Forestry Workers*

(*a*) *Seamen*

Administration at the national level is directed by a board of five members. Seamen and shipowners each have one representative on the board. The administration is partly co-ordinated with the special health insurance scheme for seamen. Any dispute relating to decisions of the national board may be brought before a Court of Appeal for settlement. In Norway, the pensions are paid through local insurance offices. Payments to retired seamen living abroad may be made through consulates.

(*b*) *Fishermen*, and

(*c*) *Forestry Workers*

Administration through NII and local insurance offices.

5. *Family Allowances*

Administration by NII and local insurance offices.

6. *War Pensions*

Administration by NII and local insurance offices.

7. *Health Insurance*

The National Insurance Institution is the central governing body of the health insurance scheme and the local insurance offices were, in fact, first established as health insurance offices.

CHAPTER 4

Health and Welfare Services

HEALTH SERVICES

Structure of the Medical Services

The organization of medical services in Norway is functional and there is a tripartite structure as in Britain, the main divisions being: hospitals and other institutions; local authority medical services; and general practice in medicine and dentistry. Voluntary organizations also provide a substantial share of medical services particularly through their hospitals and clinics.

The central government department administering the health services is the Directorate of Health, which is one of the three major divisions of the Ministry of Social Affairs. The Directorate is responsible for the health insurance scheme as well as for a variety of other services. There are separate, but co-ordinated, sections of the Directorate with special responsibilities for work in hospitals, tuberculosis, psychiatry, hygiene, drugs, and dentistry respectively.

Due to the size of the country and the fairly scanty population it was decided quite early that reliance on private medical practitioners would not be sufficient to ensure adequate standards of health and the foundations of local authority medical services were laid down by the Public Health Act, 1860.

There is now a chief medical officer in every county and one or more district medical officers in each of the 418 local health districts into which the country is divided. These county and district medical officers are employed by the state and form over 10 per cent of the medical profession. They have two major functions: to administer and develop local health services (excluding general practice); and to take care of the sick. District medical officers' duties involve the supervision of public health and nursing services (including mental health) and of medical staffs, institutions, and pharmacies. All drugs in Norway are dispensed under public control either through hospitals or municipal pharmacist shops.

In recent years emphasis has been laid on the development of preventive medicine and general public health activities, and county and district medical officers have been at the forefront of this work. Local health services are, therefore, being expanded together with more specialized hospital services. Town and other district medical officers are *ex officio* chairmen of local health committees. Town engineers are also members, while the other members are elected representatives (councillors).

Health committees make public health regulations and seek to ensure their enforcement by, for example, inspection of water supplies, places of refreshment, and food shops. The range of their duties and functions is comparable to that of local health committees in Britain and includes the care of health in schools and other educational institutions.

Apart from his general public health duties the district medical officer is obliged to give medical aid to people living in his district in return for a reasonable fee, thus helping to make up for the shortage of general practitioners in certain areas. The duties of the more senior public medical officers—such as the county medical officer—are administrative rather than medical. At county level the medical officer is chairman of a committee which considers applications for rehabilitation assistance and disability benefits. When appropriate this committee also deals with applications for social assistance under the 1964 Social Care Act. The county medical officer is assisted in his work by a 'social secretary' who is a trained social worker.

The county medical officer has important duties in connection with the administration of hospitals and other medical institutions in his area. The scope of these functions is widening as government policies give increasing responsibility to the counties for the organization and administration of local and national hospital and other institutional services.

Hospitals

About four-fifths of all hospital beds are in state, county or municipal institutions of one kind or another. Counties and municipalities have built and administer the great majority of general hospitals, while the state has concerned itself primarily with specialized hospitals—for tuberculosis, or psychiatric treatment, for example—and the medical training hospitals in Bergen and Oslo. Further teaching hospitals and medical schools are being planned. The combined efforts of public and voluntary hospitals are not adequate to meet all demands and a programme for the provision of more public hospitals has been commenced.

A rising proportion of doctors in Norway are employed in hospitals—at present just over 30 per cent—and the number of specialists in relation to general practitioners is also increasing. Nevertheless general practitioners still form the largest group—being about 60 per cent of all doctors.

General Practice

General practitioners in both medicine and dentistry are independent, fee-earning professionals. Scales of fees are fixed by agreement between the professional associations and the National Insurance Institute, and the great bulk of fees come from national health insurance sources. Scales are not strictly observed, but where a patient believes he has been overcharged he may apply to the municipal prices committee. The variations—and their degree—of fees charged, particularly by dentists, shows that this loose arrangement does not bring anything like uniformity. If the physician is independent, so is the patient, and he may go to whoever he chooses without prior registration.

The number of inhabitants per doctor (counting hospitals, public medical officers and general practitioners together) in 1961 was 877 for the whole country, but ranged from 1 doctor to every 393 persons in Oslo to 1 per 2239 in one of the western counties. The same county also had the largest number of inhabitants to dentists —2927 to 1, while Bergen was best served in this respect, having a dentist to every 907 persons. Oslo was the next best, having 1 dentist to every 1033 inhabitants.

The authorities consider that there is a shortage of doctors and regard it as a serious problem. The rural and coastal areas—particularly in the far north and in some western counties—are much worse off than the larger towns, or the south-east as a whole. This shortage exists despite the use of district medical officers to treat patients in the country or coastal areas. The possibility of compulsory service in the north has been discussed in the *Storting* (parliament) but, so far, the government has not adopted such a radical measure.

Dentists

A Dental Care Act in 1949 provided for the appointment of a county dental officer in every county (apart from Oslo and Bergen) and the establishment of a public dental service. This is additional to the existing services provided by dentists in private practice. Certain districts have a dental care committee.

In districts where the public dental service has been established, children aged 6 to 18 receive free treatment. Infants under school age and adults are charged according to a scale fixed by the Ministry of Social Affairs, but as far as adults are concerned, the scales are not strictly observed or enforced.

The school dental service has succeeded in ensuring that over 70 per cent of all pupils receive a dental examination (and treatment if required) at least once a year. Some municipalities have extended this service to pre-school children and the youths who have left school.

Other Public Medical Services

Central and local authorities separately or jointly provide a number of other important medical services, frequently within the hospital or alternative institutional framework. The most prominent services are in connection with the prevention and treatment of tuberculosis (though needs in this field have fallen dramatically since before the war); care of the handicapped; mental illness and defects; nervous disorders; epilepsy; child and youth psychiatry; alcoholism; and the health of particular occupational groups such as seamen.

Voluntary Organizations

Voluntary organizations have made a very considerable contribution to the development and continuing provision of health services in Norway. The so-called 'big Four' have been especially prominent. These organizations—the Norwegian Red Cross, the Norwegian Women's Public Health Association, the National Public Health Association, and the Norwegian People's Aid—have pioneered in preventive, curative and rehabilitative work and still play a very large part in health and welfare services. One of their most notable efforts has been the provision and running of the great majority of the 1400 health centres for mothers and young children throughout Norway. This has been achieved by the two voluntary public health associations.

WELFARE SERVICES

Social Care and Social Assistance

The origins of what has now developed into a comprehensive system of social assistance—or 'social care' as it is becoming known generically—were created by the Poor Law of 1845. The scope of provision widened as time passed, levels rose, and a variety of services in cash and kind multiplied as further needs emerged or were recognized and action was taken to meet them. Eventually a network of services had developed but, characteristically, piecemeal growth had produced uneven distribution, with gaps in some areas of need and overlapping in others. Problems of co-ordination were difficult due to the cumbersome and complicated structure of what may loosely be called welfare services. But in this field of social provision as in others, the 1960s were a decade of reorganization and expansion. In 1965 the Social Care Act became law. This was one of the most important pieces of legislation in the history of Norwegian social policy and together with the National Insurance Act, 1965, initiated a major reconstruction of social insurance and welfare services.

The Social Care Act provides a new framework for social work in connection with the family. A central aim of welfare policy expressed in the legislation is to assist the individual and the family by drawing upon whatever skills and resources are required. The individual and his or her particular needs are the principal focus of the co-ordinated efforts to be employed and the object is to equip the individual as far as possible to play a satisfying and useful role in society. Thus the philosophy of rehabilitation and help towards self-help which motivates so much of Norwegian social policy has been given greater prominence by the new legislation.

The Social Care Act requires that a social welfare board be established in every municipality. The board must have at least five members, but, this apart, the actual number is left to the discretion of the municipal council which also elects the members. The board's functions include: drawing up a joint budget for social work in the municipality; assessing social needs and preparing schemes for the development of social work services; and co-ordinating public and voluntary social services to assist the individual or the group.

The direct administration of the board's work is delegated to a social care office. In principle, every municipality should have a social care office, but the small, scattered population and meagre resources of certain areas has been taken into account. Thus, with the consent of the Ministry of Social Affairs, municipalities may set up offices jointly with other communes. Otherwise, the establishment of social care offices is proceeding by stages, in order of size of municipality, with the larger authorities setting up offices first. It is expected that all municipalities with populations of over 4000 will have social care offices by 1969, and those with more than 3000 inhabitants by 1970.

The Act defines the purpose of the social welfare boards (and therefore, of social care offices) as to 'provide information, advice, and guidance to such persons who need it in order to become self-supporting, or to overcome or adjust themselves to a difficult personal situation'. This is a very comprehensive aim and the social care offices are required to offer a correspondingly wide range of services. They do this by the direct provision of some services, but also by maintaining close links with other agencies such as the local insurance offices, hospitals, local health services, voluntary organizations, and other agencies. Where they exist, there is particularly close collaboration with family health centres.

The social care offices themselves provide family casework, guidance and advice on social problems, and some financial assistance. This may take the form of grants to help people who for one reason or another find themselves in circumstances not adequately covered by social insurance. More important because of the constructive intentions behind them are the various loans or grants available for vocational training or educational courses, or for other purposes, but all of which have as their aim that the individual should be self-supporting.

The Social Care Act (Section I, para. 3) says:

'I. Persons who are not in a position to support themselves or to provide for their own needs, are eligible for social assistance in the following forms:

(*a*) Loans, guarantees for loans, or grants towards vocational training designed to fit the person for employment, or for other purposes which may enable him to become self-supporting.

(*b*) Work with remuneration at sheltered work homes (for

certain groups of socially maladjusted persons) or sheltered workshops, residential or non-residential.

(*c*) Admission to homes for the aged, rest homes, or other suitable institutions.

(*d*) Private arrangements for clothing, board and lodging.

(*e*) Grants, or in exceptional cases, loans towards maintenance.

(*f*) Loans or grants for purposes other than those mentioned in (*a*) to (*e*), to the extent deemed necessary.'

The Act also provides that the social welfare board can give financial assistance in circumstances not covered by the preceding list. This gives greater scope and flexibility to the board in dealing with individual clients. Apart from finding places in sheltered employment, nursing homes, or other appropriate institutions, the social care office may provide—or pay for—domiciliary care for persons.

The Ministry of Social Affairs has pointed out, in its circular to local authorities on the Social Care Act, that emphasis should be placed on preventive work in connection with children and young people, and that the care of the elderly and aged should also be given a major place in the work of the social care offices.

The Social Care Act provided an opportunity for the development of a more general and comprehensive after-care service for discharged prisoners, since the legislation requires the local social care offices to give information, advice and guidance and, where appropriate, material aid to applicants with a view to enabling them to achieve self-dependency or to adjust successfully to difficult circumstances. The intentions of social care policy go beyond the proposals and largely remedial functions described in the preceding pages. There is an overriding aim, which is to improve social conditions through action at the local level. The 'Standard Instructions to Chief Social Welfare Officers' require them to make 'proposals which can bring about improvements in social conditions in the commune'. Because of its knowledge of local circumstances, and the first-hand experience gained in dealing with individual cases, the municipal social welfare board is considered to be specially equipped to take the initiative in formulating solutions to social problems. It is recognized—and emphasized—that this will involve extensive reciprocal collaboration between municipalities; between municipalities and the county or the state; with voluntary agencies and private firms.

Home-help and Home-nursing

The essential function of both home-help and home-nursing services is to provide aid in the home during times of urgent need and when suitable help cannot be obtained elsewhere. The services are provided by municipalities and follow the lines laid down by the Ministry of Family and Consumer Affairs in 1959. But these services are not obligatory and just under half the municipalities have organized both, though most of the rest have a home-help or home-nursing service. It is mainly the sparsely populated districts in western and northern Norway which are not provided for, however, and a large majority of the population live in districts where one or both these services are provided.

Finance for the services comes mainly from municipal taxation, and partly from social and health insurance funds and state grants. There is also an income from charges for services which are made on a sliding scale according to income and family circumstances, and in some cases no charge is made.

Home-nursing services are also provided by various voluntary organizations. Regulations for home-nursing have been drawn up by the Directorate of Health.

Family Care

A primary function of social care offices is to assist the family, but there are many other agencies having this aim—among them are child care committees (described below); family counselling offices, and family health centres. Family counselling offices act as advisory and referral agencies. They offer marriage counselling, advice and guidance to unmarried mothers and, where appropriate, refer clients to doctors for advice and treatment. The family health centres—interpreting 'health' broadly—operate in the field of social medicine. They offer guidance and simple treatment aimed at maintaining sound physical and mental health within the family, but with primary emphasis on the care of mothers and young children. The majority of the 1400 health centres throughout the country—roughly 1 to every 2500 persons—are run by the larger voluntary organizations (generally with financial support from the state and the local authority), and the rest are provided by the local health authorities.

Other services supporting and assisting the family include the local health committees in each municipality whose work involves special responsibilities in caring for the health of mothers and children; day institutions for pre-school children (where family circumstances are taken into account); as well as temporary domestic or nursing assistance when mothers fall sick or are otherwise incapacitated. The services mentioned are specifically concerned with supporting the family, but they operate within a much wider framework of social insurance, health and welfare services which all contribute to some degree to the maintenance of conditions which enable satisfactory family life to develop.

Care of Children

Once more, there are many services ranging through social insurance, family allowances, housing subsidies, education and labour protection, which have child care as one of their objectives, but certain services are more directly concerned with this aim and were specially created to fulfil it. The promotion of child welfare is one of the aims of municipal social care offices, but each municipality also has a child care committee (set up under the Child Care Act, 1953) which is primarily responsible for child care. Its functions are broadly similar to those of children's committees in Britain and may be classified as protective and preventive.

Child care committees are concerned with children under the age of 18 who:

(*a*) live in conditions which endanger or harm their health;
(*b*) show particular difficulty in adjusting to their environment;
(*c*) are not receiving adequate care and attention; and
(*d*) are not receiving necessary care and attention when ill.

Children may be placed in foster homes, children's homes, nursery schools, training or other special schools, or residential institutions which can provide treatment or care appropriate to their needs. They remain under the constant supervision of the child care committees which may also extend supervision to children in their own homes.

Child care committees may provide or arrange help in the form of cash, goods or services. After-care is an important part of their work.

Municipal health committees work closely with child care committees not only in connection with the health of the individual child or his family, but also by supervising and regulating standards of hygiene and health in children's institutions and foster homes. Health committees also arrange adoptions.

In the educational field educational psychologists advise pupils, teachers, and parents as a routine service, but also make assessments and recommendations about the need for teaching in special classes or schools. Psychiatric advice is also available.

There is a National Child Care Council, appointed by the government, to advise the Ministry of Social Affairs on child care questions. It is also invited to express its views on matters of principle in child care. At an intermediate level between the Ministry of Social Affairs and the municipalities come the county child care committees. These are voluntary committees set up by and composed of administrators and social workers and their aims are: to advise and guide the municipal child care committees, and to take or support initiative in establishing or developing child care services (and institutions) in their counties.

Among the other services related to child care are: youth services, police social offices, vocational guidance offices and employment exchanges. Police social offices are found in some of the urban areas and their work is aimed at preventing delinquency. This they seek to do by encouraging young people to engage in various activities, and often do so by collaborating with the local youth committee and youth clubs.

The age of criminal responsibility was raised to 14 in 1898—the Penal Act, 1842, had fixed it at 10—and a proposal to raise it to 15 was rejected by the Storting in 1965. Children under 14 are never taken before the courts for misdemeanours, and children from 14 to 18 only rarely. Instead, these older children are usually referred to the child care committees which have considerable powers under the 1953 Child Care Act and the Young Offenders Act, 1965, which superseded the sections of the Child Care Act referring to penal sanctions. Child care committees may remove children from parental care and place them in foster homes or various institutions where this is considered in the interests of the child's welfare. The legislation emphasizes—and government departments have reiterated—that restrictions on liberty which may be imposed must have positive aims of securing rehabilitation or readjustment through treatment, education or training, and these restrictions are not intended to be punitive. This philosophy is also paramount in dealing with young offenders.

Between 8000 and 9000 children under 18 are 'under care' at some time during any one year—out of a total child population of 1,000,000—and roughly 5000 of these are actually *in* care, a half of them in foster homes, a quarter in children's homes, and the rest in various other kinds of institution for observation or treatment, or otherwise not living with their families. The total numbers involved —as a proportion of the population—are much smaller than in Britain, but the new cases in any year are smaller again. The figures given above refer to the total numbers recorded as being or coming into contact with some form of care—whether at home or actually 'in care'—during a year. The number of new cases annually in the mid-sixties, from causes ranging from delinquency to loss of parents, was just over two thousand (2 per 1000 of the population 'at risk') and just over half of these were taken into care—a third of these to foster homes, rather more than half to children's homes, and about 8 per cent to approved schools. About two-thirds of the children who remain with the families are placed under some form of welfare supervision. Most 'under care' cases are short-term, and are urban rather than rural. A half are 14 or over, nearly three-quarters are over 10, and 55 per cent are boys. In connection with behaviour or adjustment problems the proportion of boys rises to 70 per cent or more.

Juvenile Delinquency

Delinquency among those under 18 in Norway is treated in the first instance as a behavioural problem and a matter for the child care committee. The Child Care Act, 1953, states that children up to the age of 18 who 'by offences against the law or by other behaviour show such poor adjustment to their environment or to the community that special measures are found to be necessary', shall be helped by the child care committee in the manner found to be appropriate.

As already noted, children under 14 are never subjected to court hearings, and older adolescents only infrequently. In 95 per cent of the court cases against children under 18, proceedings are waived or suspended. Waiving of proceedings is conditional on referring the case to the child care committee which may then decide to implement various measures under the Child Care or Young Offenders legislation. They have authority to place maladjusted children in special schools or treatment homes, but such action is not taken without background or personal reports from social worker, psychologist, doctor, psychiatrist, or others whose knowledge and judgement is of value. Parents are held closely involved in the discussions as far as possible, and the compulsory transfer of a child to a foster home or institution is only resorted to when other approaches have failed. It is rarely necessary for the child care committees to apply sanctions in the face of parental opposition.

Where proceedings against young persons are not waived, it is common for the courts to impose a 'conditional sentence'—comparable to conditional discharge in the United Kingdom—and also probation. The rules governing conditional sentence (or the postponement of execution of sentence) were first introduced in 1894. Postponement of sentence is normally for two years, but may exceptionally be for five years, and the person may be placed under supervision. The numbers placed under supervision have risen steadily since the beginning of the 1950s.

There is no highly developed probation service in Norway, but several of what are now the functions of the official probation service in Britain are performed by voluntary or semi-official organizations, as well as by the child care service. Easily the most important organization providing supervision and after-care in connection with the penal system is the Criminal Welfare Association, which increasingly resembles an English-type probation service in its early stages. It is probable that a probation service organized on a municipal or county basis will emerge before long.

In general, Criminal Welfare Associations carry out supervisory functions in all cases where there are no special grounds for arranging supervision by other agencies such as the police, child care committees, or individuals. But in these cases too, the CWA may still exercise overall supervision. The supervision is usually by permanent CWA officials or, in smaller associations, by voluntary assistants.

The Young Offenders Act, 1965, introduced youth detention and converted the work training schools into youth prisons. Since, on average, only sixty youths a year were committed to training schools in the early sixties, the numbers affected by the re-designation were also very small. Youths from 14 to 21—or in exceptional circumstances 23—may be committed to youth prison for a maximum period of two years. It is a preventive institution which aims to reform and rehabilitate. After-care of a suitable kind and duration is provided where this is considered appropriate. Here again, the social care office can be brought in as an agency which now stands centrally in the range of welfare services.

Care of the Old

The social insurance (old age pensions) and health services form the main structure of services connected with the care of old people, but they are linked with other services, and one of the functions of the social care offices is to co-ordinate and develop the various forms of personal assistance to the old. Many towns have 'health and welfare' centres, established and operated by local authorities, voluntary organizations, or both. As their name suggests, these centres offer a range of welfare services besides simpler forms of medical care. Among their activities are: 'meals on wheels'; chiropody; clubs and meetings; excursions and holidays; helping to provide or find housing; arranging home visits; referring cases and needs to appropriate local authority or private agencies; advising old people on the solution of financial problems.

Statutory and voluntary bodies arrange domiciliary nursing or, alternatively, elderly persons who are unable to care for themselves can be taken into nursing homes or geriatric wards. Local authorities and voluntary organizations such as trade unions, professional associations, or religious congregations, have built institutions and individual dwellings for old people.

A national institute for geriatric research was established in 1957. In addition there is a permanent official committee studying the problems and care of old age and producing information and reports for distribution. One of the 'Big Four' voluntary agencies (The National Public Health Association) specializes in the same field, and provides advice and guidance to local authorities and voluntary agencies on the provision of care for the elderly. As in other health and welfare activities, there is close collaboration between official and voluntary agencies working with old people.

In recent years attention has been drawn to difficulties caused by low incomes, poor housing, unsatisfactory institutions, and social isolation, and current policies are trying to overcome these problems by national and local action.

Alcoholism

Although the consumption per head of alcohol in the form of beer, wine and spirits in Norway is smaller than in the rest of Scandinavia (except Finland), and much lower than in most other European countries, alcoholism is widely regarded as a serious problem. It is doubtful if the incidence of alcoholism in Norway is abnormally high compared to other European countries—it may in fact be low—but there is more general awareness of the consequences of over-consumption, and an extraordinary amount of activity concerned to find and treat people who are regarded as immoderate drinkers.

The recurrent public debates, the number of voluntary and official organizations which exist to combat the use and effects of alcohol, the stringent laws controlling the sale of wines and spirits, and the functions of the municipal temperance committees, combine to reveal powerful moral attitudes directed at the consumption of alcohol. The unversality and persistence of feelings of disapproval and guilt can probably only be comprehended by people from other countries with strong Lutheran or Calvinist traditions, such as Scotland, most Canadian provinces, or from other parts of Scandinavia. Both alcohol and alcoholism are the objects of a number of legal, educational, medical and welfare measures and activities. Sometimes, in the treatment of alcoholics, all four components are brought to bear with a view to effecting a lasting mental and physical rehabilitation.

Temperance Committees

These were established in every municipality by the Temperance Committees Act, 1932, after it had become clear that the misuse of alcohol had social and medical aspects which needed informed treatment. They are nominated by the municipal council and consist of at least three members, one of whom should be a doctor, where possible. The main function of the committee is to work for greater temperance in the municipality by:

(*a*) Dealing with or assisting persons who misuse alcohol or other intoxicants or narcotics—and to offer advice and help to their families and others close to them.

(*b*) To support and develop educational activities relating to alcohol—in schools and by other means.

(*c*) To act as a specialist, advisory and consultative committee to the municipal authority on matters within its field of reference.

Temperance committees are empowered to take action on their own initiative with persons who, through the use of alcohol (or other intoxicants or drugs) are a danger to themselves or their environment. The committee may also intervene at the request of the person himself, his wife (or husband), parents, children or other near relations; clergyman or doctor (under certain conditions); child care committee; social care office voluntary welfare agencies; or the police—who also have a duty to inform the temperance committee of all convictions for drunkenness.

The central administration of temperance committees and their activities is carried out by the National Temperance Council. This is a committee of five members appointed by the Crown (Government). It is the state's expert committee on matters relating to the use and misuse of alcohol, while its other functions are in some degree comparable to those of the local temperance committee in the field of information and education. There is a chief medical officer for the treatment of alcoholics. He is also in charge of the central institution for such treatment. All applications for the admission of patients to the institutions are submitted to the chief medical officer for decision.

The government supports temperance work in ways other than those already outlined. It allocates substantial amounts every year to educational and information activities through the medium of temperance organizations and the National Council for Temperance Education. In addition, these organizations are paid a special subsidy towards the salaries of a number of full time peripatetic lecturers (at present seven) who travel the country lecturing to schools and organizations on the alcohol problem. Significantly, both the temperance committees and the licensing system come under the control and direction of the Ministry of Social Affairs.

CHAPTER 5

Social Work and Its Co-ordination

SOCIAL WORK

It is not easy to find precise or satisfactory definitions of 'social work' and 'social worker', there are differences of opinion about the meaning and scope of these terms, and it is probably more useful to say what social work tries to do than to look for a definition which excludes forms of service which many people regard as social work. In Norway, for example, it is accepted that no meaningful distinction can be made between social workers and administrators in many agencies and organizations.[1]

A Norwegian authority, Bernt Lund, has defined social work in the following, comprehensive, terms in an official report[2]:

'Social work seeks to bring about adjustments in the relationship of individuals and their social environment with a view to creating conditions in which their social functioning is satisfying, secure and free from conflict. . . . Social work operates in the area in which individuals and their social environment come into contact and interact.'

'Social functioning' means the fulfilment of social roles (what is expected of people) as fathers or mothers, husbands or wives, employees, workmates, neighbours, and so on. The writer goes on to say that the problems for the solution of which social work is particularly appropriate are those which hinder a person's 'social functioning', are destructive of individual wellbeing, or undermine relations with other people. Social work has two main purposes which are interlinked:

(*a*) to eliminate the causes of problems afflicting the individual; and

(*b*) to reorganize or reconstruct the client's relationship with his environment.

[1] See, for example, *Bernt H. Lund* 'The functions of senior personnel in the social services' in *Training of Senior Personnel for the Social Services* (Report) UN Geneva 1964 p. 25.

[2] B. H. Lund *Utdanning av sosialarbeidere i Norge* (Kirke-og undervisnings-departmentet Oslo 1963) p. 9. (*Training of Social Workers in Norway*, Ministry of Church and Education, 1963).

And it attempts to do so in such a way that problems do not recur. Social work tries to strengthen and support the client's own resources to enable him to solve his own problems as far as possible. The writer points out that the aims of social work are broader than this, for it also seeks to strengthen society's resources for the solution of problems through vigorous social policy.

Three forms or areas of social work are identified:

(*a*) work with the individual;
(*b*) work with groups; and
(*c*) social planning and administration which are concerned with communities of different sizes and with society as a whole.

Social work with individuals is similar in range and scope to what is practised in other advanced countries, as are the other forms of what Lund has defined broadly as 'social work'. Work with groups may have general or specific aims. The former may have preventive or ameliorative goals as in youth organizations or various kinds of work with old people in clubs, associations or centres. But social work in group settings is also concerned to identify and solve problems of individuals within the group, and in this respect, the aims can be defined as specific.

In his report[1] Lund formulated the objects of social work training in Norway:

'Social work training shall equip the student with a foundation of knowledge, attitudes and skills which furnish qualifications for working with people in a way which results in an improvement of their social functioning and also contributes to the student's personal and professional development.'

The social worker usually deals directly with the client, but many trained and experienced social workers are necessarily engaged in administration—especially in the smaller municipalities—where the small size of local offices means that it is not economical (or perhaps possible) to separate administrative and social work functions entirely. The relative numbers of trained social workers, and the proportions of time they give to 'administrative' or 'social work' duties, vary with the nature of the service in which they are engaged. For instance, the arrangements in institutions providing care and treatment for maladjusted children, mentally handicapped, nursing homes, or old people's homes are very different from those in social

[1] Lund (1963) *op. cit.* p. 17.

care offices. The institutions have a far higher proportion of personnel with advanced training in some field which might be either social work, psychology, psychiatry, education or medical nursing. Municipal social care offices, on the other hand, generally have relatively fewer of their staffs trained in some branch relevant to social work, although the officials concerned are responsible for developing social work programmes and administering the services. If these administrators have had any training it was usually in legal or commercial (e.g business administration) disciplines. Trained social workers are usually found at the lower levels of the administrative structure providing the personal services and only partly engaged in administration.

A survey of social workers in 1960[1] found that the 744 in the sample were distributed as follows:

1	General social work in municipal social administration, including social insurance and welfare services	44·1 per cent
2	Family, child-care and youth services	15·3 per cent
3	Medical social work including care of alcoholics	13·3 per cent
4	Employment and rehabilitation services	9·8 per cent
5	Personnel and welfare work in large public or private organizations	9·6 per cent
6	Care of the old	3·6 per cent
7	Welfare and aftercare services connected with prisons and police	4·3 per cent

It was not possible to make precise boundaries between the different areas of work. Some medical social work in hospitals or other health service institutions, for instance, was concerned with rehabilitation, and there might be overlaps between social work in the family—child care—youth area and care or aftercare in connection with imprisonment or the police. Similarly, it would not be uncommon for there to be a link between the care of alcoholics and prison aftercare.

Of the social workers surveyed, 62·1 per cent were employed by municipalities, 22·8 per cent by the state, 12·8 per cent by voluntary agencies or private firms, and 2·3 per cent by the counties.

[1] Bernt H. Lund, *Sosialarbeiderne og sosialforvaltinger* (Social Workers and Social Administration), Oslo 1960.

There have been changes in the number and distribution of social workers since 1960, but the main pattern in Norwegian social work is much the same, and although specialization is becoming more apparent, the process is necessarily slow. Thus the general social work in municipal employment is likely to remain the largest grouping.

The two main staffing problems in what may loosely be called the social work services are: (*a*) how to increase the flow of newly trained social workers, and (*b*) how to improve the quality and effectiveness of existing staffs, particularly those whose duties, though mainly administrative, involve collaboration with social workers or dealing directly with clients (as in social insurance or vocational guidance offices).

A number of measures have been taken to raise numbers and standard of personnel in the services.

Vocational Training Before Recruitment

Vocational training for social work is not new in Norway—the first school of social work was established in 1920 by the Norwegian Council of Women, a voluntary organization. The first state school came in 1950 with the formation of the Norwegian School of Municipal Administration and Social Work. Both schools are in Oslo, but other state schools of social work have been set up, in Trondheim in 1962, and in Stavanger a few years later. Courses at the state schools combine practical and theoretical training and last for 2½ years, and the National Council of Women's school, which formerly provided one-year courses, has now followed suit. At present only about a third of practising social workers have completed the 2½-year courses, but the proportion will rise steadily as the social services expand their recruitment and the schools increase their flow of trained social workers. The United Nations reports on training for social work show that theoretical and practical training in Norway is broadly similar to that of other highly developed countries.

Between them the schools provide ninety to a hundred trained social workers a year, but the total is rising. The number may be small, but in relation to population an equivalent output for Britain would be up to 1400 a year. About half the candidates qualify at the Norwegian School of Municipal Administration and Social Work in Oslo, a quarter at the Trondheim school, and most of the rest at the National Council of Women's school. The state school also runs a two-year course for child care workers, so the total of social workers qualifying there every year is well above fifty. In addition, the school is developing training and refresher courses and seminars for highly qualified and experienced social workers.

In Norway as in other countries, the further development and effectiveness of social work is handicapped by a shortage of social workers with advanced training and of institutions in which to train them. The report which has been referred to earlier[1] discusses the need for greater specialization in social work and, associated with it, the need for advanced training and study. The report proposed the establishment of a course of advanced theoretical and practical training and the creation of a College of Social Work, preferably as a school of the University of Oslo. Only experienced social workers would be qualified for admission. All social work training in Norway is provided at schools and institutions outside the universities, and there is little or no contact between them. This is considered to be particularly disadvantageous at the higher levels of training where the rigorous demands of academic disciplines would offer a valuable formative influence.

The purpose of the proposed college would be to extend and deepen knowledge and improve the more sophisticated skills in social work, making the individual social worker better equipped all round and also in his or her special field. But there would be wider aims, namely, to contribute to the development of social work as a whole, and to professionalization.

Lund estimated that about two-thirds of social workers who had completed the 2½-year course might be eligible for places at the college. This figure may be too high if academic standards were to be achieved and maintained—though the quality, including educational attainment of basic course students at the school, is rising—but even so, it is evident that there is a large pool of experienced social workers ready to be given advanced training.

A survey by Kluge[2] found that two-thirds of the students who graduated from the state school of social work in Oslo between 1950 and 1960 had undertaken some form of further study or training, but mostly short-term, since only 6 per cent had taken courses lasting a year or longer. Over 70 per cent, however, said

[1] Lund 1963, *op. cit.*

[2] Liv Kluge, *Norges Kommunal-og sosialskole gjennom* 10*år* 1950–1960 Oslo, 1960, pp. 26–7.

that they wanted to pursue courses of that duration. These findings were confirmed by Holter in another study.[1] She reported that virtually all those who were interviewed expressed a need for some form of further training in social work.

Apart from the courses at the state school in Oslo, advanced training in social work is little developed and takes the form of in-service training rather than systematic, full-time courses of theory and practice at educational institutions. Many Norwegian social workers go abroad for their advanced studies, and this is a common feature of the system of higher education. Part of the explanation for this is that Norway is too small to support the variety of highly specialized institutions which are required, but as the number of qualified students from basic courses increase, the provision of more advanced studies is growing in several disciplines, including those in social work education.

One institution which has offered advanced training to social workers since the early fifties is the Institute for Child Psychiatry in Oslo. Teaching includes child psychiatry, clinical psychology, and specialized forms of therapeutic education. But the training of social workers at this institute is on a very small scale, since only a few can be admitted every year.

In-service and Supplementary Training

Several courses have been launched in the 1960s with a view to increasing the effectiveness of personnel in the social work services, locally and centrally. A number of schemes have been arranged jointly by the Norwegian Social Welfare Association—which is a federation of municipal social agencies—the Ministry of Church and Education, and the Ministry of Social Affairs. The National Insurance Institution also organizes a variety of residential and correspondence courses as well as local conferences such as 'weekend schools'. During any one year about a third of all social insurance employees participate in some form of study or training. The Directorate of Labour has developed in-service training for staff whose work is connected with rehabilitation.

The courses arranged by the Social Welfare Association in conjunction with the central government departments of education and social affairs are intended to help bridge the gap until adequate

[1] Harriet Holter, *Sosialarbeiderens yrkes-rolle* (The Social Worker's Role) *Tidsskrift for samfunnsforskning*. No. I, 1960.

numbers of trained social workers can be produced by the expansion of the training schools. Courses are directed primarily at the staffs of municipal social care offices whose duties have become more social work orientated and exacting following the implementation of the Social Care Act. Under the Act, personal social services—largely channelled through or co-ordinated by the social care offices—form the main instrument for solving social problems but few of the existing staff of the offices have specific or adequate training for social work though many are experienced and competent. The new in-service training schemes are intended to equip these people to a standard where they will gain formal recognition of competence from the Ministry of Social Affairs. The schemes also serve as 'refresher' or supplementary courses for personnel who have received social work training at some time.

Efforts are being made to bring social workers and administrators up to date in their knowledge and to increase their understanding of new or complex questions through bulletins and circulars from central government departments, explanatory leaflets, or pamphlets on a variety of social problems. There are besides, three periodicals dealing with various aspects of social work and social administration. In addition, the Norwegian Social Welfare Association issues fuller summaries and discussions of official circulars and organizes conferences and short study courses at county level to consider new legislation. One important aim of these is to bring together staff and elected representatives (councillors and members of parliament) in free discussion.

A great deal of voluntary and statutory social work in Norway is carried out by personnel who have been trained at schools of nursing, training colleges for special teachers, 'child-care' schools, the Institute for Child Psychiatry, and the universities.

The majority of medical nurses are trained on three-year courses at state hospitals. About 1500 medical nurses a year complete training and a large majority of these are engaged in work directly concerned with social problems in old people's homes, residential institutions, and certain domiciliary health or welfare services.

Child-care schools train teachers for work with young children in nursery schools and day homes. A proportion of doctors, psychologists, sociologists and lawyers take posts in social work on completing their training.

The great majority of social workers in Norway are women and several factors account for this. Among them are: tradition; salaries —which are low by comparison with other occupations also requiring high standards of education and training; and a lingering popular belief that no particular qualification is required for social work (other than a well developed social conscience). These factors are diminishing in importance, however, and the status of social work, salaries, number of men, and of qualified social workers of both sexes, are all rising.

CO-ORDINATION

Fragmentation and an irrational separation of function still handicap attempts to maximize the effectiveness of social services and of the social work which forms part of them. The size and number of voluntary organizations engaged so extensively in social work makes the task of co-ordination more complex. But over the last ten years or so there has been steady progress towards a closer co-ordination in social services and social work, and a variety of measures have been adopted to bring this about. Greater co-ordination has been achieved in policies and legislation as well as in administrative arrangements.

Legislation to bring about integration and more uniform benefits in social insurance services was introduced in 1958 and extended and improved by the National Insurance legislation in 1966. This, in turn, was linked with the comprehensive reorganization—aimed at integration and co-ordination in welfare services—laid down by the Social Care Act. There is a growing insistence in social legislation on trying to match services to the needs of the individual client—and it is recognized that in this social work has a central part to play.

At the local level, municipal social care offices and the health and social insurance offices are multi-purpose agencies each deploying an increasing range of personal services to meet individual and family problems, and the trend towards assembling services in a few offices with close links between them is kept up by pressures from central and local authorities.

Liaison committees—or less formal *ad hoc* gatherings—and 'teamwork' of different kinds have spread rapidly in central and local government administration, and also help to bridge gaps between official and voluntary agencies. Three main purposes motivate these developments: better communication, and more effective co-ordination and implementation of social policies. The trend is not limited to administration, for liaison and teamwork has also been adopted within social service institutions and agencies of all kinds.

In county and municipal agencies the work of certain senior and chief officials requires them to co-ordinate a number of social work tasks which are directly under their control, and to collaborate with other agencies providing allied or related services. Leading examples are the county medical officer, the county governor, and the chief social welfare officer in a municipality. The county medical officer's duties involve him in medical, welfare, employment, and rehabilitation services, and he is a member of various committees dealing with these. He is assisted by a 'social secretary' who is a trained social worker. One of the medical officer's major responsibilities is to supervise (and help to integrate) the work of district medical officers and of health committees in the county.

The county governor is the senior public official in the county, and among his functions he is consultant, adviser, guide and co-ordinator. Social legislation has increased both his powers and the range of his duties. Under the Child Care Act, for example, he is charged with supervising child care in the municipalities and providing the local child care committees with information, advice and guidance. The county governor has also been given comparable functions in social care and is statutorily responsible for the planning, establishment and operation of psychiatric services, though the actual planning and administration is likely to be carried out by medical staff.

At the municipal level, the social welfare officer has extensive duties in connection with the numerous welfare services which are now co-ordinated in or closely linked with the social care offices.

There are proposals for the formation of county social welfare (or social care) boards to work for a higher degree of co-ordination of personal social services and to develop services by combining resources more effectively.

Nationally and locally, there are many statutory and voluntary committees whose objects include: discovering social needs; developing and improving social services; providing information, advice and guidance; and achieving more effective liaison and co-ordination within the structure of official services and between them and voluntary services. Heavy reliance on voluntary social work (and social services generally in welfare and medical fields) has created problems of co-ordination, and particular efforts are made to integrate the work of statutory and voluntary services.

CHAPTER 6

Education and Housing

Education and housing are two areas in which the state and local authorities provide a high proportion—in some respects all—of the necessary resources, but they are not social services in the accepted meaning of the term. Certain parts of the educational system, however, are clearly social services aimed at the solution of the problems of individuals or groups, and are closely associated with other social services, especially those concerned with welfare and health.

EDUCATION

The educational system in Norway is being increasingly adapted to the great variety of minority educational needs which are not being met by ordinary schools, and in this way performs some of the functions of a personal social (or social work) service.

Special schools have been established by the state, counties, municipalities, and voluntary organizations. The state has taken the leading part, leaving the municipalities freer to concentrate on the conventional forms of education for the mass of children, and has founded schools for children who are blind, deaf or partially deaf, educationally subnormal, maladjusted, or have speech difficulties. In recent years, the counties have become more prominent in the provision of special schools of different kinds to serve the municipalities in their area. These schools are financed largely from the tax revenues transferred from the municipalities to the county. Municipalities are the primary education authorities and bear 50 per cent of the cost of education (apart from what they contribute to the county), a larger share than British local authorities.

Local education committees have close links with the special schools and with child care committees. They may refer maladjusted children to special observation schools (for a maximum of two years). An education committee may also decide to expel a child from school, but this is normally done in consultation with the municipal child care committee and, probably, with the school psychologist. The child care committee then assumes responsibility for the child under powers granted by child care legislation. The welfare of the child is the paramount consideration in such cases.

Current thinking and planning in relation to education is in the direction of more and better facilities for children with particular handicaps or other problems. The 'Long-term Programme 1966–69' —which contained the economic and social planning proposals formulated by the government for the next four-year plan—drew attention to what was regarded as a major defect of the educational system, 'the lack of educational facilities for those children who have difficulty in keeping up with the normal pace of education. Modern methods of special education, based on extensive research, have shown that proper training can often be a more crucial factor for the development of such children than for others. Intensive education frequently represents their only chance of developing themselves into full members of society'. And the conclusion was that 'great emphasis must be placed upon the expansion of special education. . . .'

HOUSING

State intervention in housing in Norway has taken the forms which are familiar in many other countries and can be divided into regulation and provision. The scope and detail of regulation have both grown, commencing with legislation or by-laws concerned with fire hazards and sanitation in the 1820s and proliferating in a complex body of laws dealing with minimum housing standards; the design of the dwelling and its environment (including town and regional planning and 'green belt policy'); and rent control. Provision or assistance by the state and local authorities has been predominantly financial and very few houses (under 5 per cent) are constructed by the authorities. Instead, housing policy since the war has aimed at stimulating non-profit housing associations such as co-operatives. Almost 30 per cent of all new dwellings are built by non-profit organizations, but the proportion is higher in the larger towns, rising to over half in Oslo. Roughly two-thirds of new dwellings are erected by private builders for individual owner-occupiers and the great majority are timber-built, single-family houses. This pattern is largely accounted for by the small, scattered population and the absence of a land shortage, though good building sites are in short supply in and near the larger centres of population. In these areas a high proportion of new building consists of blocks of flats or terraced housing.

The biggest contribution to housing is made by the state through loans and subsidies. Over 70 per cent of all dwellings built since the war have received substantial financial assistance through one or other of the two housing banks (the Housing Bank for urban areas, and the Smallholders' Bank in rural areas), and the proportion remains fairly constant in respect of new construction. The first government measure to improve the supply and terms of housing finance was in 1894, with the creation of a Housing Loan Fund which was replaced in 1903 by the Workers' Agricultural Property and Housing Bank. One of the main objects of this bank was to grant loans to persons of little or no means. It, in turn, was superseded by the National Smallholding and Housing Bank in 1915.

Two new state housing banks were founded in 1946 (the Housing and Smallholders' Banks respectively) and the government considerably extended its financial and administrative responsibilities in housing.

Financial Assistance

Financial help is given mainly in the form of loans on favourable terms compared with the private market, but there are also housing subsidies for certain individuals and families. The interest rate on state housing loans was 2½ per cent from 1946 until 1957, when it was raised to 3½ per cent on new loans. New arrangements were introduced in 1966 and the interest rate was raised to 4½ per cent. The loan structure was simplified at the same time and housing loans now consist of *first priority loan* (from the state bank) at an interest of 4½ per cent, and *second priority loan* (not necessarily from the state housing banks, but guaranteed by them) at 5 per cent. Both rates of interest are below current market rates and the difference represents an interest rate subsidy. One aim of the new regulations was to reduce the amount of capital which had to be found by the average person seeking a loan. No repayments have to be made on the first priority loan during the first five years, with very low repayments of 0·5 per cent of capital in the next five years, and 1·0 per cent a year after the tenth. The amortization period is, therefore, a very long one and this helps to bring house purchase within the range of people on moderate incomes. The second priority loans are to be repaid over fifteen years on a scale rising from 5 per cent a year in the first five years to 8½ per cent in the last.

Rent Subsidies

Subject to certain conditions, families with children, elderly people, and the disabled are entitled to rent subsidies. Above a certain income limit, the subsidy varies according to income, but there are other factors influencing the level of the subsidy. The subsidy is related to the date of construction of a house as well as the interest rate on the loan and, therefore, attempts to take into account changes (almost certainly increases) in the cost of building over time. In addition, the subsidy is used as a means of enabling people to raise their housing standards and may be reduced proportionately if a 'persons per room' norm is exceeded. Where there is persistent overcrowding it may be withheld entirely.

The state meets four-fifths of the cost of subsidies and the remainder is paid by the municipality. Payment is made through the Housing Bank or, in rural areas, the Smallholders' Bank. The central department with administrative and policy responsibility for housing is the Ministry of Local Government and Labour.

Special kinds of housing—for old people, the disabled, blind or other handicapped, or for families with particularly acute problems—are built by local authorities (with government loans and grants), housing associations, or voluntary agencies.

Rent Control

In common with other countries, Norway introduced rent control during the First World War and reintroduced it at the beginning of the Second. It has remained in force since for much of the private rental market and only a small increase over the 1940 rent has been permitted so far. This is another way in which the government has sought to prevent the price of housing rising beyond the means of the average family.

From the brief description given it may be seen that financial assistance combines two elements: (*a*) general assistance in the form of loans, grants, reduced interest rates and low, controlled rents—and, in principle, this is available to the whole population; and, (*b*) specific assistance which is given through rent subsidies or special housing to individuals and groups whose needs are assessed as pressing. Thus the objects of this two-fold policy are to secure adequate housing for the whole population at a reasonable cost (this is the 'universalist' aspect of housing policy) and, where necessary, to match the assistance given more exactly to individual needs (the 'specific'—or social service—aspect of policy). These aims are common to housing policy in most countries, it is the means adopted in seeking to attain them that differ rather than the ends themselves.

SUGGESTIONS FOR FURTHER READING

Norway

As yet there is no single book available which will provide the student with a comprehensive survey of Norwegian social development and social policy, but the supply of relevant literature is both increasing and its quality improving. A growing proportion of it is being published in English by government departments, universities, research institutes, and other agencies (such as the Norwegian Joint Committee on International Social Policy many of whose publications are listed below*).

The Norwegian Embassy is usually able to help in obtaining up-to-date information about current material on social policy and administration. In the United Kingdom, Bailey Bros. and Swinfern Ltd., Warner House, Upper Thames Street, London, E.C.4, handle the publications of the Norwegian Joint Committee on International Social Policy, and in North America they may be ordered from the University of Wisconsin Press.

For convenience, the publications (which includes cyclostyled material available from official sources on application) in the following list are grouped into books, reports and journals.

Books

1. *General and descriptive*

James A. Storing, *Norwegian Democracy*, Oslo, 1963
T. K. Derry, *A Short History of Norway*, 1957
Geo. R. Nelson (Ed.), *Freedom and Welfare*, 1953
Aftenposten, Oslo (pub.) *Facts about Norway* (annually)
Donald S. Connery, *The Scandinavians*, 1966

Social Policy and Services

*Dorothy B. Skårdal, *Social Insurance in Norway*, Oslo, 1960
*K. Evang and D. B. Skårdal, *Health Services in Norway*, Oslo, 1960
*M. Langholm, *Family and Child Welfare in Norway*, Oslo, 1961
*F. Danielsen, *Care of the Aged in Norway*, Oslo, 1958
**Housing in Norway 1950–1960*, Housing Directorate, Oslo, 1962
A. Evensen, *Social Defence in Norway*, Oslo, 1965

*G. Mortensen and S. Persson, *Vocational Training in Norway*, Oslo, 1964
*H. Dolfman, *Labor Relations in Norway*, Oslo, 1957
Geo. M. Wiley, *Educational System of Norway*, Oslo, 1955
Sosiale fakta (facts about social services), Min. of Social Affairs (periodically)
A. Marthinsen *et al.*, *Veileder i praktisk sosial medisin*, Oslo, 1962
E. Storsteen (Ed.), *Sosial Handbok for Norge* (2 volumes), Oslo, 1952–53

2. *Reports and Statistics*

Social Developments in Norway, Min. of Social Affairs (periodically)
Social Welfare Statistics of the Northern Countries, Min. of Social Affairs (bienially, jointly)
Statistical Yearbook of Norway, Central Bureau of Statistics, Oslo

3. *Journals*

Kommunalt tidsskrift (Municipal journal)
Sosialt arbeid (Social Work)
Kuratoren (The Social Worker)

4. *Other sources*

Publications of the United Nations agencies
OECD, ILO, ISSA, and other bodies

CANADA

CHAPTER 1

Introduction

There are many different strands to the complex pattern of cultures and traditions that can be discerned in Canada's emergence as a modern technological nation of some 20 millions of people in 1961; 18,238,000 at the 1961 Census and estimated at just over 20 million in 1966. Canada was first settled by the French, whose defeat at the Plains of Abraham in 1759 led to the establishment of a British Colony, governed from London, but with specific obligations to the French population, contained in the Quebec Act 1774 to protect the laws and customs of France as extant at the time of the conquest. The effect of the American Revolutionary War was twofold. In the first place the presence of a strong, and now anti-British nation on the southern borders of the new country put great pressure on the new colony to preserve some kind of unity in order to remain independent. In the second place it led to the emigration of large numbers of United Empire Loyalists to the Atlantic provinces and Southern Ontario. This, together with emigration from Britain, produced a powerful and lasting tradition of Protestant English-speaking majority to offset the Roman Catholic and French-speaking population of the province of Quebec. The commercial policies of the British Government in the early nineteenth century, emphasizing free trade but renewing the support of previous protective policies, compelled the nation to press ahead with the settlement of the prairies and the west country. Thus, at Confederation in 1867, as the Report of the Rowell-Sirois Commission of 1937–8[1] puts it, 'Federal union was a plan whereby, through mutual concession, cultural and local loyalties could be preserved and reconciled with the political strength and solidarity of the whole.' The instrument in

[1] Canada, *Royal Commission on Dominion Provincial Relations.* Report Book I p. 29. Ottawa, King's Printer 1940.

which all these conflicting tendencies were reconciled was the British North America Act, 1867. This is a statute of the British Parliament, and is a document of fundamental importance to the organization and administration of welfare services to this day. The political effect of this document has been, since 1867, to establish an uneasy balance of power between the central government in Ottawa and the sovereign provinces that make up the Confederation. This balance shifts between the parties from time to time, often unpredictably, a fact which makes particular difficulties for the administration of public affairs.

Throughout the nineteenth century there was a steady flow of immigrants to Canada, not only from the United Kingdom, and especially from Scotland and Ireland, particularly in times of economic stress in those countries—of which the Irish movement in the 'Hungry Forties' is one of the most vivid examples—but also from areas of central Europe, notably from the Ukraine, South Russia and central Europe. These waves of settlement have each left a deposit of language and culture, as well as traditions of regional identity and independence, that can still be found in various parts of Canada. Two other great waves of immigrants have left their mark on the Canadian scene. The first, immediately preceding the First World War, was associated with the building of railways and the opening up of the west and included many immigrants of European origin as well as large contingents of British and American settlers. The second, following the Second World War, brought to Canada large numbers of immigrants from Great Britain and from various European countries to take advantage of the explosion of economic prosperity that swept North America in the post-war years.

In the first stages of its growth Canada was essentially an agricultural country, and its welfare problems were those of a settled agricultural community. As it became industrialized, and as transportation improved, the problems became those of town-life in the new urban centres of the early and middle twentieth century. In the period since the Second World War Canada has had to face the 'explosion of the cities' and the very rapid rise in mobility that have followed the new technological revolution. Welfare problems have become increasingly those of an urban industrial society and less and less amenable to the simple local solutions of self-help, family interdependence and action by local government, which are characteristic of static rural populations. The magnitude and speed of this change is graphically illustrated by a Table in the *Third Annual Review*[1] of the Economic Council of Canada.

EMPLOYMENT IN AGRICULTURE, MANUFACTURING AND OTHER OCCUPATIONS
(per cent of total employment)

	*United Kingdom**			*Canada*			*United States*		
	1901	1950	1965	1901	1950	1965	1900	1950	1965
Agriculture	9	4	2	40	21	9	38	13	6
Manufacturing	33	41	38	16	26	26	22	26	25
Other	58	55	60	44	53	65	40	61	69
Total	100	100	100	100	100	100	100	100	100

* For Britain, farming, forestry and fishing are included in 'agriculture'. By 1900, much of the decline in employment in British agriculture had already occurred. In 1850 this group account for 22 per cent of the occupied population in Britain.

Source: Based on data from Phyllis Deane and W. A. Cole, *British Economic Growth* 1688–1959, and Economic Review, National Institute of Economic and Social Research; *Historical Statistics of Canada*, pp. 59–65, and *Canadian Statistical Review; Historical Statistics of the United States*, pp. 72–4, and U.S. *Statistical Abstract* 1965, pp. 216–20.

This important Report has a significant passage in which it is pointed out that rapid economic growth of this kind creates problems and has social costs which have still to be met:
'Illustrative of the issues which have become the subject of increasing social concern are: the problems of poverty in the midst of affluence; the needs for better access to high standards of health care and to opportunities for maximum educational advancement for all individuals in the society; increased air and water pollution in an age of greatly advanced scientific capabilities for dealing with these problems; increased urban congestion and blight concentrated especially in centres of highest average income and wealth; and the greatly increased needs for recreational facilities and enlarged cultural opportunities in conditions of reduced working time and increased

[1] Canada, The Economic Council of Canada *Third Annual Review*. Ottawa, Queen's Printer, 1966, p. 19.

leisure. . . . A more equitable distribution of rising opportunities, income and wealth has thus become a prominent objective of modern industrial economies along with other basic economic and social goals.'

These problems and expectations are still undergoing painful assessment in Canada and the welfare structure is constantly being amended to take them more fully into account. The organization and administration of social services in Canada are indeed liable to change greatly in the near future, as greatly as their political and economic context may require.

SOCIAL STRUCTURE

Canadian geography is an important factor in the design of its welfare administration. A population of some twenty millions is spread across a country 3000 or more miles in breadth, from Newfoundland to British Columbia, and is mostly concentrated in a narrow strip on the southern border, with heavy concentration in the two major provinces of Ontario (6,250,000 in 1961) and Quebec (5,260,000 in 1961). In spite of the marvels of modern communication, which brings the whole country within hours instead of days of travel between its several parts, and the electronic linkages of radio, telephone and the computer, it is still true to say that each of the major regions is in some degree isolated by geography from the others, except the large central region where the isolation is due more to cultural and political traditions than to geography.

Each of the provinces, in its turn, has considerable geographic obstacles to the administration of services to people. In British Columbia the mountain and river systems create long and tenuous lines of communication in all areas except in the populous southern areas. The Prairie provinces have relatively small populations spread over very large areas of land, with only one, or at best three, nodal points of concentration in larger cities, which increasingly tend to contain most of the provincial population. For example, Manitoba with a land area of 211,775 square miles had a population in 1961 of 921,600, of which 476,000 lived in the area of Metropolitan Winnipeg. Ontario has a large conurbation spreading for 100 miles or more along the north shore of Lake Ontario, from Niagara Falls to Oshawa, supported by a hinterland of medium-sized urban areas and well-settled agricultural areas and an enormous area to the north where the mineral and forestry wealth of its primary industries is to be found, but where the population is thinly spread and not easy of access. In much the same way the province of Quebec has its urban and industrial strength along the St Lawrence River, supported by expansive rural areas, strong in tradition and politically powerful but with a declining economic importance and social significance. The Atlantic provinces have their populations mainly in the seaports, although the decline in fishing and seagoing trade has made them the depression areas of Canada with the highest level of social problems and the lowest level of available resources. All of them are now engaged on a determined effort to industrialize, and to develop their largely untapped natural resources. They, too, tend to have wide areas to administer, with poor communications and thin-settlements of population outside one or two major cities.

POLITICAL STRUCTURE

Canada's political structure is complex but has had, and continues to have, an important influence on the development of its social services. It is a constitutional monarchy in which the Queen of England is also Queen of Canada. The royal functions are exercised for the whole country by a Governor-General. Until the appointment of Mr Vincent Massey in 1952 this position was invariably held by a distinguished public figure from Great Britain, but it seems likely to be held in the future by a Canadian. The post is almost entirely ceremonial in its official duties but there is no doubt that an experienced Governor-General can be of great service to the Prime Minister of the day and his Cabinet, and there are ample opportunities for the Governor-General to give social and cultural leadership to the country. The last occupant of this post[1] and his wife, for example, were responsible for the establishment in 1965 of the Vanier Institute of the Family to engage in research and study of the social needs and problems of the family in modern society. In the provinces the Crown is represented by a Lieutenant-Governor, again a ceremonial appointment with potential usefulness on an informal basis if the holder is a person of wisdom and experience.

The Federal Government reflects the same type of Parliamentary structure as Great Britain, with a House of Commons, elected at general elections and exercising the real legislative power. The

[1] General Vanier died in 1967.

majority party forms the Government and the familiar apparatus of a Prime Minister and his Cabinet answerable to the House of Commons provides the main political direction of public affairs, with Cabinet Ministers, as in the United Kingdom, exercising the chief executive office of a Department of State. The Canadian Senate is less powerful and much less respected than the House of Lords, but it has provided, on occasion, a useful check on legislative haste and a forum for discussion of important issues of policy. The recent pattern of establishing a Senate Committee to study an issue of social policy has produced, so far, two very important documents of welfare policy: the reports of the Senate Committees on Employment in 1962 and on Aging in 1966. Both documents have had a considerable influence on public policies.

The provincial governments, with the exception of Quebec, are all unicameral, and vary in strength according to the size and resources of the province. They also have governments from the majority party in the legislature after a general election. Clearly a province like Prince Edward Island, with a total population in 1961 of 104,600, more nearly resembles an English County Council, while a province like Ontario, with six and a quarter million people in it, has a very considerable volume of public business to control and direct. Nevertheless, each of the ten provinces is a sovereign power within the terms of the British North America Act, and can act independently of the others and of the Federal Government. Local government varies considerably from province to province, and comes entirely under the jurisdiction of the relevant provincial legislature. The early provinces which were settled by United Empire Loyalists and British immigrants have invented systems of municipal government in the English tradition, with cities, towns, villages, counties and elected municipal organizations. There is a strong tendency now either to abolish local government (a process now in progress in the province of New Brunswick) or to create metropolitan local authorities for the 'big city' areas like Montreal, Toronto and Winnipeg and to reorganize and strengthen local government by creating larger operating units. Generally speaking, in welfare matters there has been an overall tendency for the provinces to undertake and finance welfare services to an increasing degree and to leave less responsibility to their municipalities. In Newfoundland there was no tradition of municipal government at the time of union with Canada in 1949, and welfare has remained a wholly provincial responsibility.

It would not be appropriate here to give a history of the political kaleidoscope of Canada's party system or of the constantly changing balance of forces between one party and another. It is, however, important to note that the general tendency has been for the provinces to elect governments of a different political complexion from the federal party in power in Ottawa. There is, therefore, an almost continuous tension between the government in Ottawa and the governments of the provinces. During wartime, and especially in World War II, the national government tended to take over powers of taxation, direction of the economy and management of the internal affairs of the county. The post-war period, and notably the years from 1945 to 1955, was therefore a period of strong federal initiative and provincial adaptation to the federal lead. This pattern has in recent years been challenged by the provinces, especially by the province of Quebec. As the balance of government function moves from the conduct of a war, managed, so to speak, by the nation, to the provision of services, such as roads, natural resource development, education, health and welfare, so the provincial budgets rise till they now aggregate more than the national budget, and political leadership gravitates to the provinces who claim constitutional rights to have been invaded by the Federal Government. The province of Quebec, which for a long period after World War II was almost an autarchy looking backwards to the past, suddenly in 1960 elected a Liberal Government determined upon modernization of the province's affairs, and the return to the province of its political independence and the direction of its economic and social development in accord with its own French Canadian traditions. This was a dramatic, and for the government in Ottawa an awkwardly intractable, demonstration of the sovereignty of the provinces, but other provinces, notably Ontario, had been making the same point in less dramatic terms, for some years. This phase of readjustment of political power between federal and provincial governments is not yet over and it may yet lead to substantial changes in the pattern of social services. For example, at a federal-provincial conference in September 1966, called to deal with the allocation of fiscal resources, the federal Minister of Finance proposed that certain important 'shared' programmes in health and welfare should be returned entirely to provincial jurisdiction in return for the release to the provinces of increased revenues from taxation.

It is clearly essential to clarify the constitutional position.

The Constitutional Background

The British North America Act 1867 has been, in the present century, a continuing source of conflict and confusion, and nowhere has this situation been more evident than in the field of public health and welfare services. Section 91 of this Act defines the classes of subjects that fall within the 'exclusive Legislative Authority of the Parliament of Canada', in addition to the general power 'to make Laws for the Peace, Order, and good Government of Canada, in relation to all Matters not coming within the Classes of Subjects by this Act assigned exclusively to the Legislatures of the Provinces'; but the only 'Classes of Subjects' so designated that have any relation to health and welfare are the census and statistics (Subsection 6), and quarantine and the establishment and maintenance of Marine Hospitals (Subsection 11).

Section 92 of the British North America Act 1867 is almost as vague, when it states, under the general power: 'In each Province the Legislature may exclusively make Laws in relation to Matters coming within the Classes of Subjects next hereinafter enumerated; that is to say . . .' and the only relevant subsection is Subsection 7: 'The Establishment, Maintenance, and Management of Hospitals, Asylums, Charities, and Eleemosynary Institutions in and for the Province, other than Marine Hospitals.'

Other sections which have come to be important in the determination of health and welfare responsibilities are Subsection 13 (Property and Civil Rights); Subsection 16 ('Generally all Matters of a merely local or private Nature in the Province'). The absence of any specific reference to the control of insurance has led to continuous and as yet unresolved conflict.

It was assumed in 1867, or so it seems, that health and welfare were the responsibility of the provinces and this assumption has hardened in time, through custom and legal interpretation, into established doctrine. As one writer succinctly put the matter:

'. . . judicial misconstruction of sections 91 and 92 has nullified, with only a few exceptions, the residuary power of the Dominion and has transferred this power to the provincial domain, under the guise of property and civil rights.'[1]

On the one hand, 'gradually the "Peace, Order and good Government" power of the Dominion became by judicial interpretation

[1] D. A. Schmeister, *Civil Liberties in Canada*. Toronto, Oxford University Press, 1964, p. 9.

emptied of practically all meaning, except perhaps in the event of war or other national emergency'[1]; on the other hand, the cost and complexity of health and welfare services, and the growing disproportion between the fiscal capacities of the federal and provincial levels of government have made absolutely essential an expanding measure of federal responsibility for these services.

This situation has been met in two ways. The first has been for the Government of Canada to obtain an amendment to the British North America Act 1867 to permit the Federal Government to undertake certain social services. The need for this step was sharply focused by the decision of the Judicial Committee of the Privy Council in 1937, in which it was held that the Employment and Social Insurance Act, 1935, was *ultra vires* because it was in pith and substance 'an insurance act affecting the civil rights of employers and employed in each province'. Two amendments affecting health and welfare have so far been made to the British North America Act 1867. In 1940 an amendment was made to Subsection 2 of Section 91 to add a new subsection '2A Unemployment Insurance' after the words 'The Regulation of Trade and Commerce'. The only other amendment to the British North America Act was made after a careful study of old age security by a Joint Committee of the Senate and the House of Commons.[2] This further confused the constitutional question by adding to Section 94 of the British North America Act, which is a very general section dealing with a restricted power to achieve uniformity of 'Laws relative to Property and Civil Rights'. After consultation with and agreement by the province, a new subsection was added:

94A 'It is hereby declared that the Parliament of Canada may from time to time make laws in relation to old age pensions in Canada, but no law made by the Parliament of Canada in relation to old age pensions shall affect the operation of any law present or future of a Provincial Legislature in relation to old age pensions'.

This amendment, drafted in these restrictive terms to satisfy the jealousy of the provinces of their rights under the British North America Act, has already produced complications. In 1963 the Province of Ontario introduced a Pension Benefits Act providing

[1] L. M. Gougin and Brooke Claxton, *Legislative Expedients and Devices Adopted by the Dominion and the Provinces.* A study prepared for the Royal Commission on Dominion-Provincial Relations. Ottawa, The King's Printer, 1939.

[2] Canada, *Report of the Joint Committee of the Senate and the House of Commons on Old Age Security.* Ottawa, King's Printer, 1950.

for compulsory retirement plans for industrial employees through private insurance coverage. The Province of Quebec established in 1963 an inter-departmental committee which undertook a most comprehensive study, and gave notice in the Quebec Legislative Assembly on 23 August, 1963:

'That it is expedient for the Legislature of the Province of Quebec to pass as soon as possible an act to establish a public and universal retirement fund based on actuarial calculations, and maintained by compulsory contributions.'

These two provincial actions demonstrated that the amendment of 1951, in the words of the Quebec study, 'presents a new problem in the matter of the division of powers, because it apparently divides the same subject by entrusting it partly to federal jurisdiction and partly to provincial jurisdiction'.

After prolonged political discussion and negotiation, the dilemma has been resolved, for the present at least. A motion was passed by the Canadian Parliament on 19 June, 1964, requesting the Parliament of the United Kingdom to repeal the existing section 94A of the British North America Act and replace it with an amendment in somewhat wider terms. The new Section 94A gives the Federal Parliament the authority to legislate with respect to supplementary benefits irrespective of age, including benefits for widows and dependent survivors, thereby extending the powers which existed in theory in the original 1951 version of the section to establish a contributory social insurance programme for old age pensions. The parallel rights of the provinces to act in the same field are retained in the new Section 94A. The United Kingdom Parliament passed the required amendment on 31 July, 1964. In August 1964 the Federal Government issued a White Paper[1] on the Canada Pension Plan in which it set out its proposals for a universal contributory social insurance scheme to cover retirement, death benefits and benefits for dependent survivors, including widows and orphans of insured persons.

This proposal, after negotiations to reconcile the proposals with those of the province of Quebec, was passed in April 1965. The constitutional significance of this plan is that it plainly recognizes that social insurance is an area of shared jurisdiction in which the provinces have prior rights. The Canada Pension Plan includes a provision that a province may establish its own plan, and be

[1] Canada. Department of National Health and Welfare. *The Canada Pension Plan.* Ottawa, The Queen's Printer, August 1964.

exempted from the provisions of the federal plan if its benefits are 'comparable to those provided under this Act'. The only province that has established its own plan is the Province of Quebec.

The second method used to secure federal participation in health and welfare has been the use of what has been described as a legislative expedient.[1] This device was first employed in 1926, nominally on constitutional grounds. It seems to have been adopted by the federal government of the day primarily to avoid taking full fiscal responsibility for old age pensions. The federal government, using its undoubted power to expend the general revenue at will, makes available grants to any province on condition that the province pass social legislation—in this case to provide non-contributory old age pensions—which includes and is not contrary to the conditions specified in the federal legislation; and then make an agreement with the federal government under which the province will obtain the federal moneys under specified detailed conditions. Although it has been argued that the judgement of Atkins, L. J. in the case already cited[2] may invalidate federal social legislation of this kind, the device has been extensively used since 1926. This device has recently been directly challenged in a report of considerable importance[3]:

Recommandation 14

Le gouvernement du Québec devrait poursuivre et intensifier ses efforts pour que le gouvernement du Canada se retire des programmes conjoints d'assistance sociale et compense, par un élargissement des champs de taxation, les charge accrues qui en decouleraient pour la Québec.[4]

The grounds on which this recommendation is justified are significant:

L'article 92 *de l'Acte de l'Amérique du Nord brittanique reconnâit en effet aux provinces le droit de légiférer en matière de sécurité sociale. Pendant longtemps, celles-ci, à l'inclusion du Québec, ont joué un rôle*

[1] L. M. Gongin and Brooke Claxton. *op. cit.*, p. 21.

[2] p. 165.

[3] Québec, *Rapport du Comité d'étude sur l'assistance publique*. Québec, Juin 1963. (Report of the Study Committee on Public Assistance.)

[4] The Quebec Government should pursue and intensify its efforts in order to obtain the withdrawal of the Federal Government from joint social assistance programs and have the Federal Government compensate, through extension of taxation fields, the Province of Quebec's increased expenditure arising therefrom.

passif en ce domaine, se contentant uniquement de suivre le gouvernement fédéral en adhérant à des programmes conjoints. Trop souvent, elles n'ont songé qu'à récupérer les sommes qui leur revenaient. En un mot, la législation sociale québecoise devrait être le fruit d'une pensée propre, plutôt que le point de rencontre de plusiers lois diverses plus ou moins liées les unes aux autres et inspirées d'un contexte bien différent de celui du Québec.[1]

If the position taken in the 1963 Report of the Quebec Study Committee on Public Assistance Legislation accurately reflects the official position of the government of that province, and there is good reason to believe that it does, and if this position is supported over the next decade by other powerful provincial governments, the whole fabric of social legislation may have to be rewoven in the light of a new balance of constitutional powers. This will be reflected in part by constitutional amendment and in part by reinterpretation of the constitution in new and as yet unfamiliar ways.

SOCIAL LEGISLATION

In the context of this uneasy equilibrium of constitutional powers, social legislation in Canada can be grouped into three major categories:

1 Federal legislation in respect of a limited number of federally operated programmes, uniform for the whole country.

2 Federal-provincial legislation, in respect of programmes operated by the respective provinces under provincial legislation framed within the terms of an agreement between the federal and each of the provincial governments.

3 Provincial legislation, in respect of programmes operated by, and financed and controlled by the respective provinces, or administered in some instances by municipalities within the province under provincial legislation.

[1] *Op. cit.*, p. 124. Section 92 of the British North America Act confers on the provinces the right to pass their own social security legislation. All the provinces, including Quebec have long played a passive role in this field, and have been satisfied to follow the lead of the Federal Government by agreeing to joint programs. Too often, their sole concern was centred on recuperating sums reverting to them. In a word—the social legislation of Quebec should be the product of its own thinking, instead of a meeting point of several different statutes more or less inter-related and inspired by a context quite different from that of Quebec.

Within each of these three categories a distinction will be made between those programmes which are designed to ensure a regular income to individuals and families who have been, for some reason, unable to earn an income, or are the dependents of someone unable to earn an income; and those that are intended to make certain services available to individuals in need of them. Services in the first category are generally described as income-maintenance services; in the second category they are generally classified as health or welfare services. If this division is employed within the classification by levels of government that arises from the federal nature of Canadian government, there emerges a convenient and relatively simple device for the organization and presentation of the maze of legislation covering the whole kaleidoscope of human needs.[1] Income-maintenance and welfare services will be described in Section 2 and health services in Section 3. A final section will deal with problems of administration, staffing and financing the social services generally.

[1] In this connection, the author's research assistant, Mr John Wismer, spent three months of concentrated labour identifying and examining over 500 pieces of legislation which might be deemed to fall within these categories. Neither he nor the author is satisfied that everything of significance has been uncovered and classified.

CHAPTER 2

Income-Maintenance and Welfare Services

FEDERAL LEGISLATION

(*a*) *Income-Maintenance*

Family Allowances

As in Britain, the Family Allowance Act 1944 was passed as a prelude to post-war reconstruction. Although no amendment was made to the British North America Act, and there have been rare suggestions that the 1944 Act is technically *ultra vires*, its validity has never been formally challenged. Under it allowances are paid to the mother in respect of every child under sixteen years of age who was born in Canada or who has been resident in the country for one year or whose father or mother was domiciled in Canada for three years before the birth of the child. The monthly allowances are $6 for each child under ten years of age and $8 for each child over ten but not over sixteen years of age. There is no means test but allowances are not payable in respect of a child who does not fulfil the educational requirements for school attendance of the province of residence or in respect of a girl who is married and under sixteen years of age. The allowances are not regarded as taxable income of the family, but the tax exemption in the Income Tax Acts for children eligible for family allowances is lower than the exemption for dependent children not eligible for family allowances. An auxiliary provision under other legislation now enables the Department of National Health and Welfare to pay family assistance for a period up to one year at the same rates as family allowances in respect of each child under sixteen years of age resident in Canada who is maintained by an immigrant who has the status of landed immigrant or a Canadian citizen returning to Canada until the child becomes eligible for the normal provision of family allowances.

Youth Allowances. In July 1964 the Federal Parliament passed a Youth Allowances Act which provides for the payment of allowances of $10 a month to parents in respect of dependent youths aged 16 and 17 who are maintained by their parents and are in full-time attendance at any educational institution, or prevented from attending by reason of disability.

Old Age Security Pensions and the Canada Pension Plan

Following the amendment to the British North America Act in 1951, a system of universal old age security pensions was introduced. Under this Act every person aged 70 or over who meets the residence requirement is entitled to a flat-rate benefit of $75 a month, payable in Canada, or, if the recipient has resided in Canada for twenty-five years since age 21, anywhere outside Canada. This latter provision permits older Canadian residents to retire to a less rigorous climate and retain their pensions. The residence requirement is ten years immediately preceding entitlement; if the person has been absent during any of the period of required residence he must be resident for the one year immediately preceding entitlement and must have had residence in Canada for twice as long as the period of absence during the normal required period of residence. A person with forty years' residence in Canada since age 18 will be eligible even if he is non-resident at the time of application. The flat rate benefit became available at age 69 in 1966 and will become available at age 68 in 1967 and so on until by 1970 it will be payable at age 65 to all eligible residents of Canada. In 1968 and thereafter the amount of $75 will be adjusted in line with the Canada Pension Plan Index.

The Canadian Pension Plan[1] provides for compulsory coverage from January 1966 of almost all employees and self-employed persons in Canada. This is essentially a compulsory contributory scheme into which all covered persons, and, if they are employed, their employers, will pay contributions. The contribution rate established in the Bill is 3·6 per cent (in the case of employees 1·8 per cent payable by the employer) of each contributor's annual earnings between the exempted amount and the maximum pensionable earnings. The basic exemption was set in the Act at $600 a year for 1966 and 1967, and the maximum pensionable earnings was set at $5000 a year for the same period. In 1968 and thereafter these basic figures will be adjusted by reference to movements in the Consumer Price Index (to be reflected in a specially constructed 'Pension Index') and from 1976 onwards on an Earnings Index based on average earnings.

[1] Canada. Department of National Health and Welfare, *The Canada Pension Plan*. Ottawa, The Queen's Printer, 1966.

Combined with the Old Age Security benefits, which will remain in effect, the benefits for older people will thus all have a flat-rate component and an earnings-related component. The basic benefit of the old age pension will be the present flat-rate of $75 a month adjusted after 1968 by the Pension Index and available by 1970 at age 65. The supplementary retirement benefit will, at the maturity of the plan in 1976, and on the assumption that the consumer price index and wage levels remain steady, range from $25 a month to $104 a month, at age 70, making the maximum $179 a month when combined with the flat-rate benefit. The supplementary retirement benefit will be available at approximately lower rates, and upon satisfaction of a test of retirement, between ages 65 and 69, and without a test of retirement from age 70. The retirement will fall to 65 by 1970. The objective of the whole scheme is to make the retirement pension of an amount equal to 25 per cent of the average earnings of the contributor.

The plan provides for benefits to *disabled contributors, widows and orphans of deceased contributors, and a death benefit*. In each case there will be a basic flat-rate benefit and an earnings-related supplement except in the case of the death benefit, which is a lump sum payment. In the case of a person so disabled as to be unable, by means of his disability, to support himself, the basic benefit will be $25 a month and the supplementary benefit is calculated to produce 75 per cent of the retirement pension which would have been paid on the same earnings record.

Widows' pensions will be paid to widows over 45 years of age, with provision for pensions to women widowed between age 35 and age 45 with *pro rata* reductions in the rate of benefits according to the age at which the beneficiary is widowed. Below age 35 no widow's benefit is payable. The basic flat-rate of widow's benefit at age 45 will be $25 a month with a supplementary benefit based on her husband's contribution record that will raise the benefit to $34 a month at the bottom of the scale up to $64 a month at the top. When the widow reaches age 65, or at latest age 70, the flat-rate component of her widow's pension will be replaced by a flat-rate component of the old age pension.

A widow with dependent children will receive the full widow's pension at whatever age she is at the time of her husband's death, and in addition will receive orphan's benefit of $25 a month for each dependent child up to four children and thereafter $12·50 for each subsequent eligible child. When the children cease to be dependent, she will receive a widow's benefit. Widows who have contribution records in their own right which entitle them to old age security and retirement benefits at age 65, or at latest age 70, will be able to combine these with their widow's pension rights. A disabled widow will, from 1968 on, be entitled to a full widow's pension.

Orphans' benefits will be $25 a month for each child, with a limitation on the total benefit, the benefits for fifth and subsequent eligible orphans being $12.50.

Death benefits will be paid if the deceased person has contributed for at least three years, for at least one-third of the years in which he could have contributed, or for at least ten years. The amount of death benefit will vary according to the contribution record, with a maximum of $500.

The Canada Pension Plan provides for an automatic adjustment of contributions and benefits, including the benefits available under the Old Age Security Act according to changes in the Consumer Price Index and the average levels of wages. The Canada Pension Plan will be a partially funded plan, contributions exceeding outgoings in the early stages by very considerable amounts. The funds thus accumulated, estimated at more than $4 billions in the first ten years, will be available on loan to the provinces in proportion to the contributions received from the provinces which will thus have access to capital funds that many of them need for social capital expenditures associated with rapid population growth and urban and industrial expansion.

Now that the Canada Pension Plan has been enacted, Canada has covered most of the major contingencies of income loss in a highly industrialized society, except the loss of income due to inability to work owing to illness.

Old Age Benefits 1966 and Canada Assistance Plan The full effects of the Canada Pension Plan upon the patterns of welfare in Canada are not yet clear. It was very quickly realized, for example, that the Canada Pension Plan did not give any additional aid to those who were already retired nor to many of those who would retire before the plan reached maturity in 1976. In December 1966 the federal government introduced an Amendment to the *Old Age Security Act* to provide a 'guaranteed income supplement' to recipients of the flat-rate benefit who have not received much, if any, improvement in their incomes as a result of the *Canada Pension Plan.* The passage of the *Canada Assistance Plan* in July 1966 will materially affect provincial and municipal welfare services, but in precisely what ways it is impossible to foresee with any accuracy. The Canada Assistance Plan is dealt with further in a later section relating to federal-provincial shared programmes.

Government Annuities and Occupational Pension Schemes Mention should be made here of two other legislative provisions through which support and assistance is given to individual and group pension plans of individual Canadians. The Government Annuities Act, first passed in 1908, provides an opportunity for the purchase of annuities up to a maximum income of $1200 a year through the Annuities Branch of the Department of Labour. For many years, as an encouragement to individuals to save for their old age, the interest rates under this plan were more favourable than those available in the commercial market, and in effect were subsidized from the public funds. These annuities were used as the basis of many private and occupational pension funds, which have developed very rapidly in Canada, as in other countries, over the past twenty years.

Occupational pension funds created in response to pressures at the bargaining table during industrial wage discussions are subject to concessions under the Income Tax Act, the contributions of individuals and employers being deductible, within certain limits, from income before taxation. In 1956 the federal government withdrew its previous measures to supervise these plans by regulation under the Income Tax Acts, on the assumption, it is believed, that this activity might be unconstitutional. There is now a substantial move, referred to later in this section, to develop provincial legislation for the expansion and regulation of occupational pension funds.

Unemployment Insurance

The Unemployment Insurance Act was introduced in 1940 in anticipation of post-war readjustments in the labour market. After numerous amendments it was rewritten in 1955, and in 1962 was the subject of intensive enquiry by a special Committee of Inquiry,[1] as a result of which it is almost certain to be amended in the near future. Its present form is that of the classical model of a contributory social

[1] Canada. *Report of the Committee of Enquiry into the Unemployment Insurance Act.* (Gill Committee), Ottawa, The Queen's Printer, 1962.

insurance, somewhat distorted by subsequent additions of political rather than actuarial origin. The Act requires all persons employed by the hour, day or at piece-rate, and all those who receive $5,460 a year or less at weekly, monthly or yearly or commission rates, to be insured by their employers with a limited list of exempted classes. The main classes exempted are employees of the public services, self-employed, the armed forces, teachers, private domestic servants and those in certain types of agricultural, horticultural and forestry employment. About 71 per cent of non-agricultural employees are covered (1963). Equal contributions to the Unemployment Insurance Fund are paid by employees and employers on a sliding scale related to wages, in twelve different classes. The Government contribution is equal to 20 per cent of the joint contributions of workers and employers, together with costs of administration. Benefits are related to average wages, and represent between 35 per cent and 50 per cent of wages. Duration of benefit rights is one week of benefits for every two weeks of contributions up to a maximum of 52 weeks. Grafted on to the basic scheme is a system of seasonal benefits for those whose normal benefit rights are exhausted in the period between 1 December and 1 May, and a further elaboration to provide benefit rights to fishermen. These two additions, together with heavy unemployment in 1961 and 1962, have drained the reserves of the Unemployment Insurance Fund almost to vanishing point.

The Act is administered by a Commission of three members and contains provision for local appeal tribunals and the appointment of an official Umpire as a last court of appeal against administrative decisions.

Ex-Service Men's Pensions and Other Financial Benefits

Canadian legislation for the benefit of ex-service men is among the most generous of any of the benefits provided for the participants in World War I and World War II. The Pension Act provides for pensions in respect of war-caused disability, injury, disease or death of members of the armed forces. The Civilian War Pensions and Allowances Act provides similar benefits for certain groups of persons whose service during World War II in the Allied cause exposed them to risks of disability and death: these groups include merchant seamen, ferry pilots, salt-water fishermen and others who served in organized ways in the war effort. These Acts are administered by the Canadian Pensions Commission. Disability pensions are based on an annual rate for a man 100 per cent disabled, for all ranks up to the rank of colonel, of $2,160, with supplements for dependent children up to 16 years of age for boys and 17 for girls, and, where appropriate, for dependent parents. Pensions are payable to widows of entitled veterans and their dependent children, and, in some circumstances, to dependent parents. The War Veterans Allowance Act, which is administered by the Department of Veterans Affairs, provides an income-maintenance benefit on a means-test basis to older ex-service men (over 60) and women (over 55) who are unable to maintain themselves because they are unemployable for reasons of mental or physical health. Provision is made for the payment of allowances to the widows and orphans of eligible recipients of War Veterans Allowances.

Assistance to Indians in Need

Under the British North America Act 1867, responsibility for the administration of Indian Affairs is a federal responsibility. Public assistance is granted by the Department of Indian Affairs and Northern Development to Indians who are not able to maintain themselves and their families. Steps have been taken in several provinces to provide for the inclusion of Indians for welfare benefits and services under the relevant provincial programmes, with federal reimbursement to the province in some instances, but there is no basic intention of transferring to the provinces the ultimate responsibility of the federal government for Indians and Eskimos. Indians in all parts of Canada are, when eligible, paid family allowances, old age security pensions and benefits under the various federal-provincial programmes and other welfare services under provincial and municipal jurisdiction.

Financial Aid to Farmers

Although Canada is now a highly industrialized country with its population classified at the 1961 Census as 12,700,390 Urban Population and 5,537,857 as Rural Population,[1] agriculture is still one of its basic industries. Income-maintenance for an agricultural community must be concerned not so much with the payment of an income as with the retention of the farmer in his productive capacity as a producer. There are, therefore, on the statute books a number of federal Acts designed to assist and protect the farmer whose crops

[1] *Canada Yearbook*, 1962. Ottawa, The Queen's Printer, 1963, p. 1197.

have failed or whose income is inadequate; to enable him to put in seed for the next year's crop and, meanwhile, sufficiently improve his income. Chief among these is the Prairie Farm Assistance Act 1939, creating a Prairie Farm Emergency Fund to assist, with money payments, farmers in need in areas of low-crop yield in the Prairie Provinces and the Peace River Area of British Columbia. This Fund is created by a levy from the farmers of 1 per cent of the value of sales of grain crops and additional funds from the federal Consolidated Revenue. Payments are made to farmers on the basis of acreage and crop yield. Other legislation dealing with such matters as Crop Insurance, Agricultural Rehabilitation and Development, Farm Credit and Farm Improvement Loans, belongs more properly to agricultural legislation than to welfare, although it has significant implications for the maintenance of farm incomes.

(*b*) *Welfare Services*

Since constitutional interpretation and practice restrict the federal government's powers in the welfare fields, federal provision of direct welfare services to individuals is quite limited, except in relation to programmes that have been sanctioned by custom or constitutional amendment. In the administration of family allowances and old age security, the Department of National Health and Welfare maintains in each of its administrative regions a small welfare section to deal with welfare problems that may arise, as for example when the administration of family allowances reveals a serious family problem. As a general rule the practice is to refer the problem to the appropriate local private agency or municipal or provincial welfare department.

1 In 1962 the federal government introduced a programme of *welfare training and research grants* intended to stimulate research and to assist the expansion of programmes for developing qualified staff for the rapidly growing welfare services. For the most part these grants are dealt with in co-operation with the provinces, but certain grants, notably those for the encouragement of research, assistance to professional schools of social work, and providing national scholarships and fellowships, are dealt with at the national level. The government also passed legislation in 1962 authorizing the establishment of a National Council of Welfare whose functions are vaguely advisory to the Minister on welfare matters. The first appointments to the Council were made in 1965.

2 *Welfare services to Indians*, including housing, the care of neglected children, rehabilitation of handicapped Indians, and community development on Indian Reserves, all fall within the purview of the Department of Indian Affairs and Northern Development. Increasingly, however, arrangements are being sought to bring Indians within the framework of the normal welfare services of the respective provinces in which the Indians live.

The federal government is also responsible for the education of Indians, either by paying the cost of tuition in private schools or in the public schools of the various provincial school systems, or by operating special schools for Indians not able to use the regular school system, either because the Indian children still live on Indian reserves, belong to migratory bands, require residential education or are confined to hospital.

The Indian Act has been very much criticized in recent years as being out of date and too paternal in its provisions for the care of Indians. Joint Committees of the Senate and the House of Commons sat in 1959, 1960 and 1961, and a final report was presented to Parliament in 1961 recommending many changes in the legislation all directed to the emancipation of Indians to full and responsible citizenship 'without prejudice to the retention of the cultural, historical and other economic benefits which they have inherited'.

3 *The welfare of Eskimos* is, in the same way, the responsibility of the Department of Indian Affairs and Northern Development, and includes not only family welfare services, but also vocational training and adult education, housing subsidies and loans, and other means intended to assist the Eskimo to adjust to membership in a twentieth century industrial society.

4 *The National Employment Service*. The Unemployment Insurance Act 1940 not only established a contributory unemployment benefit scheme for the great majority of employed workers, but also created the National Employment Service. Public employment offices are established throughout Canada to provide a free employment service where workers seeking new jobs and employers in search of workers have the resources of an integrated national network of offices at their disposal. Applicants for unemployment insurance benefit are required to register for employment at the local employment office, but any one may use these offices. Among the special services available are departments which deal with the particular employment needs of young workers entering the labour market, women workers, disabled

and other workers with special needs, and executives and professional workers with specialist qualifications. Until the spring of 1964 the National Employment Service was operated, in parallel with Unemployment Insurance, by the Unemployment Insurance Commission. On 24 February, 1964, the Government announced the transfer of the National Employment Service to the direct jurisdiction of the Department of Labour. In 1966 it was transferred again, this time to the newly created Department of Manpower and Immigration.

Veterans' Welfare

Perhaps the largest range of welfare services comes within the responsibilities of the federal Department of Veterans Affairs. Many of the provisions of the legislation for the benefit of war veterans, known collectively as the War Veterans Charter, are now reaching the end of their usefulness. The payment under the War Service Grants Act of gratuities on discharge and the use of re-establishment credits to discharged veterans are now rapidly diminishing. Training under the Veterans Rehabilitation Act of veterans for civilian occupations has largely ceased except for activities associated with the training of persons with pensionable disabilities. The Children of War Dead (Educational Assistance) Act makes it possible to assist children of service men who have died in or as a result of service, including service in peace-time, to continue their education for four years beyond the achievement of high school leaving standard. This ensures that, when they are able to benefit, these children may continue their education at least to the attainment of their first degree at a university. The Veterans Land Act has provided financial assistance and loans to enable the ex-service men to settle on the land as full-time farmers, or as part-time farmers, or as commercial fishermen, or to open up new land as pioneer settlers, or to build their own homes on urban lots. The War Veterans Allowance Board not only administers the financial payments to eligible ex-service men but also provides counselling and other social services to the recipients.

Public Housing

Unlike most other industrial nations, Canada has not developed large-scale public housing programmes as an integral part of its overall welfare services. The pattern has been rather to make money more easily available than normal market conditions would allow in order to stimulate private home construction. The basic legislation is the National Housing Act 1954. The 1964 and 1965 amendments to this Act constitute the last major revisions of legislation dating back to 1935. The chosen instrument for the administration of this Act is the Central Mortgage and Housing Corporation. The chief service is the provision of insurance of mortgage loans granted by lending institutions for the construction of approved types of building to individuals, builders, co-operative housing associations, farmers and other groups of individuals. Loans are made directly to certain limited classes of applicants, including limited dividend companies for low-rental housing, non-profit organizations for the construction of housing for elderly persons, and universities for the construction of student residences. The Central Mortgage and Housing Corporation also has an extensive programme of research into many aspects of housing, building construction problems, house design and Community Planning.

Fitness and Amateur Sport

The federal Fitness and Amateur Sport Act 1961 provides funds 'to encourage, promote and develop fitness and amateur sport'. Grants are made to national organizations to strengthen their capacity to take a more active part in international and national sports; grants are also made to the provinces to assist them with community programmes. Fellowships, scholarships and bursaries are available for professional studies in physical education, recreation and medical aspects of fitness. Grants may also be made for construction of facilities, though this is likely to be restricted to national projects. The Department of National Welfare is responsible for the administration, aided by a National Advisory Council on Fitness and Amateur Sport, and committees of experts.

FEDERAL-PROVINCIAL LEGISLATION

The legislation in which the federal government provides substantial funds and other supports to provincial governments which, in their turn, are prepared to use their constitutional powers to enact and administer legislation that conforms to the requirements of the federal act, leads to the 'shared programmes' which have been one of the major sources of progress in Canada's social welfare expansion since this device was first used in 1927. The *Canada Assistance Plan* which was enacted in July 1966 is the most sophisticated, and the most flexible of these federal initiatives to assist in the development of better social services without infringing on provincial constitutional rights. However, the new balance of political power between the federal and the provincial governments is not yet established, and at the federal-provincial conference on tax-sharing and fiscal matters in September 1966 the federal minister of finance proposed that the provinces, in return for the release to them of certain tax resources, would accept full responsibility for the operation of three 'shared programmes'—the health grants programme, the hospital insurance and diagnostic services programme and the Canada Assistance Plan. In view of the uncertainty of future developments it seems best to recapitulate first the 'shared programmes' as they existed in 1966 and then to set out the Canada Assistance Plan as it was enacted in the middle of 1966 in an effort to co-ordinate and improve the existing shared programmes. The implications of all these moves and countermoves for the administration of social services will be dealt with later.

(*a*) *Income-Maintenance*

Old Age Assistance

When the federal government introduced the Old Age Security legislation in 1952 to replace the previous Old Age Pensions laws, it followed the precedent set in 1926 of providing federal financial support for a federal-provincial programme, this time of means-test assistance to old people aged 65 or over. The federal share of the cost is prescribed as 50 per cent of $75 a month or of the amount of the assistance benefits actually paid, whichever is the lesser. The federal share is paid from the Consolidated Revenue Fund. The Old Age Assistance Act authorizes the federal government to make an agreement with any province to provide a payment of assistance up to a maximum figure on conditions under the provincial legislation that are 'in accordance with this (i.e. the federal) Act' and the regulations made under it. The Act itself prescribes the basic conditions of eligibility, which include residence in Canada on approximately the same terms as the Old Age Security Act, maximum limits of income and the exclusion from benefit of recipients of financial assistance under other programmes supported by federal funds. The Act also specifies in considerable detail the provisions of the agreement which the provinces must meet, including transferability of recipients' rights between provinces, protection of the recipient against loss of voting rights as a condition of assistance, proofs of age of recipients, maintenance of records, the treatment of real property in the assessment of income and other conditions. The provinces are given a guarantee of ten years' notice by the federal government before the termination of an agreement. Provision is made for the establishment of an Advisory Board composed of two representatives of the federal government and of each of the participant provinces to review the regulations under the Act. The Act is accompanied by the most detailed federal regulations prescribing, among other things, the form of applications, the frequency of investigation and review of cases, the acceptable proofs of age, residence, the ways in which other income, real and personal property are to be assessed, the recovery of assistance payments improperly made to recipients, and the conditions under which assistance payments may be paid to trustees on behalf of a recipient who is incapacitated and unable to look after his own affairs. All the costs of administration in the province are paid by the provincial governments.

Clearly the significance of Old Age Assistance as a programme will diminish rapidly as the Canada Pension Plan and the progressive reduction in the age of eligibility for Old Age Security to 65 come into effect.

The Blind Persons Act 1952

The Act as amended follows the same pattern as the Old Age Assistance Act, with some important differences in detail. The federal share of the assistances is set at 75 per cent of $75 a month or of the actual assistance paid, whichever is the lesser. The minimum age of eligibility is 18, and the upper limits of assets under the means test are somewhat more generous than those provided in the Old Age Assistance Act. The other terms of eligibility, such as residence, are the same as in the Old Age Assistance Act.

The Disabled Persons Act 1953–54

This Act also takes the same basic form as the Old Age Assistance Act 1952. It makes provision for assistance to the 'totally and permanently disabled'. The federal share of the assistance is set at 50 per cent of $75 a month or of the actual assistance paid, whichever is the lesser. The age of eligibility is 18 and the upper limits of assets under the means test are the same as those provided in the Old Age Assistance Act. The recipient must fall within the definition in the Regulations: 'A person shall be deemed to be totally and permanently disabled when suffering from a major physiological, anatomical or psychological impairment verified by objective medical findings which is likely to continue indefinitely without substantial improvement and, as a result thereof, such person is severely limited in activities pertaining to normal living.' The Regulations set out in extended detail the form of the medical evidence which must be provided and require such further medical review or investigation at least once a year as the nature of the recipient's disability may require. The interpretation of 'disability' leaves open a wide area for variations of opinion between the different provinces and for disputes between the provinces and the federal government in specific cases.

The Unemployment Assistance Act 1956

This uses the same legislative expedient of providing for payment of money from the Consolidated Revenue Fund for the purpose of sharing expenditures on assistances made by a province or a municipality in the province which has signed an agreement with the federal government in accordance with the terms specified by the Act. It takes a somewhat different form from the other three Acts already discussed. It provides that the federal government contributions 'shall not exceed fifty per cent of the unemployment assistance costs in the province in respect of which Canada has, under the agreement with the province, undertaken to contribute'. No maxima or minima of the individual benefits are prescribed and no detailed regulations are included for the calculation of the income and assets of individual recipients.

The determination of conditions required for eligibility for assistance is left entirely to the provinces, which in some instances pass the task of administration on to the municipalities. The operative general condition in the agreement, which is set forth as Schedule A to the federal Act, is that recipients must be 'unemployed persons who are in need' (including their dependents). Excluded from the classes of recipients for whom the federal government will share the cost of benefits are inmates of institutions, recipients of benefits under other programmes in which the federal government shares, payments for medical care, funeral expenses and travelling expenses, and costs of administration. The exclusions have, however, been modified by the permission to include 'payments made to or on behalf of persons who are inmates of homes for special care', by which are meant nursing homes, hostels for indigent transients, homes for the aged, poor houses, almshouses, and hostel facilities provided for the aged within housing projects constructed under the provisions of the National Housing Act, provided that the recipients are unemployed and in need, and the payments do not 'exceed what an individual might reasonably be expected to pay for accommodation of a comparable kind and quality in the same locality'; and that these inmates 'would not normally be cared for in general, acute, chronic or convalescent hospitals, tuberculosis sanatoria, mental institutions, institutions for incurables, orphanages or child welfare institutions'. The room for differences of interpretation and for administrative confusion provided by this loophole is ample; that it works at all is a tribute to the patience, ingenuity and wisdom of the administrators.

Another loophole is the permission to include, as eligible expenditures in the provincial claim for sharing by the federal government, supplementary allowances to recipients of monetary benefits under other programmes, specifically Old Age Security, Unemployment Insurance, Old Age Assistance, Blind Persons Allowances, and Disabled Persons Allowances, provided that an individual needs test is applied in each case to determine the amount of supplementation. The federal government is thus liable to share 50 per cent of the cost of allowances which, in the judgement of the provinces, are necessary to make good the deficiencies in other programmes of income-maintenance under other federal legislation.

A further complication is the exclusion from federal participation of benefits paid to recipients of Mothers' Allowances. This relates to a provincial programme for the assistance of needy mothers with dependent children which was Canada's first categorical assistance programme and until recently was in operation in all provinces. The provinces have now begun to merge this programme into their general assistance programmes. Where this has been done—as it has in seven provinces—the federal government, in sharing costs under the Unemployment Assistance Act now, therefore, has to impute the amount which is attributable to the presence on the assistance rolls of needy mothers with dependent children.

Agreements with the provinces were limited to a maximum of five years duration; in practice, all the provinces now have agreements under the Act which are carried over from year to year.

In effect, the federal government has become a partner in general assistance through the Unemployment Assistance Act. The attempt to establish some measure of federal control by legislative devices over all the main details of assistance payments has given rise to considerable criticism both in principle[1] and in administrative practice.[2]

The Canada Assistance Plan 1966

The Canada Assistance Plan was seen by the federal government as a logical corollary to the Canada Pension Plan. It was intended that Canada Pension Plan would gradually absorb from the assistance rolls not only the under-supported older people by better and earnings-related benefits but also a significant proportion of those who require long-term income supports, through the provisions for Widows, Orphans and Disabled Benefits in the Pension Plan. This would leave, essentially, the persons with special needs and the families and persons in need of services and short-term financial support to be provided for at the provincial and local levels of government. It was also intended that by transferring the heavy burdens of long-term financial care more to the national level, the provinces would be able to expand specialist services and to improve their administration.

The basic intention of the Canada Assistance Plan is to make it possible for the provinces to abolish all the separate categories of the present legislation and to establish a single programme of assistance to cover the needs—both for income-maintenance and for welfare services—of all those whose needs are not met, or in the assessment of the province are not adequately met, by other programmes. The federal government establishes no ceilings in legislation to the amounts in which it would share, but the Canada Assistance Plan requires that need must be determined by an individual needs-test of each applicant or family. The federal government will no longer exclude recipients of Mothers' Allowances

[1] e.g. See Québec, *Rapport du Comité d'étude du loi d'assistance publique*. Québec, 1963.

[2] Canada, *Royal Commission on Government Organization*, Vol. I. Ottawa, The Queen's Printer, 1962.

or the cost of children in the care of the provincial child welfare authorities from the shareable expenditures, and will extend the range of institutional care towards the costs of which the federal sharing arrangement will apply, as well as making provision for 'work-activity projects' to encourage training and rehabilitation of the unemployed and for Indian welfare. For the first time in the history of federal provincial shared programmes, the Canada Assistance Plan makes provision for federal sharing of the costs of improved administrative arrangements and for the development of welfare services such as home-maker and home-help services, day-care and social counselling services and the better use of voluntary services available in the local community.

The Canada Assistance Plan has been brought into effect in most provinces insofar as amendments to provincial legislation have been made to permit the province to conform sufficiently to the new Act to include as shareable items for federal financial participation as much as possible of the hitherto 'non-shareable' items, notably Mothers' Allowances and child welfare payments. There are no signs yet that the concerted reorganization of public assistance at the provincial level which the Plan might have initiated has been seriously undertaken. In accordance with its declared policy, the Province of Quebec has 'opted out' of all the shared programmes in return for revenue concessions and intends to develop its own welfare programmes in its own way. Part of the delay in the other provinces is undoubtedly due to the relative slowdown in the economy in 1966, producing much less optimistic views about expanding fiscal revenues; but part must be attributed to the uncertainty generated by the uneasy political situation in which the struggle for political power and tax-revenues is not yet decided. The full implications of the adoption of an individualized needs-test for all benefits, of the inclusion of service benefits as 'shareable' expenditures, and of federal support for improved standards of administration have not been studied in any detail.

The Administration of Federal-Provincial Assistance Programmes

The administration of the categorical assistance programmes for Old Age Assistance, Blind Persons' Allowances and Disabled Persons' Allowances is the responsibility of the provinces within the limits of the federal legislation. Each province, therefore, has its own enabling Acts and Regulations for each programme.

Consequently there are wide variations relating to the economic and social conditions of the respective provinces.

In all provinces the administration of the categorical allowances is undertaken by the provinces without recourse to the municipalities.

The situation is quite different in the case of the Unemployment Assistance programme. Here the majority of the provinces have, until recent years, retained some measure of municipal responsibility. In Newfoundland aid has always been a provincial responsibility. In 1960 the government of Quebec relieved its municipalities of responsibility for contributing to the costs of aid to needy persons in either their own homes or homes for special care. In Ontario and Alberta, as well as in several other provinces, there has been a continuous shift of responsibility for long-term assistance cases from municipal to provincial responsibility. In all provinces the provincial governments, by the use of different legislative expedients, have accepted a very large share of the costs of Unemployment Assistance. This is true even in the province of Ontario, where local responsibility and administration still remain with the individual municipalities; but where, more recently, these are being shifted to the county and district level on a consolidated basis.

The federal-provincial agreements require that a condition of established 'residence' in the legal sense for assistance shall not prevent a person accepted in one province from receiving assistance if he moves to another province. Within some provinces there is still adherence to municipal resident requirements with varying degrees of severity. The conditions to be met under the tests of need, while conforming generally to the federal legislation in respect of the categorical programmes, are entirely in the hands of the provinces under general assistance (or as it is variously known in the different provinces, social assistance, social aid, or general welfare assistance). Provinces are permitted to supplement other allowances through the use of general assistance and to recoup 50 per cent of the cost of supplementary benefits from the federal government provided that each individual case is examined on some assessment of need, which takes account of the recipient's needs and resources. No distinction is made in the federal legislation between 'employable' and 'unemployable' persons as a condition of sharing the costs of assistance—simply that recipients must be unemployed and in need.[1]

[1] A parallel with national assistance (now non-contributory benefits) in Britain, which can only be paid to persons who are not in full-time employment.

(*b*) *Welfare Services*

Since in none of the major federal-provincial programmes of income maintenance before the Canada Assistance Plan does the federal government share in the costs of administration, the 'service' elements of welfare services to individuals do not come under federal-provincial arrangements. There are, however, a number of special programmes in which there is a joint interest.

Mention has already been made of the federal *welfare training and research* grants administered by the Department of National Health and Welfare. The larger part of the training grants, including those for bursaries to students in professional schools of social work, in-service training programmes, and experiments in staff development, are made on a matching basis with the provinces.

There are also a number of provisions in the *National Housing Act* which depend upon federal-provincial partnerships. In some provinces, for example, the province will provide all or part of the 10 per cent of equity which must be provided outside the federal financial support. Loans are also available under the National Housing Act to assist municipalities with projects for control of water and soil pollution, sewage treatment and trunk sewer: 25 per cent of the federal loan assistance is not reclaimed if the project is completed by an approved date. The federal government, under Section 35 of the Act, can share with the provinces on a 75–25 per cent sharing basis, in the costs of creating low-rental housing projects, and in the costs of land assembly and the preparation of the land required for residential construction. Grants are payable under Part V of the Act to assist municipalities in making the necessary surveys and studies preliminary to civic plans for urban redevelopment and urban renewal plans. Under Section 23 the federal government can share up to 50 per cent of the cost of acquisition and clearance of areas selected for the renewal and redevelopment of run-down and 'blighted' parts of the cities. All of the ten provinces except Prince Edward Island have passed the necessary complementary legislation to allow them to participate in joint federal-provincial housing and land assembly projects. Thus far, however, there has been nothing approaching the large-scale public-housing and renewal projects of Britain and other European countries.

The *Vocational Rehabilitation of Disabled Persons Act* 1961 marks the beginning of co-ordinated efforts to restore and re-educate disabled persons for useful and productive membership of society.

Responsibility for this Act lies with the federal Department of Labour, with the assistance of a National Advisory Council on the Rehabilitation of Disabled Persons. While there is a National Co-ordinator, and a national programme of research and publication, the core of the Act is the provision authorizing agreements with the individual provinces for a period not exceeding six years to enable a federal contribution of 50 per cent 'of the costs incurred by the province in undertaking in the province a comprehensive program for the vocational rehabilitation of disabled persons'. The definition of 'comprehensive' is kept fairly general to include assessment and counselling services, rehabilitation, training and placement services, the use of voluntary societies, the training of counsellors and administrators of rehabilitation programmes, and the co-ordination of all activities in the province relating to vocational rehabilitation of disabled persons.

Although it more properly belongs with Labour Legislation, or perhaps even more properly with Educational Legislation, mention must be made here of the *Technical and Vocational Training Assistance Act*, 1960. Although education is constitutionally reserved to the provinces, the federal government has been involved in sharing the costs of vocational training as far back as the 1920s and 1930s. In its most recent form, the legislation provides massive federal aid to provinces for the expansion of vocational training facilities and assistance to students taking technological and vocational courses of study. Under the provisions of 'Program 6' for disabled persons this Act has provided a valuable collateral resource to the provinces in developing their programmes under the Vocational Rehabilitation of Disabled Persons Act 1961.

PROVINCIAL LEGISLATION

(*a*) *Income-maintenance*

With the entry in 1956 of the federal government into partnership with the provinces in the cost of general assistance, and with recent legislation of the 1960s, there is only one income-maintenance programme over which the provinces retain sole jurisdiction: Workmen's Compensation. The provinces, however, as the constitutionally responsible authorities, have not only been left with full responsibility for the administration of public assistance but have exercised their right to operate it with a wide variety of interpretation within the general framework of the federal legislation.

Workmen's Compensation

Workmen's Compensation in Canada is largely derived from the Ontario Workmen's Compensation Act 1914. The basic principle is that an injury, death or industrial disease arising out of employment is assumed to be a risk of employment. Employees lose their right of action against their employer for an injury from an accident during employment. All claims are made against the Workmen's Compensation Board of the province. Unless the claimant opts to proceed against a third party for negligence, the Boards take over the right of the injured person to prosecute actions for liability against third parties. All except a very few employers are required to be covered by the Workmen's Compensation Act of the province. A federal Act provides for the protection of federal employees on the same terms as those prevailing in the province of usual employment of the worker. Seamen are covered by federal legislation, the Merchant Seamen Compensation Act (Canada).

Each provincial Workmen's Compensation Board maintains its Workmen's Compensation Fund, sustained by a compulsory levy on the industries in the province, which are rated by general classes in accordance with the hazards of the industrial group and the past experience of claims in respect of that class of industry. Excepted classes, for example charitable organizations, may apply to be accepted by the Workmen's Compensation Board to be covered. In Quebec and Ontario, the public authorities and large public utilities, such as railways and telephone companies, pay to the provincial Workmen's Compensation Boards the costs of compensation and medical care, as well as a proportionate share of administrative expenses actually paid out in respect of their employees.

The Acts require the reporting of all except minor injuries. Full medical care, either in the home or in hospital, and rehabilitation services are given in respect to the compensate condition. In general these services are provided by the normal medical and hospital services of the community, but the Workmen's Compensation Boards provide consultation services and exercise surveillance of the services rendered.

There is a brief waiting period before compensation is paid, varying from one day in three provinces to five days in others, but if the disability continues beyond the waiting period, compensation is payable from the date of injury. Compensation for loss of earnings[1] is generally based on average earnings up to a ceiling income, which varies from province to province. Additional allowances are made for dependent children, normally up to 16 years of age, but with discretion, up to 18 or 19 years for educational reasons. The Acts also prescribe minimum payments. The normal rate of compensation in all provinces is 75 per cent of earnings, with pro-rated reductions for partial disablement. For minor disablements (10 per cent disability or less—5 per cent in Alberta) provision is made for lump-sum payments at the discretion of the Workmen's Compensation Boards.

Death benefits include burial grants, widows' and dependent children's allowances, and in certain circumstances allowances for other dependents.

These Acts thus fulfil the intent of the author of the first Ontario Act of 'getting rid of the nuisance of litigation' from workmen's compensation. There are no provisions for appeals to the courts against decisions of the Workmen's Compensation Boards, but cases may always be submitted for review and readjudication.

Some of the Workmen's Compensation Acts also provide for safety education and accident prevention services.

Portable Occupational Pensions

Until 1959 the Department of National Revenue required occupational pension plans under private auspices to meet certain minimum conditions in order to allow the contributors, employers and employees, to claim certain exemptions under the Income and Corporation Tax Acts from the taxation of their contributions. In that year the federal government withdrew these limitations, in the belief that they might infringe on the undoubted fact that control of insurance is a constitutional right of the provinces. The province of Ontario in 1963 passed the Pension Benefits Act, which requires the employer of fifteen or more workers to enrol them in a pension plan with an approved private insurer which meets certain minimum conditions. These conditions require that minimum pension rights acquired by a worker over 30 years of age shall be vested in him, and therefore become 'portable', that is to say, are carried by the

[1] Differing from the British Industrial Injuries Scheme in which the disablement pension (but not the short-term industrial injury benefit) is basically related to loss of faculty.

worker if he changes his employment, thus building up a right to a supplementary pension on retirement for a large number of workers now in regular employment to add to their statutory benefits under Old Age Security Allowances and the Canada Pension Plan. Benefits beyond the minimum scale prescribed in the Ontario Act must be vested at age 45. The Act also contains provisions designed to ensure the solvency and proper management of these private pension plans most of which are occupational plans created as part of the overall contract negotiations between the unions and management. This legislation, which was significantly amended in 1965, now limits the functions of the Pension Benefits Act of Ontario essentially to the control and regulation of private pension plans, particularly in regard to portability of pension rights. It is being used as a model by other provinces.

Mothers' Allowances

The purpose of Mothers' Allowances, which until recent years were in effect in all ten provinces, is to provide an income, on a means test (or needs test, as the case may be), to mothers who have dependent children in their care. In those provinces where the Mothers' Allowances have been, or are being, merged in the general assistance legislation, the basic conditions have been renewed in the new legislation. The conditions of eligibility, therefore, vary somewhat from province to province. The allowances are paid to needy mothers where the breadwinner of the family is dead, or is physically or mentally disabled and unable to support the family. Mothers in this category also include those who have been deserted, a term variously defined but usually meaning that the husband can be shown to have left the home without support and to be undiscoverable or unable to meet a court order for maintenance. Other eligible needy mothers as defined in some provinces include those where the breadwinner is in a penal institution or who are divorced or legally separated, and unmarried mothers. In Ontario, Quebec and Nova Scotia these allowances are available to Indian mothers who are otherwise eligible. In some instances the father of the family is eligible under certain circumstances where the mother is not in the home to benefit under this legislation. In some provinces the allowance includes an additional amount if the disabled father is being maintained in the home, while in others this fact is taken into account in the budgetary calculations for the allowance. Allowances may also be paid to foster parents, who are restricted in a number of provinces to the grandmother, aunt or sister of the child. Children are covered under this legislation up to the age of 16 in the provincial laws, with provision for extension beyond that age while the child continues his education, or, if incapacitated, until he becomes of the eligible age (18 years) for Disabled Persons Allowance.

The probability is that the detailed regulations of this categorical allowance will be increasingly merged into the provisions of the general assistance legislation, and this process will be expedited by the inclusion of Mothers' Allowances in the 'shareable' category of the Canada Assistance Plan.

Widows' Allowances

The provinces of Quebec and Ontario have recently added a new category to public assistance with the introduction of allowances to widows and unmarried women of 60 or more years of age, under provisions similar to Old Age Assistance available to persons between 65 and 69, with the major exception that the residence requirement is one year. These allowances will, in time, tend to disappear under the expanding influence of the Canada Pension Plan provisions for Widows' Benefits.

School Allowances

In 1961 the province of Quebec introduced the Schooling Allowances Act, which provides for the payment to parents of an allowance of $10 a month for each child over the age when they cease to be eligible for Family Allowances, providing the child is being maintained by his parents and is continuing his education at school or university. In 1964 the federal government passed the Youth Allowances Act, which makes similar provision for Canada as a whole, and permits a province to make its own provision, with appropriate fiscal adjustments. The province of Quebec, therefore, continues the operation of its '*Allocations Scolaires*' under the Act of 1961.

(b) Welfare Services

Child Care and Protection

The administration of laws for the protection and care of children by the state, or by private agencies by virtue of public legislation, falls within the sole jurisdiction of the provinces as affecting civil rights, while the administration of these laws is, in all provinces, the responsibility of the departments of public welfare. Every province has legislation, either in the form of a Legitimacy Act, or a Children of Unmarried Parents Act, or within the terms of an over-all Child Welfare or Children's Protection Act, which defines the status and protects the interests of children born out of wedlock. All provinces provide for the identification, where possible, of the putative father and impose upon him obligations for the maintenance of the child, although in practice this legislation is difficult to enforce.

In every province there is extensive legislative provision prescribing the status and the procedures connected with the care and protection of children. In most provinces these duties are now the administrative responsibility of the public welfare departments, but there are still in existence, especially throughout Ontario and in a few urban areas of some other provinces, private Children's Aid Societies with legal responsibilities for child care services under provincial supervision. There are increasing indications that the pioneer work of the voluntary societies, dating from as early as 1893, has now achieved its purpose and that the basic responsibilities for child care will become public responsibilities throughout Canada in the not too distant future.

The general pattern of child care legislation is for a child to be brought before a court as a child in need of protection (in some provinces) or as a 'neglected' child (in other provinces). Although there are differences between the various provinces, all the relevant legislation sets out detailed definitions of 'neglect' which must be proved to the satisfaction of the court. An interesting feature of some of the provincial child care legislation is the recognition of 'emotional deprivation' as a cause of neglect. Where there is provision for Juvenile and Family Courts, or in Quebec for 'social welfare courts', cases are heard in these courts. Where special courts of this type are not in existence the cases are heard in the ordinary civil courts (magistrates' courts). The legislation in all provinces provides for cases concerning children to be heard in private and for the identity of those concerned to be protected.

The legislation provides for children to be made wards, either of the Minister (in Saskatchewan, Ontario, and Quebec) or of an officer of the Crown such as the Superintendent of Child Welfare (Alberta and Newfoundland). In the other five provinces 'wardship' is granted to either the appropriate officer of the Crown or the local Children's Aid Society where there is one. 'Wardship' may be temporary for a period (limited in some provinces to a maximum period) to enable the child welfare workers of the public department or the Children's Aid Society to attempt to improve conditions in the home sufficiently to permit the child's return to his own home. There has been a small number of cases in recent years where wardship has been taken to permit the competent authority to give consent to medical procedures, such as blood transfusions, when the parents refused consent and the child's life was judged to be endangered by the refusal. On the other hand 'wardship' may be permanent, that is to say it will remain with the competent authority or designated person until the child reaches the terminal age prescribed in the legislation or is adopted, whichever first occurs. The terminal age varies but is generally 18 years, or, in the case of a female, marriage if before the age of 18, with provision in some provinces for continuation of wardship of children to age 21 in certain cases to permit the completion of the child's education. The precise legal meaning of the term 'wardship' is not entirely clear but it appears to cover all the rights and obligations of a 'guardian of the person' with responsibility for the care and custody of the child. The laws of the province of Quebec are somewhat different, being derived from the traditions and practices of Roman Law, with a strong emphasis on the infrangible character of the family as the essential unit of the social order.

The competent authority, in making arrangements for the care of the child, may place it in supervised 'foster home' or consider placing it in a home for adoption, or arrange for its adoption, or place it in an institution for special care. Legislation in some provinces prescribes limitations which must be observed if possible in the selection of foster homes, particularly in order to ensure that the religion of the foster home is the same as the official religion of the child. Illegitimate children are held to have the same religion as their mothers. Renewal of temporary wardships is a matter for action by the courts and, although this is not always entirely clear in the legislation, termination of wardship is also a matter for court action.

In addition to the children brought into care under statutory provisions because of demonstrated neglect, there are also considerable numbers of children under the protective care of child care agencies, especially of voluntary agencies, where the agency either is giving service, while the child remains in the home, in order to strengthen the family life, or is looking after the children during a temporary crisis, such as hospitalization of the mother. This protective service is increasingly being recognized as a legitimate function of child care on which public financial expenditure is justifiable. There are some tentative developments also of preventive services in a few places; these are intended to forestall unsatisfactory home conditions liable to lead to neglect or potential neglect of children.

All provinces have legislative provisions controlling the adoption of children. While adoptions by private arrangement are still possible, the adoption order must be made by the court and there is a growing extension of provisions that require a report based on the best interests of the child to be made by the competent child welfare authority before the decision of the court is taken. Adoption laws require the consent of the parents, or in the case of illegitimate children, of the mother, except in a limited number of specified cases if the judge deems the dispensing of the consent to be in the best interests of the child. General conditions limiting the ages and circumstances of adoptive parents are to be found in the legislation, and provision is made also for periods, varying from six months to one year, of adoption probation before the legal confirmation of adoption is completed by the court. The legal status of the adopted child in the adoptive family is defined and his retention of rights, if any, of inheritance from the natural parents is also specified. The child welfare authority is responsible for the investigation and approval of adoptive homes for children in its care whom it places for adoption. Provisions are made in all adoption legislation to prevent the adoption of children for monetary rewards.

All provinces have legislation for the inspection and control—and in some provinces for the licensing—of institutions which provide care for children, whether they are boarding homes or day-care centres. Provisions in the provincial legislation also provide for the payment of both capital grants and maintenance grants to approved voluntary societies for the operation of approved charitable institutions for the care of children, such as orphanages and homes for special types of care. In addition there are in a number of provinces provisions for the establishment and operation by the province of 'Training Schools' or 'Industrial Schools' for boys and girls to which the courts may commit children brought before them for neglect, or, more often, charged with 'delinquency'. In some provinces these training schools come under the jurisdiction of the department of public welfare; in others they come under another department, as for example the Attorney-General's department or, in Ontario, a

Department of Reform Institutions. A child committed to one of these correctional institutions becomes a ward of the appropriate child welfare authority or, in some provinces, of the superintendent of the institution to which he is committed.

Juvenile Delinquents Act

The Juvenile Delinquents Act was passed in 1908 by the federal government. This Act, when proclaimed by a province, sets out a number of acts which when committed by a child constitute an offence known as a delinquency. The national Act defines a 'child' as a boy or girl apparently or actually under the age of 16, but leaves the provinces discretion to adopt some other age limit. In Alberta the age is 18 for girls and 16 for boys and in Saskatchewan, Ontario, New Brunswick, Prince Edward Island and Nova Scotia the age specified in the provincial legislation is 16; in Newfoundland it is 17; in British Columbia, Manitoba and Quebec it is 18. The Act becomes effective only in those provinces or parts of provinces for which it is expressly proclaimed. When a child is found by the court to have committed a delinquency he is dealt with by the court not as an offender 'but as one in a condition of delinquency and therefore requiring help and guidance and proper supervision'. Charges of juvenile delinquency are normally heard in a juvenile court, if one exists, or by a magistrate sitting as a juvenile court judge. Cases are for the most part heard in private and under less formal conditions than in the ordinary courts. The judge usually has, as an integral part of the court staff, one or more full-time or part-time probation officers, and has wide discretionary powers to prescribe appropriate supervision and treatment, including the use of probation, appropriate to the needs of each child found to be a delinquent. There are wide variations in the application of this legislation in different parts of Canada. For example, in some places the municipality is responsible for the establishment and maintenance of a juvenile court; probation services, while greatly improved, are still uneven and sometimes non-existent.

The Care of the Aged

As in other Western industrial nations, the care of the aged has increasingly engaged the attention of the legislators, as the numbers of older people in the population increased, and as the provisions and protections available in a static rural society for older dependent people have disappeared in the growth of dynamic urban industrial society. Suitable living accommodation is one of the major needs of older people and is the subject of legislation federally and in all provinces. As already mentioned, the federal National Housing Act contains provisions for federal assistance on a substantial scale to low-rental housing projects. Thus housing for elderly persons of low income can be and is sponsored by non-profit organizations and municipal authorities. These provisions are matched in most provinces by provincial legislation of the same kind, as for example The Elderly Persons Housing Aid Act and The Homes for Aged Act of the province of Ontario. More recently there has been concern for the social needs of older persons, illustrated by the passing, in 1962, in that province of a Social and Recreational Centres Act and, in 1966, an Act to encourage the establishment of smaller 'Rest Homes' in local communities.

A long tradition of institutional care of dependent elderly people is exemplified by the existence of provincial or municipal 'Homes for the Aged', which are, in some provinces, the refurbished Poor Farms or Poor Houses of an earlier generation. There has been a great deal of reconstruction and new building in all provinces under legislation which enables a province to provide or to assist local municipalities in the provision and operation of homes for old people. For the most part these homes provide accommodation for those who are eligible, under the federal legislation and its provincial counterparts, for Unemployment Assistance as residents in homes for special care.

The supervision of private homes and accommodation in a number of provinces includes a system of licensing. In other provinces the objectives of ensuring minimum standards of accommodation are sought by the use of public health acts and regulations, conditions of approval as recipients of grants from public funds, as in Ontario and Quebec, or in several provinces by municipal ordinances under the Municipal Acts of the provinces. Regulations under these various legislative provisions are often very detailed.

Boarding homes, rooming houses and other forms of care for older persons are subject to systems of inspection and license in some provinces, for the most part by municipalities or under provincial legislation affecting institutions of all kinds.

The Ontario Elderly Persons Social and Recreational Centres Act 1961–62 authorizes the provincial government to assist voluntary organizations with 30 per cent of the cost, provided the project is also supported by the relevant municipality with at least 20 per cent of the cost, of erecting or adapting premises for use as social and recreational centres for elderly persons. The Community Programmes Branch of the Department of Education provides advisory services on educational and recreational activities for older people under Education legislation.

In the province of Quebec the institutional care of old people is by long tradition the special province of the religious orders and private social agencies, who are assisted under provincial legislation with capital grants and maintenance allowances.

Rehabilitation

As in many other countries, the task of providing services intended to restore to his maximum capacity for self-care and if possible employment a person who is physically or mentally disabled is one of considerable complexity and involves a wide range of legislative provisions and administrative arrangements. Some of these are mentioned elsewhere. Disabled ex-service men and women are provided with a wide range of medical and social services by federal government under the various Acts comprising the Veterans Charter; similarly, the provincial Workmen's Compensation laws make extensive provision of income during disability and for the restoration of an eligible disabled worker. The Special Services divisions of the Canada Manpower Centres assist handicapped persons by providing employment counselling and selective job placement services and by participating in vocational training plans. The various income-maintenance programmes, especially those covered by the federal and related provincial Disabled Persons Acts, make it possible for the province to provide income to the totally and permanently disabled.

The Agreements made under the federal Technical and Vocational Training Assistance Act and the Vocational Rehabilitation of Disabled Persons Act are the instruments which enable the provinces to use existing health and welfare services according to the specific needs of the handicapped individual. As mentioned earlier, the latter Act makes provision for a National Co-ordinator in the Civilian Rehabilitation Branch of the federal Department of Labour. All provinces have matched the federal action by appointing a co-ordinating official for rehabilitation services.

CHAPTER 3

Health Services

The provision and administration of health services in Canada are, as they are in the welfare services, in a state of rapid and almost continuous change. A *Medical Care Act* was passed by the federal Parliament in December 1966 and the federal government is committed to the implementation of medical care not later than 1966. In the case of health services, therefore, the services as they operated in 1966 are recapitulated first and an extended note is made of the new legislation and its possible implications for the future. The general administrative implications of the new developments are referred to later in this chapter.

FEDERAL

The federal government has limited jurisdiction in the field of health. Although in matters relating to health the British North America Act is as vague as it is about welfare, custom and practice have allocated primary responsibility for health to the provinces, except in respect of those special groups of persons who are accepted as federal responsibilities and certain aspects of health which are either specified in Section 91 of the British North America Act or arise out of national or international health obligations.

The Department of National Health and Welfare was constituted in 1944, when the health functions of the federal government were transferred from the then Department of Pensions and National Health. The Food and Drug Directorate of the present department administers the Food and Drugs Act and the Proprietary or Patent Medicine Act, under which the government exercises control over the safety, quality and the labelling and advertising of all food, drugs, cosmetics and therapeutic devices made or sold in Canada. The list of drugs for sale on medical prescription only is maintained by the federal government under this legislation. Under the Narcotics Control Act the federal government is responsible for the regulation and supply of narcotic drugs. Penalties for the illegal import and export of these substances and for trafficking in them were sharply increased in the revision of this legislation in 1961. The Directorate also administers the Poison Control Centres established in the principal hospitals and the Canadian Adverse Drug Reaction Reporting Programme.

The federal government is responsible for the administration of the Quarantine Act under which all traffic entering Canada is inspected to prevent the entry of infectious diseases. Under the Canada Shipping Act it provides medical, surgical, hospital care and other treatment for sick mariners from vessels using Canadian Ports, for which purpose it maintains clinics in most of the major port cities. Under the Leprosy Act the federal government maintained a leprosy hospital at Tracadie in New Brunswick, which was closed in 1966.

The medical examination of immigrants to Canada, as required by the Immigration Act, and the provision of medical care to immigrants in transit or awaiting employment are undertaken by the national health branch of the department; and assistance may be given to needy immigrants requiring hospital or medical care during their first year in Canada, usually by an arrangement for sharing costs of the necessary services with the province in which the immigrant resides.

The department undertakes hospital and medical care, as well as public health services for Indians and Eskimos, and acts as the provincial department of health for the North West Territories. The department also services certain other federal departments in health matters, particularly the Department of Transport in all matters of Civil Aviation Medicine and the provision of a diagnostic and emergency medical service to federal government employees in Ottawa.

The Department of Veterans Affairs has an extensive Treatment Services Branch, whose primary responsibility is to examine and treat ex-service men and women for their pensionable disabilities. Certain other categories of ex-service personnel are eligible for treatment by the department, including recipients of War Veterans Allowances, and eligible war pensioners of other Allied countries who are now resident in Canada. Services are also provided, on request, to other persons for whom the federal government is responsible, including the Royal Canadian Mounted Police, and members of the armed forces. The Department of Veterans Affairs operates nation-wide hospital services, dental services, and domiciliary care. The prosthetic services of the Department of Veterans

Affairs were transferred to the Department of National Health and Welfare in 1966.

FEDERAL-PROVINCIAL

The National Health Grant programme was inaugurated by Order-in-Council in 1948 to provide federal assistance to the provinces to expand and improve their facilities and services for health care. This programme was estimated to cost about £55 million in 1965–66. These grants are paid to the provinces as grants-in-aid of approved projects under nine major classes: hospital construction; general public health; rehabilitation services; mental health; professional training; public health research; tuberculosis control; cancer control; and child and maternal health.

In 1957 the Hospital Insurance and Diagnostic Services Act provided federal financial assistance to enable the provinces to establish hospital insurance programmes for hospital care in active treatment, chronic and convalescent hospitals. Federal assistance does not extend to institutions providing custodial care, to mental hospitals or tuberculosis hospitals. All ten provinces and both territories now have 'hospital insurance' coverage, although not all of them have adopted the contributory insurance method of requiring individual premiums to be paid by individuals and families as a prerequisite of service. Saskatchewan, Manitoba, and Ontario require the payment of premiums, while the other seven provinces support their plans from the general revenue, or from earmarked taxes within the framework of the general revenue.

The legislation provides that provinces must make available basic services[1] of hospital accommodation and meals in public wards; medically necessary nursing services; laboratory, radiological and essential diagnostic procedures; drugs, biologicals and related preparations when administered in hospitals; radiotherapy and physiotherapy service when available; and other services as provided in the particular federal agreement under the Act. Among the other services are included, in some provinces, out-patient service, rehabilitation services and certain other specified diagnostic and treatment services.

The federal department provides a wide range of consultant and advisory services to the provinces and to specific fields of medical

[1] In North America, as in most other countries, hospital care is concerned only with the essential items of hospitalization. Medical care by surgeons and physicians is organized and financed quite independently.

activity. Among these are the Child and Maternal Health Division; the Dental Health Division; the Epidemiology Division, concerned with research and advice on communicable and non-communicable diseases; Research Development and Planning and Evaluation; the Medical Rehabilitation Division, which deals with the medical aspects of the allowances programmes under the Disabled Persons Act and the Blind Persons Act; the Mental Health Division, which provides advice on programmes and grants for mental health; and consultant services on nursing, and nutrition. Several divisions of the federal health department carry out specific statutory responsibilities as well as extending consultant services to the provinces; for example, the divisions of Public Health Engineering, of Radiation Protection and of Occupational Health.

In addition to the hospital services programme, the Health Insurance and Health Resources Branch of the Department of National Health and Welfare administers the federal aspects of the Health Resources Fund, set up in 1966 to make available $500 million over a fifteen-year period for the expansion of medical and dental schools and the teaching hospitals, and the recently passed Medical Care Act which authorizes federal contributions towards the cost of provincial medical care insurance plans. This Branch also includes a Health Facilities Design Plan.

The Dominion Council of Health is composed of the Deputy Minister of National Health, the deputy minister (or chief health officer) of each province and five appointed representatives of interested groups, such as the universities, labour, agriculture and women's organizations. It serves as an advisory body to the federal government and a co-ordinating device for federal-provincial relations in the field of health.

The Royal Commission on Health Services

In June 1961 the federal government appointed a Royal Commission with very broad terms of reference to report 'upon the existing facilities and the future need for health services for the people of Canada and to recommend such measures, consistent with the constitutional division of legislative powers in Canada, as the Commissioners believe will ensure that the best possible care is available to all Canadians. . . .' The Hall Commission's Report[1]

[1] Canada, *Report of the Royal Commission on Health Services*, Vol. I, 'Major Analyses and Recommendations'. Ottawa, The Queen's Printer, 1964.

was published in June 1964 and recommends a comprehensive universal health service, financed through compulsory health insurance, and administered by the provinces.

Meanwhile some of the provinces have gone ahead in their several ways to establish medical care programmes partly in anticipation of federal action on the Hall Commission's Report, and partly to occupy what is recognized as an increasingly important area of provincial jurisdiction.

Reference is made in later paragraphs to the specific arrangements in the several provinces. The federal government passed legislation in December 1966 to provide federal financial contributions for provincial programmes, and is pledged to make it effective in 1968. As a prelude to action in this field the federal government established in 1966 a Health Resources Fund of $500 million over a fifteen-year period, the basic purpose of which, in the words of the Prime Minister 'is to help to meet the greater need to provide trained people to provide medicare services'. The money will be used 'to provide and equip research establishments, teaching hospitals, medical schools and training facilities'. Grants from the Fund will not be available to meet operating costs of such establishments. The Medical Care Act 1966 makes provision for federal sharing of 50 per cent of the cost of provincial medical care programmes providing that the plan is operated on a non-profit basis by a publicly responsible authority appointed or designated by the province, that the plan is available on uniform terms throughout the province, that not less than 90 per cent of the insurable residents of the province are entitled to service (95 per cent after 1970) and that no unreasonable barriers of provincial residence or waiting periods be introduced to limit coverage. The plan is strictly confined to the services of a medical practitioner and it is too early yet to determine the administrative and medical problems that will arise in its operations. They will undoubtedly be great as the provinces attempt to fashion provincial plans to take advantage of federal funds for their own plans which, in their present forms, do not conform to the federal requirements, being in some cases more restrictive in coverage and more extensive in range of benefits. There is, however, power in the Act to extend the range of services if a province so decides and the federal government agrees. The Act also permits provinces considerable latitude in the detailed development of plans. Meanwhile the current burden of medical care rests on the provincial governments.

PROVINCIAL

Public Health

As the primary jurisdiction for health services, each province has an extensive range of legislation for the provision of health services and the supervision of health services in the province. Although there are variations, due to the social, cultural and economic factors, all provinces now maintain basic public health services. Legislation exists to provide for inspection and control of sanitation, food supplies and sanitary conditions in areas such as parks, streets, theatres and other public places. Air pollution, water pollution, and radiation are all features of a rapidly developing industrial community which require health controls and for which legislation is in force or under study in most provinces. The supervision and control of health conditions in industry falls more properly within the field of labour legislation, under such acts as Factory Acts, Shops Acts and Mines Acts, while the Workmen's Compensation Acts, already mentioned, deal with such matters as accident prevention and health hazards in industry. The control of communicable diseases, requiring the reporting and supervision of cases, research and diagnostic services, is one of the oldest established areas of provincial legislation, and is usually undertaken in co-operation with local health authorities. Health education is a major activity in all provinces. All provinces maintain public health laboratory services, to carry out the examination of food, milk and water supplies and assist local health authorities with facilities for bacteriological and pathological examinations in the fulfilment of their duties under the public health acts of the province. Dental health services are, for the most part, directed at preventive care, more especially in connection with education and care of the dental health of children. Water fluoridation is being developed under provincial legislation in seven provinces, usually under the direct operation of municipalities and local health authorities.

Public health services are organized at the local level either under the jurisdiction of the municipalities or of health units, regions or districts comprising a number of municipalities.

Medical Care for Special Groups

All provinces accept responsibility for the care of the mentally ill. With very few exceptions, mental hospitals are provincial institutions.

Psychiatric wards in general hospitals and out-patient services for the mentally ill are being rapidly developed. Legislation relating to the care of the mentally ill makes provision for the protection of the civil liberties of patients by requiring specific procedures for certification and committal of mentally disturbed persons, although it is still true that in certain provinces committal procedures do not give adequate protection. Institutional and out-patient provision exists in nine provinces for the treatment and education of mentally retarded patients. There are a number of institutions in six provinces which provide special care for emotionally disturbed children.

All provinces have legislation for the control and treatment of tuberculosis and venereal disease, and many provinces now accept responsibility for the care and treatment of certain long-term diseases, such as cancer, poliomyelitis and cerebral palsy. Assistance is given to voluntary organizations in the provision of services for other diseases of a chronic and disabling nature, such as heart conditions, diabetes, paraplegia, blindness and deafness; and to agencies such as crippled children's societies and generalized rehabilitation agencies for the physically disabled of all ages.

Medical Care for Assistance Beneficiaries

For several years a number of provinces have financed most of the cost of providing personal health services for persons without financial resources. In general this care is limited to recipients of various types of public assistance. In other provinces provision for such financing continues to be the responsibility of the municipality. The extent of medical care available to the indigent varies. Physician service in home and office is financed in Ontario. Virtually complete medical care is available in British Columbia, Alberta, Saskatchewan, Manitoba, and Nova Scotia. Typically, payment is also made for dental and optical services and for prescribed drugs.

Various provinces have, in addition, introduced legislation concerned with medical care provision for the whole population.

Public medical care for the whole population has existed in a modified form for some considerable time in three provinces. In Newfoundland the Cottage Hospital plan has for a long time provided general physician and hospital care, financed in part by contributory premiums and in part from public funds, for about half the population situated in the sparsely populated areas of the province. More recently the province accepted responsibility for free medical and surgical care in hospital for all children under 16 years of age. In Manitoba and Saskatchewan there has been for many years a pattern of medical care services provided by a doctor under contract with a municipality or group of municipalities. In addition, a comprehensive contributory programme of physicians' services has been in operation since 1946 in an area (the Swift Current health region) of Saskatchewan.

In 1961 the government of Saskatchewan passed a Medical Care Insurance Act establishing a tax-financed medical insurance programme for the whole population. After a vigorous controversy the Act was amended in 1962 to meet certain objections of the medical profession. All residents of the province except those covered under other public programmes are compulsorily covered by the plan. The patient has free choice of doctor, and four methods of payment are available. The doctor can charge the cost directly to the Medical Care Insurance Commission; the patient can enrol as a member of an approved voluntary medical care plan, which will pay the doctor and be reimbursed by the Commission; the patient can pay the doctor's bill and himself collect from the Commission; or, lastly, the patient can make a private arrangement with his doctor outside the plan. The Commission accepts responsibility for payment of 85 per cent of the fee schedule.

In October 1963 Alberta introduced a Medical Plan, the purpose of which was to make comprehensive medical care insurance available to all residents through the existing private health insurance industry. Approved policies, with minimum standard policies for basic benefits must be offered without exclusions because of age, health conditions, or cancellation of previous policies, and must provide guaranteed basic services, on a renewable contract. Provision is made for public supplementation of persons of low income. A number of special agencies were established under the Act to regulate the operation of the Plan.

British Columbia passed a *Medical Grant Act* in March 1965 which established a new agency called the British Columbia Medical Plan, to make medical insurance available to all persons in the province and to provide subsidies to enable persons of low incomes to belong to the plan.

The Ontario Medical Services Insurance Act was passed in June 1965. This Act controls the medical insurance industry by prescribing maximum premiums, benefit levels, types and levels of medical benefit and conditions of coverage. It also provides for the subsidization of the premiums of all persons of low incomes through a government department which will act as the carrier of all subsidized contracts.

All three provinces have defined low income persons for the purposes of subsidization of their premiums through definitions based on the taxable income—or the fact of an income below the income-tax limits—of the individual or head of the family. This has created a new type of means test which may prove to be administratively too complex and illogical to survive. It remains to be seen whether the introduction of the federal *Medical Care Act of 1966* will lead to further complications of this fractionated approach to medical care, or whether the gradual pressure of demand will lead to a more genuinely national programme of medical care, operated as a partnership between the federal and provincial governments. All medical care programmes are necessarily complex and it may well be that by permitting parallel developments of independent plans in the private field, the inevitable breakdowns and complications will be less damaging because confined to the separate plans and will be dealt with more effectively because they do not endanger the whole national network but only a single province—or even only an individual carrier. No province appears yet to have achieved adequate coverage of its population through private plans to meet the conditions of the federal Act and the prospect appears to be a long period of experiment. This period will undoubtedly see political, financial and professional manoeuvres, and the emergence and disappearance of a chaos of administrative expedients in a series of determined efforts by the medical profession and the private insurance industry to retain substantial control of the field; in these manoeuvres there will be varying degrees of support from individual provincial governments. A shift in the balance of political power, or an economic recession, might easily lead to a hasty reversal of positions and the emergence of a National Health Service, largely operated and supported by governments at provincial and federal levels.

CHAPTER 4

Problems of Administration, Staffing and Finance

THE ADMINISTRATION OF HEALTH AND WELFARE SERVICES

It will already be evident that, in order to conform to the constitutional, fiscal and political forces operating in Canada, the administrative arrangements are both complex and repetitive. Since the health and welfare programmes have grown up, so to speak, out of the social and political pressures of the changing situation and are not developments of any predetermined plan of action, there is also a tendency for the administrative direction of particular programmes to be placed in the hands of government departments or agencies that reflect the balance of forces at the time of this establishment rather than in some pattern based on administrative logic. A similar situation existed in the United Kingdom until the Beveridge Report of 1942 took an over view of the results of a similar haphazard growth in Great Britain and set forth a comprehensive and logical basis of reorganization. Even if his proposals were not all adopted and circumstances have changed the design, the need for some underlying consistency in organization was clearly established and has reached its present expression in a Ministry of Social Security, and in the separation of functions between the responsibility of central government for income maintenance services and the local authorities for welfare services and short-term emergency aid. Canada did not have a Beveridge Report and her political and constitutional situation has not permitted such a logical arrangement of functions. Welfare programmes which emerged in the period of federal initiative and responsibility during and after the Second World War will be found operated by or largely under the direction of the federal government, while programmes that have developed in periods of provincial strength will be found operated at the provincial level of government, even if financial support for them is drawn substantially from federal tax resources.

At the federal level the government department most concerned with health and welfare services, is, naturally, the Department of National Health and Welfare, established in 1944 originally to carry out the federal government's health functions and to administer the Family Allowances programme. For all practical purposes this department is really two departments with a single minister and common research division and service divisions. It has a Deputy Minister for Health who heads the permanent staff of the Health Branch and a Deputy Minister of Welfare who heads the permanent staff of the Welfare Branch.

The Welfare Branch has become responsible for the federal government's responsibilities in the several new programmes as they have developed. Family Allowances, Youth Allowances and Old Age Security benefits are wholly administered by this Department, through Regional Offices in each of the provinces. The Canada Pension Plan will be administered by the Department, although the collection of contributions will be the responsibility of the Department of National Revenue. The Department is also responsible for the administration of the shared programmes in which the federal government provides financial reimbursement of approved provincial programmes of Old Age Assistance, Blind Persons' Allowances, Disabled Persons' Allowances and, through the Unemployment Assistance Act, those provincial programmes of general assistance and supplementary benefits that are eligible for federal support: when, and if, the Canada Assistance Plan is implemented, it will replace these shared programmes and the Department will be responsible for the federal participation in the new programme.

The federal government has not been able, for obvious political reasons, to exercise the kind of control through detailed conditions attached to grants-in-aid that is characteristic of federal-state relations in the United States. It has, however, been able to exercise considerable influence on the character and operation of programmes in addition to fairly strict control of expenditure to ensure that the requirements of the legislation are observed and proper account is kept of public funds. Perhaps the most striking example of the type and extent of the federal government's influence is the requirement that the benefits paid under the Canada Assistance Plan must be calculated 'on the basis of a test established by the provincial authority that takes into account that person's budgetary requirements and the income and resources available to him to meet such requirements'. This stipulation will require provinces to establish procedures for the assessment of individual need and not to regulate benefits by arbitrarily established standards of presumed adequacy.

Another important means of influencing both policy and administration that has provided opportunities for leadership by the federal authorities has been the holding of frequent federal-provincial conferences. The conferences may be of several types. They may be formal meetings of plenipotentiaries, usually deputations headed by the respective Ministers; or they may be meetings of key civil servants to discuss highly technical and procedural matters, or to prepare for more formal meetings, or they may be meetings of government officials, experts from various fields outside government, or representatives of community groups, or some or all of these in varying combinations. Furthermore, the senior staff of the federal department spend a great deal of time 'on the road' consulting and conferring with provincial departments. This network of formal and informal consultations has done much to offset the effects of long distances and political differences which might otherwise tend to isolate the federal and provincial administrations from each other. It contains within it the seeds of a dangerous possibility that informal conversations of this kind may commit the respective parties in fact, if not in theory, ahead of legislative action and out of sight of the public accountability of the parliamentary system.

The federal department also has a number of formal advisory bodies. The Dominion Council of Health and the Canadian Council on Nutrition are essentially composed of the senior civil servants or technical experts and are primarily technical bodies, whereas the National Council of Welfare has substantial lay representation and the National Advisory Council on Fitness and Amateur Sport, and the Advisory Council of Consumers are primarily 'citizen bodies' of a more or less representative character which provide channels of communication between the Minister and his officials and their respective publics.

The Unemployment Insurance Commission, which now administers unemployment insurance throughout Canada is an example of a special agency created in 1940 to provide an instrument of federal administration at a time when there was no federal government department of welfare and when it appeared desirable to keep its operations—especially those connected with selective service and the deployment of labour—at one step removed from direct political control. Now that its employment service functions have been transferred to the Department of Manpower and Immigration, there appears to be no justification for the continued separation of income-maintenance through Unemployment Insurance from income-maintenance through the Canada Pension Plan and income-maintenance through Old Age Security, Family Allowances and Youth Allowances.

A number of other federal government departments are also engaged in welfare activities. These are, notably, the Department of Veterans' Affairs, operating health and welfare services for ex-service men and women, and the Department of Indian Affairs and Northern Development. The federal participation in public housing, such as it is, is undertaken through a Crown Corporation—the Central Mortgage and Housing Corporation—which reports to the Minister of Labour. Federal participation in the complex field of Vocational Rehabilitation is undertaken through a National Co-ordinator of Rehabilitation in the Department of Labour. While these departments are responsible for specific groups for whom the federal government is responsible, such as Veterans, Indians, Eskimos and new immigrants, there is some conflict between these departments in the design of their service programmes and in their competition for qualified staff. There is no pattern of a federal Cabinet Minister generally responsible for oversight and co-ordination of the social service ministries of the kind which has developed since the Second World War in the United Kingdom. As the various social services expand and compete with one another for priority on the Cabinet agenda and in the National Budget, some co-ordination of federal health and welfare policies and commitments is clearly needed. Whether this will lead to administrative reorganization, as it has in the United Kingdom, or be solved at the level of inter-departmental action, it is impossible to foresee. As the complexities of medical care become more and more demanding it may be desirable to detach the health functions of the department and create a Ministry of Health as a separate department of state: while this may be essential to handle the volume and variety of business in this field, its separation into a new ministry will also create new political and administrative complications.

At the provincial level the situation is less complex. The main burden of administering public health, and now hospital and medical services, falls on the provinces; and every province has a Minister of Health with a separate department.

Public health services are normally the responsibility of the municipalities, but many provinces have grouped municipalities together in Health Units in order to ensure a large enough constituency to justify the appointment of a full-time Medical Officer of Health and a balanced public health staff.

Every province also has a Minister designated as the responsible executive of welfare services, although his title may vary and he may hold it (in two provinces in 1966) in conjunction with some other ministerial function. The only extra-departmental administrations at the provincial level are the Workmen's Compensation Boards, which are by established tradition non-political administrative boards.

The provincial departments of welfare all administer those programmes relating to categories—Old Age Assistance, Blind Persons' Allowances and Disabled Persons. This is usually done through regional offices of the Department. The nature of these Regional Offices varies very considerably. In the big cities the Regional Office is likely to be a large office, with separate divisions responsible for the various programmes and a substantial number of field staff to undertake the necessary home visits and investigations. On the other hand, in an area like Newfoundland or Northern Manitoba, or up the valleys of British Columbia, where the case-load is spread very thinly over a large area of territory, often difficult of access, the Regional Office is likely to be a general purpose office with a small staff who carry out most, if not all, of the functions of the service in the field. All the provinces have located in the Department of Public Welfare, or its equivalent, a number of other functions. The most common of these is the oversight and direction of child welfare services—in most provinces, the actual conduct of child welfare duties—and of homes for the aged and other welfare institutions. In Saskatchewan the care and treatment of offenders in provincial correctional institutions comes within the duties of the Welfare Department; in several provinces, notably in Ontario, there is a special branch concerned with the co-ordination of services for the rehabilitation of disabled persons.

The operation of the general assistance programme is less uniform. In some provinces, such as Newfoundland and New Brunswick, this is included in the functions of the provincial department. In others, especially British Columbia and Saskatchewan, there are arrangements for municipal participation, which may vary from municipal responsibility in a large city like Vancouver, to the operation of the service by the provincial department but with costs shared with municipalities, as in other parts of British Columbia. In other provinces, where there are strong traditions of municipal responsibility, like Ontario and Nova Scotia, the operation is left largely in the hands of municipalities, with provincial subsidy of the costs. Even in these cases the actual cost falling on municipal governments is quite low. Since the provinces are now assured of 50 per cent of their costs from federal participation, the net arrangement is usually 50 per cent federal cost, 30 per cent or 40 per cent provincial, and 20 per cent or 10 per cent municipal cost. These proportions are achieved by a number of different and rather complex formulas and the overall effect has been to circumscribe the initiative of the municipalities—never a very strong point, in any event. The new formula of the Canada Assistance Plan, if adopted, should tend to simplify these complex financial relationships, since all benefits will be assessed on the same formula and financial support from the federal government will be available for the whole range of benefits and services and also for new administrative costs. This contrasts markedly with the situation where federal cost-sharing is only available towards actual benefits paid out in cash, and is not available for services or for administrative expenses. Some provinces, for their part, are making strenuous efforts to modernize their municipal structure, which still reflects their agricultural origin rather than their twentieth century reality—Ontario, for example, has over 900 municipal units, but these are being encouraged by the province to combine into county administrative welfare units, while Nova Scotia and Saskatchewan are attempting other methods of rationalizing the municipal disarray, and New Brunswick has replaced its municipalities by the provincial service.

The structure of welfare administration in Canada thus illustrates clearly a number of the dilemmas of any modern welfare service. Since the desired outcome of the service must come at the level of the applicant, it is essential to have a responsive and responsible local administration; but the realities of tax-resources and the necessity to have an organization of sufficient size to justify a full-time and qualified staff all tend to push the operative responsibility for service upward in the governmental heirarchy. The need for adequate accountability for public funds, which, as can be seen, tend increasingly to come from federal government and provincial resources, tends to create a complex system of audits and controls that limit the adaptability of local services to local needs. It also tends to set up political and financial strains between the various levels of government. The simplifications proposed by the Canada Assistance Plan may alleviate some of these strains, but they may also, as events have already shown, produce new strains because they will make more evident the dependency of municipalities upon provinces and of provinces upon the federal government; and dependency is always an uncomfortable and often a politically indefensible posture.

Appeals Procedure in Welfare Administration

The Canada Pension Plan contains a section providing for a system of appeals against administrative decisions, and the Canada Assistance Act requires the provinces to establish a procedure by which dissatisfied applicants can appeal against decisions by officials. This brings into prominence a feature of Canada's welfare administration that has been inadequately provided in the past, and, so far, is inadequately provided in the present. There is much discussion, beginning in the academic world but now spreading to the legal and political fraternities, of the need to establish some institution akin to the Ombudsman of Scandinavian practice. The problem is well known and is endemic to all welfare administrations, namely that tens of thousands of individual decisions and computations are made daily by officers of the welfare services. Inevitably there is an element of discretion in most of these decisions and equally inevitably there are inconsistencies, misunderstandings and errors, quite apart from the possibility of deliberate abuse and distortion. The individual citizen has no effective redress against a complex and sophisticated bureaucracy that tends to defend its own decisions, except in cases of gross error. The Unemployment Insurance Act of 1940, since it was largely modelled on the earlier British legislation, does make its provision for appeal tribunals and for the office of Official Umpire: the result is a clear-cut procedure increasingly being ossified in its own precedents and a voluminous case-load. In the United States there is a long tradition of using the law courts for test cases in the welfare field but there is no similar tradition in Canada, and, in any event, the adversary procedures of legal action are too lengthy and inappropriate for the highly specialized regulatory instruments of welfare administration. The appeals procedure of the Canada Pension Plan is for appeals to the Minister of National Revenue in matters relating to contributions and contribution records; appeals on matters relating to benefits are first made to the Minister of

Health and Welfare; and from his decision to a Review Committee, to which the applicant and the Minister each appoint a member and these two then appoint a third person who will be Chairman; there is a right to appeal from the Review Committee to the Pensions Appeal Board, with permission of the Chairman. This procedure is clearly heavily loaded against the applicant and is likely to be cumbersome and not understood by the dissatisfied appellant. It is not yet clear what provision the provinces will make in their implementation of the Canada Assistance Plan. There is considerable reluctance on the part of provincial administrators to let the appeal procedure pass out of the control of their departments. The appearance of a genuinely independent Ombudsman, operating in ways that are relatively simple and understood by applicants, would almost certainly lead to significant changes. Appeals are provided for in legislation providing benefits for Veterans (ex-service men and women) and here, as in most other legislation where it is significant, matters of medical assessment are almost entirely in the hands of the medical panels employed in the review of medical evidence. There is no provision in the various provincial Workmen's Compensation Acts for an outside appeal system, the theory being that under this legislation a case is never closed and can be reviewed at any time. The provision in legislation under the Canada Assistance Act that administrative decisions in the provincial and local services must be open to review is a substantial advance in principle but it is too early to determine what the result will be in practice. The public discussion of the need for an Ombudsman—now used as a generic term to mean any system of access to independent outside review of administrative decisions by government servants—is likely to continue.

STAFFING THE WELFARE SERVICES

In Canada, as in almost every other country, there is great concern about the need for more and more adequately qualified staff to administer the various welfare services. As a general pattern Canada has, until recently, followed the American evolution of social work as a highly qualified profession, primarily concerned with social treatment and inherited largely from the practice of private social agencies. Membership of the professional associations is confined to university graduates of a professional course of study, after the first degree, at a School of Social Work. This pattern has proved wholly inadequate to the need. While a much higher proportion of the college-age group in Canada goes to college and obtains a first degree than is the case in Great Britain, it is still only half the equivalent group in the United States. The total number of qualified graduates leaving the universities barely provides sufficient manpower to replace losses from the field due to death, retirement and separation from the service. While the Federal Civil Service has developed fairly adequate classifications and pay scales for social workers, the provincial Civil Service Commissions have only begun to do so in recent years and municipal authorities, with one or two notable exceptions, continue to follow the principle that long exposure to municipal service is the best training for most public services under municipal control. Meanwhile the range of services looking for qualified social work staff continues to expand. The expansion of medical care, mental health services, school social services, improved child care services, rehabilitation services and anti-poverty programmes merely accentuate an already impossible situation. There have been recent developments that suggest that the situation may change rapidly in the future. As a result of the Welfare Training and Research Grants programme of the federal government there has been a considerable expansion of facilities in the eight existing Schools of Social Work in Canada, and the establishment of two new Schools. Even more significant has been the growing interest of Canada's universities in the possibility of designing appropriate undergraduate curricula and the emergence of technical colleges and community colleges as a major element in the post-high school educational system of the Canadian provinces. There are signs that the lessons learned in Great Britain in the establishment of courses under the guidance of the Council for Training in Social Work in that country, will be adapted to the very different educational systems of Canada's ten provinces and that new patterns of social welfare training will emerge in the next few years of a more indigenous character than has hitherto been the case. Equally significant, perhaps, is the growing expansion in provincial departments of welfare (which are the main centres of operational responsibility) of staff development divisions with programmes of in-service training and other methods of continuous upgrading of welfare staffs.

FINANCING THE SOCIAL SERVICES

The significance of a nation's social services can in some degree be gauged from the extent and distribution of its expenditures in these services and from the relation of these expenditures to other calls upon the national income. Canada's expenditures on government income-maintenance, health and welfare services have risen from $164 a head in 1959 to $215 a head in 1964 and the total expenditure in 1964 at all levels of government was estimated at about $4 billion. This was about 12·3 per cent of net national income or 9·3 per cent of the gross national product. In other words, in proportionate terms, Canada spends on health and welfare from the public purse a little more than the United Kingdom and something less than some other countries, notably West Germany and Israel, where the figures run from 13 per cent to 14 per cent of gross national product. The proportion spent on health services has shown a steady increase in recent years as the Hospital Insurance and Diagnostic Services Act 1957 came into its full operation throughout the country and will undoubtedly increase again as the *Medical Care Act of 1966* becomes effective in 1968.

The major cost at the federal level of government falls in the universal benefit (or 'demogrant') services: family allowances in 1963–4 took $538 millions; old age security allowances for the same year took $808 millions, unemployment insurance distributed $366 millions; ex-service benefits were $256 millions, and the Prairie Farm Emergency Fund took $10 millions. Thus, of $2·8 billions of federal expenditures, $1·8 billions were devoted to wholly federal programmes. The shared federal provincial programmes took another $339 millions. Workmen's Compensation Boards spent $112 million without counting medical costs and provincial mothers' allowance programmes required $37 million.

The proportions between expenditures at the three levels of government shows clearly that while the national government revenues carry the major part of the burden, there was a slow but steady drift towards an increase in the proportionate burden of the provincial governments.

Herein lies one of the major administrative problems of social services in Canada. The constitutional jurisdiction for these services is now plainly admitted to be with the provinces. The municipalities, confined to the use of the property tax, find their revenues inelastic

Percentage Distribution of Government Expenditures on Health and Social Welfare by Level of Government, Years ended March 1959–64.*

	Percentage distribution			
Year ended 31 March	*Federal*	*Provincial*	*Municipal*	*Total*
1959	73·9	22·2	3·9	100·0
1960	71·7	25·0	3·5	100·0
1961	70·4	26·4	3·2	100·0
1962	70·0	27·1	2·9	100·0
1963	69·1	27·9	3·0	100·0
1964	68·5	28·5	3·0	100·0

* *Source:* Canada. *Canada Year Book 1966.* Ottawa, The Queen's Printer, 1965.

and their capacity to expand services strictly limited by this fact. The provinces, burdened with mounting expenses for education, housing and urban development, roads and similar services, are engaged in a continuous struggle with the federal government for access to tax-fields, the most productive of which—income and corporation taxes—were pre-empted during World War II by the federal authorities, who are unable to give them up because of standing commitments, including massive universal benefit programmes, made in the post-war period of social and economic expansion. The result is a complex and never-ending series of fiscal battles between federal and provincial governments. The growing political power of the provinces in recent years has intensified the struggle, which is further complicated by the uneven distribution of wealth as between the 'rich' central provinces and the 'poor' provinces of Eastern Canada. Quebec's persistent determination for cultural and political reasons, to be master in its own house, has further compounded the complications.

The provinces are compelled, for fiscal and political reasons, to follow the lead of the federal government in the establishment and maintenance of health and welfare programmes, but resent with varying degrees of bitterness any attempt on the part of the federal government to control the details of the programmes, and, indeed, sometimes they take exception to being forced, by the existence of federal grants, into programmes to which they give a low priority in their assessment of their respective provincial needs.

The continuous adjustment and management of this situation is not simply a question of financial arithmetic or even of administrative efficiency. It requires great political finesse as well as administrative expertize. As the Canada Pension Plan matures and the Canada Assistance Plan takes effect, and as the Medical Care Act of 1966 comes into force, the weight of total expenditure is likely to shift, perhaps to a point where the federal government level will carry as much as 75 per cent of total expenditures on these social services. If, however, this leads to reduction of provincial revenues for other purposes, or if attempts are made to prescribe in more than the most general terms for the operation of programmes, there is likely to be strong resistance and mounting resentment on the part of the provinces.

The sources of finance of the various programmes are also a source of some administrative complexity. Health costs, family allowances, youth allowances and the funds for the shared programmes and for most welfare services come from general revenues of both federal and provincial governments. Unemployment insurance is financed by weekly contributions from employers and employees with a separately managed Unemployment Insurance Fund. The Canada Pension Fund will be raised by contributions from employers and employees, and self-employed workers, while Old Age Security is paid from a Fund sustained by an earmarked portion of personal income tax, corporation tax and sales tax; this fund will now also receive a subvention from federal general revenues to meet the cost of the guaranteed minimum income supplements to old people.

At the provincial level the position is equally complex. Workmen's Compensation Boards are sustained by levies on employers of labour. The costs of Public Health and the various wholly provincial health services, like the mental health services, are met from provincial general revenues. Hospital costs are met in several ways, four provinces using their general revenues, two provinces using general revenues together with daily charges to patients, one province depending wholly on a sales tax, one province relying on individual insurance premiums with subsidies from sales tax and general revenues and two depending mainly on individual premiums, with some subsidy from general revenues. Those provinces that have entered the field of medical care so far have depended, in one case, on premiums as the main source of finance and the others on subsidization from special contributory funds or general revenues of private insurance carriers. This melange of financing may change under the influence of new legislation, especially the Medical Care Act 1966. Welfare costs of provincial governments are almost entirely derived from the general revenues of the provinces, except that in some provinces there are relatively small costs derived from private charitable sources, particularly in some child welfare services, and in a number of special service programmes where governments give grants to specialist private agencies or make fee for service payments to the agencies or assist them with both types of payment. There are, indeed, very few private agencies today that do not depend in substantial degree on funds drawn in various ways from the public purse.

All of these complex inter-relationships in the financing of the services have marked effects on the design and operation of the services, and on the extent, nature, accessibility and effectiveness of each particular service. So far the Canadian social services have not worked out satisfactory or sophisticated administrative devices for ensuring at one and the same time a reasonable degree of local and provincial initiative, an adequate level of quality of service and reasonable uniformity of accessibility and availability; and an adequate accountability for the control of public funds. The main instruments are those of the accountant, and the principal checks are those made in financial audit. The problem of other forms of audit—such as for example a 'social audit' to ensure validity, accessibility, universality and uniformity—or of 'quality audit' to ensure reasonable levels of adequacy of service and levels of benefit—remain to be tackled as major problems of public administration.

IN CONCLUSION

Canada, then, has a varied and diverse pattern of health and welfare services. The complexities and problems of administering them are those common to all countries where the major task is to convert the general intentions of major policy into the multitudinous and infinitely varied decisions that relate general policy to the specifics of individual human situations. The problems are further complicated by the federal structure of the country, with shifting balances of political power, fiscal capacity and economic resources, as well as by geographical and administrative difficulties inherent in the broad range of natural conditions and the uneven strengths of the various partners to Confederation. The fact that its pattern of social services has remained unsettled during the past twenty or twenty-five years is probably to Canada's advantage while the country continues to grow and change so rapidly, and while the resources of new technologies make possible the development of new administrative techniques that can be harnessed to the tasks ahead.

SUGGESTIONS FOR FURTHER READING

Canada

The most comprehensive and accurate reference for students is *The Canada Year Book* published annually by the Queen's Printer in Ottawa. Not only does it contain essential demographic, financial and other statistical material, but it also has substantial descriptive chapters on all facets of Canadian life. The *Canadian Labour Gazette*, from the same source, contains regular statistical series, summaries of new legislation and notes on important judicial and administrative decisions in matters relating to the social services.

The *Department of National Health and Welfare* issues a number of authoritative reference papers from time to time which supplement the standard references.

Most of these official papers can be seen, and in some cases obtained through the Canadian High Commissioner's Office in London.

The Canadian Welfare Council publishes eight times a year a journal entitled *Canadian Welfare* (*Bien-etre Canadien*), which maintains an authoritative commentary of information and comment. The Council also publishes a steady flow of studies in detail, policy statements and position papers based on national resources of information and an up-to-date knowledge of the health and welfare services of Canada.

The Canadian Labour Congress similarly publishes material in this field giving the viewpoint of organized labour on issues of social policy.

For independent scholarly analysis, comment and interpretation, the student is referred to relevant sections of:

Michael Oliver (ed.), *Special Policy for Canada*. University of Toronto Press, Toronto, 1961

John T. Saywell (ed.), *The Canadian Annual Review*. University of Toronto Press, Toronto (annually)

John Fotheringham (ed.), *Transition*. McClelland and Stewart, Toronto, 1966

J. M. S. Careless and R. Craig Brown (eds.), *The Canadians* 1867–1967. MacMillan of Canada, Toronto, 1967

PART II

THE COMPARATIVE ANALYSIS

CHAPTER 1

Social Policy and Social Planning

The four areas chosen for comparative analysis in this final section: social security policies, systems of co-ordination, social policies for the aged and for the family, have already been reviewed within the whole complex of social services in France, Norway and Canada. They were studied in context first in order to emphasize the interdependence of all social services, and of social services on the society in which they are developed. To retain this perspective, an attempt will be made to compare the overall situation in the UK and in the other three countries before embarking on the comparative analysis of these four somewhat arbitrarily chosen areas of social policy and administration.

What comparisons if any can be made of the total social effort, of the collective action for social welfare of the countries under consideration? In practically every country in the Western world, and indeed in most under-developed countries too, post-war governments have taken a broad view of the factors which promote social welfare. All recognize the inter-relationship of social and economic development, the effect of fiscal policies on the redistribution of incomes and the general standard of living, and the contributions which voluntary organizations and 'occupational welfare'[1] as well as the public social services, make to the welfare of its citizens. To take the broad view, to appreciate the interdependence of economic and social development does not, however, make the task of government any simpler and its implications are not always apparent in governmental policies. It vastly complicates the task of any student of social administration who attempts to draw comparisons of social expenditure in different countries.

What should or should not be included under 'social expenditure'? Comparisons are made from time to time of the resources devoted to certain obvious categories of social expenditure, e.g. social security services, and these are related to the gross national product,

[1] It is assumed that the reader is familiar with R. M. Titmuss' essay on welfare services provided by employers. The Social Division of Welfare published in *Essays on the Welfare State*, Allen & Unwin, 1958.

the national income or to *per capita* income. Some of these figures will be used—with caution—later, but no attempt will be made to define and compare total social expenditure. Even if meaningful, comparable figures could be obtained for a particular year, they would not be very revealing as social needs and resources are constantly changing. As the case studies have shown, an assessment of the direction in which a country is moving in response to these changing circumstances is of more interest and importance than any attempt to quantify the incidence and distribution of its social expenditure at any given time.

There are, however, three sets of comparative figures which are of some value in that they indicate in a very general way the potential needs to be met and potential resources. Table 1 gives the population structure in each country for 1965, and thus broadly indicates the proportions of the potentially dependent, inactive groups in the population. These figures could of course be modified and refined by taking into account the average school-leaving and retirement ages in each country and the various calculations made of the size of its working population. Table 2 compares the *per capita* income in each country in 1965, and should be related to Tables 3 and 4, which give some indication of rates of growth in recent years for these and some other countries.

These are factors which will influence, but in no sense determine, the action which governments will take in relation to them. The other factors which have significantly influenced the development of social policy in the three countries studied have already been indicated. But one characteristic feature which is revealing of their approach rather than of their aims is the attitude the different

Table 1

Population Structures (Percentages)

	(0–15) *1965*	*(15–65)* *1965*	*(65+)* *1965*	*Net reproduction rate*
U.K.	23·3	64·7	12·6	1·336 (1962)
France	26·2	62·0	11·8	1·373 (1964)
Norway	23·0	65·0	12·0	1·375 (1963)
Canada	33·7	58·7	7·6	1·660 (1964)

Source: Demographic Year Book 1965.

Table 2

Per Capita Income in 1964 (in US $)

U.K.	1698
France	1579
Norway	1882
Canada	2106
U.S.A.	3002

Source: Yearbook of National Accounts Statistics 1965. Table 9B.

Table 3

Index Nos. of *Per Capita* Product at Constant Prices

	1958	*1964*
U.K.	100	119
France	100	126
Norway	100	129
Canada	100	114

Source: As above. Table 179.

Table 4

Annual Rates of Growth in Total Output

Compound per cent rates of growth in gross domestic products

	1950–60	*1960–65*
U.K.	2·8	3·2
Norway	3·4	5·5
France	4·3	5·1
Germany	7·9	4·8
Italy	5·9	5·1
Belgium	2·9	5·2*
Netherlands	4·7	4·6*
Sweden	3·3	5·3
U.S.A.	3·3	4·5

*Figures available only up to 1964.

governments have shown towards any kind of economic and social planning, and their achievements in this field. Here we have an important new factor in the development of social policies in the post-war era. How far a country is going to be able to take account of its changing needs and resources, and to relate economic development to social development in a fruitful way, is going to depend more and more on its ability to plan successfully.

All four countries have attempted with varying success[1] a measure of economic and social planning if only for certain limited goals. Two common and closely related goals have been full employment and a comprehensive social security system. Both these goals, and in order to implement them, others, such as the introduction and development of a national health service and the reinvigoration of depressed 'development' areas, have been accepted by successive post-war governments in this country. But the actual planning for these goals has mostly been on a comparatively short-term basis, static and piecemeal. The UK's inexperience in overall national planning of the total economy became only too apparent when it produced its first national plan in 1966.[2]

In the European countries whose economies were so severely dislocated, and where the physical damage suffered during the war was so obvious, a high degree of government planning and control of the total economy was clearly essential and widely accepted. The experience of Norway and France is similar in this respect. Their first national plans concentrated in the early post-war years on heavy investment programmes to rebuild their shattered economies. At the same time some attempt was made through new or improved social security schemes to share out what was allowed for private consumption; substantial social development was delayed until the reconstruction period was over and a steady rate of expansion of the national economy was established. In Norway, in spite of greatly increased private consumption and considerable social development, high rates of investment have been maintained. For one advantage of a national plan is that it concentrates attention on the way in which the *marginal increase* in gross domestic production over the

[1] The whole process and techniques of planning in a small country like Norway with its 3·7 million population and unitary government may seem scarely comparable or relevant to the UK with its population of 50 million, or to Canada with its 18 million and a federal government. The UK and France are not however so different on these scores at least.

[2] The National Plan 1966–70.

period of the plan is to be distributed, as between economic and social investment, and consumption. Thus the inter-relation between economic and social investment, and between investment and consumption, receives constant emphasis, and economic growth and social development are seen to go hand in hand.

To take one example of this kind of planning: the French Fourth Plan (1962–5) envisaged that the assumed 24 per cent increase in gross domestic production over the four years of the plan should be distributed as follows:

	Increase in milliards N.F.	*Percentage increase 1965–1961*	*Percentage of total increase*
Economic investments	10·0	28	16
Social investments:			
Housing[1]	3·0	25	5
Collective equipment[2]	3·5	50	5
Administrative expenditure	3·0	22	5
Private expenditure[3]	43·0	23	67
Miscellaneous	1·5	—	2
	64·0	24	100

[1] 25 per cent increase in housing investments should make it possible to construct 350,000 homes in 1965.

[2] National education (with a special emphasis on technical and higher education), sports equipment, public health, scientific research, cultural equipment, town and country equipment, public works.

[3] Selective action was explicitly planned in favour of the lower income groups: an increase in assistance for old people and in family allowances.

The proportion of the anticipated increase in total resources to be devoted to the three essential elements of a planned economy (economic and social investment and expenditure) are determined first. Economic considerations are paramount here for the balance between investment and consumption must be related to whatever growth target has been set. If the anticipated rate of growth is not achieved then the absolute amount of money available for social development and consumption is proportionately (to the shortfall) less, and many private and public plans for improving standards of living may have to be foregone. When there is such a serious falling short of the target as the UK has experienced in the very first years of its five-year Plan, new priorities may have to be established as between the totals devoted to economic and social investment, and as between the different projects planned under these two broad headings. If such a situation were anticipated it might reasonably deserve the name of contingency planning. If not anticipated in the original Plan, it is more likely that the new priorities will be determined by the kind of political pressures and *ad hoc* decisions, which planning seeks to minimize.

Working within the framework of a basic National Plan of this kind, social planning will be concerned with the development of social security schemes to ensure that the non-active dependent groups get a fair share of the anticipated increase in private consumption, and with determining the priorities for social investment. In the past social planning has appeared to play a secondary role. The typical National Plan was constructed by economists, and reconstruction followed by economic expansion (increased productivity measured in market terms), seemed in themselves to be sufficient aims, and in the immediate post-war years were generally accepted as such. But experience has shown that increased national affluence does not in itself bring about the general improvement in the standards of living, which is surely the ultimate aim of any collective action of this kind. Once the period of war and reconstruction are past, social benefits and social investment, which do not derive from a market economy, must be seen as an integral part of the 'economics' of the Plan. In other words, increased opportunities of benefiting from such social provisions as hospitals, homes, low cost housing and pensions, must be regarded and presented, as are wages and interest rates, as an incentive and reward for the savings and the hard work of the whole population on which increased productivity ultimately depends.

On the other hand national planning demands that the social planners have an equal regard for the economic implications of their decisions about the priorities to be given to various forms of social investment and of the redistribution of incomes and expenditure likely to flow from their social security arrangements. One factor in this kind of social accounting, which is often forgotten, is that most increases in social investment (in capital expenditure on new hospitals, houses, schools, etc.) inevitably lead to new or increased social expenditure on current account. Improved development resulting from new investment is immediately reflected in higher working costs. Higher standards of accommodation and equipment naturally expected of a new hospital, clinic or Home, the extended coverage of a facility previously available to the few only, and even new preventive measures uncovering unrecognized, unmet needs, can all lead to greatly increased current expenditure on the social services. This correlation is particularly apparent in the health factor, and in France, where medical costs are largely met out of insurance funds, has led to an ever-increasing expenditure on medical benefits by the Funds. This, according to M. Clement Michel, Director of the National Federation of Social Security Funds of France,[1] has led to demands from certain quarters that medical consumption must be cut down, even while the case for increased social investment in new and improved hospitals and clinics remains undisputed. Indeed, the Fourth and Fifth Plans give an increasing priority to capital investment in the health services.

In the making of social policy there is no escape from decisions about priorities; to make social policy is in fact to make such decisions. In underdeveloped countries, where resources are very limited and even many of the basic services have still to be provided, the decisions which have to be taken are simpler if more painful. In the richer, industrialized countries they are infinitely more complicated, and if they are to be made on any sort of rational basis require the collection of an enormous amount of data to establish the case for, and the implications of, any particular development. The case to be established is not for doing something *per se* (except in emergencies and crisis when the need for immediate action is obvious), but for doing one thing rather than another, or for doing one thing before another. The essence of national planning, whether it be of a major service such as the hospitals, of a complex service like the National Health Service or Education, or of the whole economy as with a National Plan, is the ordering of priorities, the phasing of desirable developments in a prescribed order, while allowing for some flexibility in what Norway calls 'rolling' planning.

In studying the development of social policies in our own, as in other highly developed countries, it is always interesting—and important—to ask what has determined these decisions about priorities in the past and how this process is likely to be carried on in the future. The case studies were written with the avowed purpose

[1] An article in *Droit Social*, June 1964, reprinted in the *ISSA Bulletin*, May, June, July 1964.

of helping the student to answer such questions, and to encourage him to ask the same sort of questions about the way in which these decisions have been and are being made in this country.

The social scientist and social administrator contribute to this decision-making by collecting, expounding, interpreting and commenting on the relevant data. This data consists of hard facts about *present* needs and the human and material resources (of manpower and social equipment available), and the 'soft' or estimated facts about changes in needs and resources which can be anticipated as the result of natural processes or of planned development. This is a formidable task in itself, when one thinks of the whole gamut of social need and social resources, and of the expectations of those who live in, and support, the Welfare or near-Welfare States of today.

However, once a nationwide service has been established, once the State is committed to meeting certain defined areas of need (whether this be the protection of child labour or the guaranteeing of a minimum income), more comprehensive and reliable data becomes available as a by-product of the continuing operation of the service itself. The Canadian Department of National Health and Welfare and the British Ministry of Social Security (previously the Ministry of Pensions and National Insurance and the National Assistance Board) are good examples. More data is always needed of course, particularly if new developments are proposed, and the extent to which government departments, voluntary organizations and independent research workers are co-operating in this vital task is always worth noting.

However extensive and accurate the knowledge thus collected it will still only contribute to more rational decisions about priorities in so far as it is understood and accepted by those whose function it is to plan and those who make the final political decisions. The way in which this knowledge is presented to the general public and to those who have a more direct influence on the determination of priorities is almost as important as the facts themselves, however indisputable. For attitudes and even value judgements are only influenced by new knowledge if it comes in a form which is acceptable—and digestible.[1] The seminal influence of major reports, surveys

[1] A major recommendation of the Laroque report, *Politique de la Vieillesse*, was that the government should accept responsibility not only for continuing research into problems of old age, but for the dissemination of information and public education on these issues.

and for more popular consumption, of course, the press, should never be underestimated.

This is very largely a question of communication without which there can be no effective planning, whether at local, regional or national level, whether for the whole economy or for a particular service. The systems of co-ordination which have been, or are being, developed in various countries to achieve better vertical communication between different levels of administration for the formulation of national policies, and better horizontal communication between different departments and social workers for the more effective operation of their services, will be considered in more detail in a later section.

CHAPTER 2

Social Security

DEFINITIONS

Social security policies are at the heart of that 'collective action for social welfare' which constitutes the social services. Social security is, however, a term applied more easily to policies than to particular services. The income-maintenance services—insurance and assistance schemes, pensions and family allowances—constitute the major means by which social security policies are achieved. But other services are involved too. Social security today means more than the guarantee of a minimum income, it means that medical care, rehabilitation, training and employment services are available as needed irrespective of income. Beveridge recognized this when he made the provision of some kind of national health service and of a full employment policy basic assumptions of his social insurance scheme. Even a more narrowly conceived economic security will not be achieved unless certain basic health and welfare services are freely available, at least for those who are living on or near the guaranteed minimum income.

The Universal Declaration of Human Rights (Article 25, Third Assembly of the United Nations, 1948) underlines this interdependence of income-maintenance and other services, and at the same time expresses the higher expectations of the post-war world, by referring not to the guarantee of a minimum income but to the citizen's right to a 'standard of living'.

'Everyone has the right to a standard of living adequate for the health and well-being of himself and his family, including food, clothing, housing, medical care and necessary social services, and the right to security in the event of unemployment, sickness, disability, widowhood, old age or other lack of livelihood in circumstances beyond his control.'

If accepted, the citizen's right becomes the state's duty, and presumably every country which subscribed to this declaration has accepted a responsibility for promoting social security policies. As students of social administration we are, however, more interested in actual policies—in policy-in-action rather than in policy-aspirations. In order to see what is being achieved, and how, in this area of social security, it will be necessary to look at both the 'strategy' and the 'tactics' traditionally or experimentally being employed in the financing and administration of income-maintenance schemes in various countries—at the different ways in which the national income is being redistributed and the incomes of the inactive or dependent members of the population are being maintained.

STRATEGY

Each country has its own peculiar combination of insurance and assistance schemes and of universal benefits for certain risks. In the countries studied, as in many other Western countries, it is easy to discern certain common trends in the historical development of those schemes. Looking forward one can also discern interesting similarities and differences in the ways in which each country is attempting to co-ordinate its income-maintenance schemes and to relate them to those other social services which contribute to the broader aims of a social security policy. Basically there are three main ways of distributing cash benefits:

the *assistance* method—giving only to those in need, involving some form of means test;
the *insurance* method—giving only to those who have contributed, or on whose behalf contributions have been made (however tenuous the actuarial relationship between contributions and benefit);
universal benefits—giving to all residents or citizens, not because they are in need or have contributed, but simply because they fall into clearly defined categories, usually of age (children's allowances and old age pensions are the most usual form taken by these 'demogrants', as they have been called[1]).

The assistance method was developed first and dates from the time when the State only aimed, and indeed could only afford, to

[1] E. Burns, 'Social Security in Evolution. Towards What?' In *Social Science Review* No. 2. 1965. For a broadly similar definition of these three major types of social security measures (but termed social insurance, social assistance and public service) see *The Introduction to Social Security Programmes Throughout The World*, 1967 (pp. VII–X), published by The U.S. Department of Health, Education and Welfare.

relieve those in greatest need—the destitute. Social insurance came later, when the State became concerned, and could afford to help, the working classes generally by giving statutory recognition and support to their own mutual aid, or to their employers' occupational welfare scheme. It reflects the middle-class attitude towards savings and the respectability of 'insurance'.[1] Universal benefits are a much more recent development and could be regarded as a response to the concept of a Welfare State to which all contribute and from which all benefit. They are dependent on national rather than class or occupational solidarity, although the immediate reasons for introducing any system of universal benefits vary, and are usually different in the case of old age pensions and children's allowances. Many countries have already adopted, or are slowly moving towards, a system of universal benefits for particular categories of persons as the logical extension of the development of their insurance or assistance schemes.

Although for the purposes of analysis it is important to remember the basic distinction between assistance and social insurance (the former involving some kind of test of means, the latter a proof of eligibility derived from contributions), this is a very crude distinction and it is the variations on the theme of assistance or insurance which are of more interest. Those variations are many and some of them will be explored later; they are the techniques or tactics of a social security policy. But again for the purpose of comparative analysis, it is possible to discern two broad lines of development in both methods of administering social benefits. In each case one line leads to an entitlement to benefit which becomes ever more uniform, more automatic, more generalized, until the benefit becomes almost indistinguishable from a universal one. The other line of development is in the opposite direction, and provides benefits ever more closely related to the need, or to the actual contributions, of the recipient. Along this line, the social insurance schemes retain some of the complexity and the high degree of differentiation of commercial insurance, while the assistance schemes become more flexible, more individualized and tend to be closely related to, if not actually integrated with, social work and other welfare services.

In countries where both these lines of development of the assistance and insurance idea have been carried farthest, and where some

[1] A theme elaborated in *Lloyd George's Ambulance Wagon*, The memoirs of W. J. Braithwaite, London, 1957, and in T. H. Marshall, *Social Policy*, London, 1965.

universal benefits have been introduced, a common strategy is emerging. Such countries would seem to be working towards an overall pattern of social security consisting of a basic universal benefit, supplemented by a wage-related, actuarially calculated, insurance benefit for the better off; and for the relatively poor and underprivileged, by an assistance scheme which emphasizes needs rather than means, and which attempts to meet the individual's needs with services as well as cash allowances.

The broad lines of this development are shown in the following diagram:

THE NEW STRATEGY

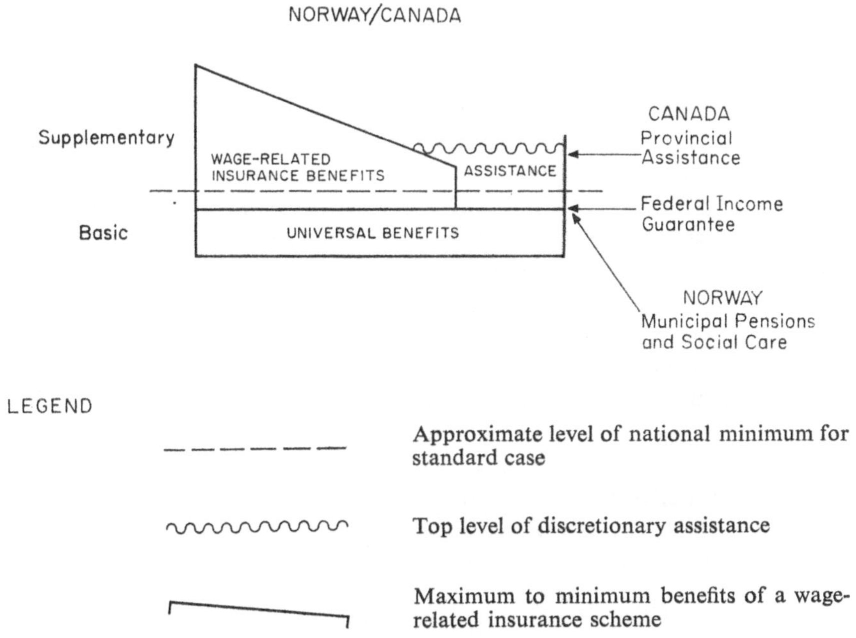

Norway, with her National Pension Plan and Social Care Act of 1965, has already adopted this strategy, though the legislation is still too recent to have been fully implemented. Sweden and Denmark have developed a similar approach.

Canada, with the Canadian Pension Plan of 1965, is going in the same direction.[1] Further federal legislation enabling the provinces to adopt a more rational and effective administration of their assistance schemes can be seen as all part of the same policy.

Two of the countries of the European Economic Community are also adopting the same strategy, at least as regards pensions. Luxembourg already has a State guarantee of a uniform minimum 'subsistence' pension, completed by a contributory pension which allows the individual pensioner a standard of living comparable to that which he had reached during his active life. Italy has recently (1965) introduced a 'social pension' of a uniform minimum amount to be paid from a 'Social Fund' established for the purpose. It is the basis of the new two-tier pension now provided by the three principal pension schemes (for wage-earners, farmers and artisans) and constitutes the first stage of a basic revision of the principles and structure of Italy's pension system. The ultimate objective is a universal pension and full state financing of the Social Fund, but the interim arrangements described more fully in the *Exposé sur l'Évolution de la situation sociale dans la Communauté en* 1965 are particularly interesting.[2]

As the insurance basis of its national insurance scheme (with its comprehensive coverage and uniform benefits) became more and more of a myth, Britain seemed to be moving in the same direction. But it has not yet moved sufficiently far away from Beveridge principles to turn its basic flat-rate insurance into a universal benefit, or to carry through a satisfactory reorganization of its tentative wage-related insurance supplements.[3] However, the basis for an uncategorical general assistance scheme, which can focus on meeting individual needs in a flexible way is already there in the Supplementary Benefits Commission of the Ministry of Social Security, even though relationships with the local authority's social work and welfare services have yet to be worked out more carefully.

[1] As regards old age pensions, Canada is near to having a three-tier system:

flat rate universal benefit plus wage-related supplement
plus occupational pension
or flat rate universal benefit plus federal income guarantee
plus provincial assistance

[2] The chapter on social security from the *Exposé* is reproduced in *ISSR*. No. 1. 1967.

[3] Now (in 1967) Government thinking would appear to favour a different solution—the American policy of a single comprehensive wage-related statutory insurance scheme, with a basic minimum ensured by the benefit formula.

In the terms of the original diagram Britain's present strategy would appear to be:

GREAT BRITAIN

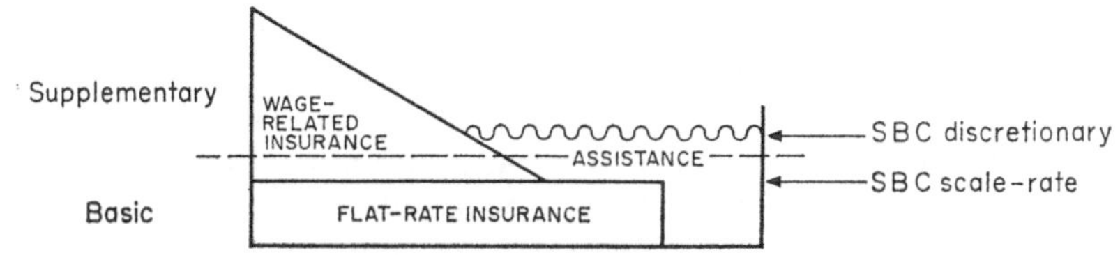

There is little evidence that France will ever adopt the new strategy. Her insurance schemes, including family allowances, have such a firm occupational basis, and the Government is so reluctant to finance any social benefits out of general taxation, it would seem unlikely that basic universal benefits, as here defined, will ever be introduced on any significant scale. Her social security schemes are likely to continue to be based on occupational rather than national solidarity, with a local social aid service to deal with residual need. The governmental role is confined to ensuring that all are attached to appropriate social security schemes, and to a fairly tight administrative control of these institutions. A unique feature of these institutions is that they all provide for their members not only insurance benefits but assistance allowances, as well as other health and welfare services. This policy could be expressed in the terms of the original diagram in this way:

FRANCE

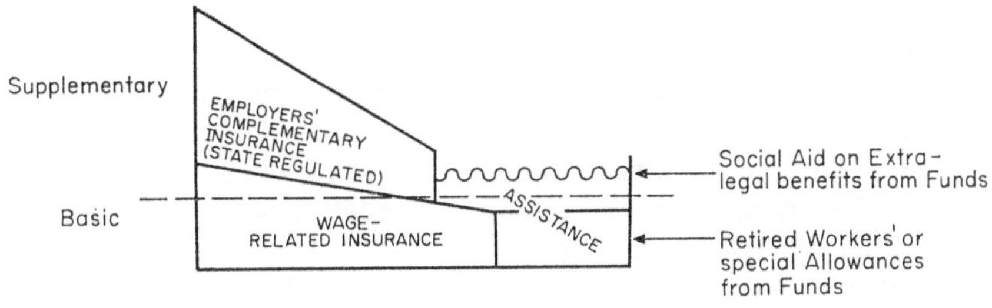

With the exceptions mentioned above, the other countries of the European Economic Community tend to conform to this model rather than to one based on universal benefits.

A fourth model could be constructed for Australia and New Zealand, where the hated English Poor Law was never established and social insurance never took root. Instead, income security against the main social risks has been provided by broad categorical assistance schemes[1] of the income tested type—with a generous means test and flat-rate benefits. Universal benefits now provide family and maternity allowances in both countries, and a pension for the over seventies in New Zealand. Supplementation of this somewhat inflexible system of flat-rate benefits (related to average needs) is left to the local authorities and voluntary organizations in New Zealand, and to the States, local authorities and voluntary organizations in Australia, where the basic schemes are administered and financed by the Commonwealth government. An 'emergency benefit' picks up some of these who do not fall into any category.

AUSTRALIA/NEW ZEALAND

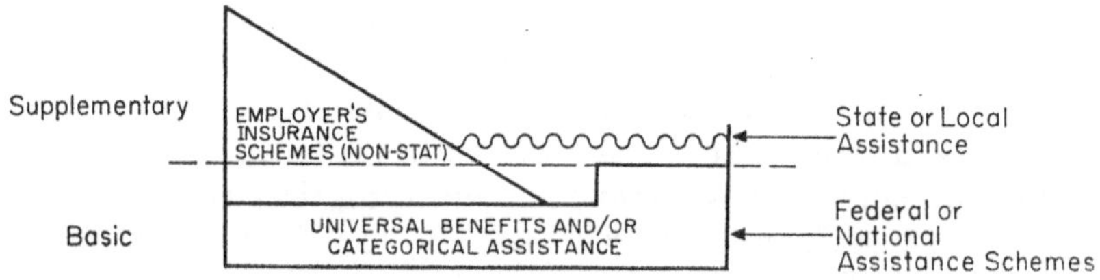

TACTICS

Thus, it would appear that although the aims which inform social security policies are very similar—all these countries subscribed to the Declaration of Human Rights—there are some quite important differences in the particular combination of social security techniques used to implement them. These differences stem in large measure from each country's particular experience in applying these techniques. Every modern industrial society has to deal in one way or another with the threats to the economic security of its citizens presented by unemployment, sickness, disability, heavy medical costs, loss of the breadwinner, large families, and old age. But there can be no appraisal of how far a country has succeeded in implementing

[1] An income conditioned old age pension was introduced as early as 1898 in New Zealand, and in N.S.W. in Australia in 1900 (replaced by a Commonwealth Invalid and Old Age Pension Act in 1908).

its avowed social security policies without looking more closely into the *way* in which it provides adequate cover against each and all of these 'social risks'.

Social Insurance and Universal Benefits

Since *contributory insurance* of one kind or another plays such an important role in most social security systems this technique will be explored first. Under contributory insurance are grouped all those schemes which provide benefits because of the beneficiary's, or his employer's contributions. No means test of any kind is involved. The analysis will be clearer if the different schemes are looked at first from the point of view of the beneficiaries then from that of the government and of the redistribution of the national income involved.

Industrial Injuries

In the industrial injuries or worker's compensation schemes in all the countries studied it is enough that the claimant for benefit is in a form of employment covered by the scheme. There is no requirement that he must have been covered by his own or his employer's contributions for any particular length of time. In most countries, as in Britain, practically all employees are covered by a general or some special scheme. The Norwegian general scheme is an unusually comprehensive one, covering the armed forces and other public servants, such as the police, who are usually provided for under separate schemes. It also covers students, school children, whose contributions are paid by the State; and self-employed persons who may join voluntarily.

Short-term injury benefits are usually wage-related and calculated on the same formula as ordinary sickness benefits. Long-term disability benefits or pensions are also related to wages as well as to the degree of injury or incapacity suffered. The only difference between an *occupational* disability pension and an *invalidity* benefit under the ordinary health or pensions insurance scheme, is that the length of time in covered employment, or the number of contributions paid, never enter into the formula for its calculation. In Britain, on the other hand, both the short-term industrial injury benefit and the long-term disablement pension are flat-rate benefits, although set at a higher rate than the standard benefit for ordinary sickness.[1]

[1] Since 1966 there is a wage-related supplement to the industrial injury benefit, as also to the *short-term* sickness, unemployment benefits and widows allowance.

Britain is again out of step in that flat-rate contributions to the industrial injuries fund are made by employees as well as employers. In most other countries the onus for financing the whole scheme is placed on employers, whose contributions in the form of a pay-roll tax are set at a rate which will meet the total cost of the benefits in cash and in kind (medical care and rehabilitation), paid out year by year. An assessment is made of the accident rate or risks of each industry or firm and the employer's contribution premium is rated accordingly. In France, typically, not only differential rates but in special cases fines or rebates are used as additional incentives to accident prevention. In Britain and Norway the industrial injury fund does not have to carry the costs of medical treatment and rehabilitation as in France and Canada, since these services are already provided on what is virtually a universal basis by the National Health Service and Ministry of Labour in Britain, and by the National Health Insurance scheme in Norway. In Canada, on the other hand, the emphasis in Workmen's Compensation legislation has, from the first, been on full and comprehensive medical care as a primary objective, accompanied by adequate compensation for loss of wages.

Sickness and Unemployment

Where contributory insurance schemes are used to provide economic security against the risks of *temporary* loss of income due to sickness and unemployment, or to the *permanent* loss due to retirement on account of age or invalidity, or to the death or absence of the chief breadwinner, the calculation of benefits and the contribution requirements vary from scheme to scheme and from country to country. The salient features of these various schemes were described in the case studies. It only remains to indicate some of the more interesting similarities or differences in the use made of social insurance techniques in the four countries.

Eligibility for *short-term benefits* usually turns on a minimum number of contributions made since entry into insurance or within a fairly recent period. This requirement may be as light as the two weeks' premiums, which entitle a Norwegian employee to receive the basic sickness benefit, or as demanding as the six months since entry into insurance and 50 out of 52 paid or franked contributions in the last contribution year, required under the British scheme. Since everyone pays premiums to the National Health Insurance

Scheme in Norway, and there are no contribution requirements whatsoever for entitlement to the medical benefits, the (cash) sickness benefit is also practically a universal benefit. It is not high, however, and is widely supplemented by voluntary insurance or employers' arrangements for paying reduced wages. In all countries, eligibility requirements for unemployment benefit are stiffer (30 weeks' contributions over the past year or 45 in the past three years in Norway), and strict limits set to the maximum period for which it may be drawn.

Old Age

Long-term insurance benefits, and more particularly those provided under supplementary insurance schemes, naturally require a longer contribution record. But there are very great variations here too, largely depending on whether the pension scheme is funded, partially funded, or run on a distributive, pay-as-you-go basis. In Norway and Canada, whose new pensions are made up of a basic, universal, flat-rate pension and a supplementary, wage-related insurance benefit, and where extensive funds for investment are to be built up in the early years of the scheme, maximum pensions only go to those who have paid contributions over a substantial number of years. Forty years are required in the Norwegian plan, although special concessions are to be made to those who are over 30 at the start of the scheme in 1967. Once a social insurance scheme is being run on a pay-as-you-go basis, the case for 'blanketing-in' those who were approaching retirement at the inception of the scheme, and who were therefore not able to contribute for long, can be justified actuarially as well as on grounds of social justice. The more comprehensive the scheme, the more 'social' in the sense that a redistribution of income is already being brought about by a weighting of the benefit formula in favour of the lower-paid workers, or the married man (by granting dependents' allowances), the easier it is to do this.

The development of Old Age and Survivor's Insurance (OASI)[1] in the USA is a peculiarly interesting example of a partially funded scheme, which has moved steadily away from the criteria of commercial insurance ever since it was introduced by the Social Security Act of 1935. Successive amendments have socialized the benefit formula and extended its coverage, until in 1950 a 'new start' was enacted, which not only allowed newly covered workers to draw a

[1] Now OASDHI: Old Age, Survivors' and Disablement and Health Insurance.

pension after having paid contributions for as few as six quarters (eighteen months), but permitted all those who were insured before 1950 to have their pension based either on their entire period of covered employment or only on their employment after 1950. At the same time the annual increment of one per cent for each year of coverage was abolished. Nevertheless, it remains a wage-related scheme and the method of determining the amount of benefit still yields relatively larger benefits to the individual with long and continuous coverage.

In Britain, when everyone was brought into a 'national' insurance scheme in 1948, the retirement pension at the full rate was awarded to any late entrant, who had contributed to the scheme for ten years before retiring at 65 or 70. Thus, since 1958, practically every one coming up to retirement age is entitled to the same basic pension. The numbers involved,[1] and the frequent raising of the standard benefit rate to keep pace with the cost of living over twenty years of steady inflation, hopelessly undermined the original actuarial basis of the scheme. The flat-rate contributions have been raised with every increase in the benefit rate, but such increases were always limited by what the lowest paid workers could afford. There was no opportunity of tapping higher incomes by raising the wage-ceiling on which contributions are paid as can be done in the wage-related schemes of the USA or France. Consequently when the scheme finally went into the red in the mid-1950s it was clear that Exchequer subsidies on an ever-increasing scale were going to be needed if the fund was to continue to meet even its existing commitments.

To avoid this, the Conservative government grafted on to national insurance a very dubious 'national superannuation' scheme.[2] This meant that more contributions could be extracted from all who were not in the lowest income range: a percentage contribution was to be paid by all employees on earned income from £9 to £15 (later raised to £18), with the promise of a superannuation supplement, strictly related to what each individual had contributed, when he came to draw his basic pension. This solved the immediate problem of the Exchequer subsidy, and according to the report[3] in which the actuarial basis of the new pay-as-you-go scheme was set out, would settle the financing of the whole national insurance scheme for some

[1] 6,190,000 by 1965; about 6½ million by 1967.
[2] The National Insurance Act, 1959.
[3] National Insurance Bill, 1959. Report by the Government Actuary.

years to come. There was no attempt to cover up the fact that this was to be done at the expense of those whose 'superannuation' contributions were to bring them in such a poor return on retirement.[1]

Taking a long-term view of the development of the country's social security policy, this was tactically and strategically disastrous. For what the government failed to recognize was that since 1958 the national insurance scheme, at least so far as retirement pensioners are concerned, has become to all intents and purposes a universal benefits scheme. Assuming that the *compulsory* contributions have been paid, everyone who 'retires' at 65 is entitled to the same pension, which bears no relation to how long, or how much, the individual has contributed. By eliminating any meaningful relationship between contributions and benefits, and wages, it has lost most of the psychological advantages of contributory insurance without reaping the advantages of a scheme of universal benefits. For the latter can pay benefits to *all* of pensionable age immediately,[2] can be financed from whatever mixture of poll-tax and progressive taxation seems desirable, and is administratively simpler and cheaper than any form of insurance or assistance.

The disadvantage of *universal benefits*, not always recognized by those who have advocated them in the past,[3] is that they are usually very minimal. The amount of money which any society is prepared to redistribute in this somewhat indiscriminate way to *all* children, or *all* old people, is unlikely to allow for more than a minimum benefit. In Canada, the universal pension of $75 a month is reckoned as insufficient and, as in Norway and New Zealand, was not given until the age of 70, until recent amendments which will reduce the age to 65 by 1970. Those retiring before this age, those with special needs and those who have been used to a higher standard of living (and one way or another this involves a very high proportion of retired persons) will need to supplement their universal pension with some kind of insurance or assistance benefit. In other words, it will

[1] No guarantee was written into the scheme that the superannuation supplements would be revalued in relation to the cost-of-living at the time they were drawn. Those who were able to contract out of this bad bargain (because they were contributing to an occupational scheme) have to pay a larger basic contribution, since by contracting out they avoid the element of subsidy to the basic scheme in the superannuation contribution.

[2] The more generous the blanketing-in arrangements the less argument there is for excluding the older groups.

[3] See R. Mendelsohn, *Social Security in the British Commonwealth. Op. cit.*

not be possible to avoid the two-tier system, which is in fact being developed in every country where the basic pension is a universal one. It is perhaps significant that Norway, Canada and New Zealand had no experience of contributory pensions before they moved from an income conditioned old-age pension to a universal one.[1] All have retained some kind of supplementary assistance scheme to meet special needs.

Even those countries like France and Britain who have not yet adopted, and perhaps never will, a universal pension, appear to be developing a somewhat similar two-tier strategy, and not only for old age benefits. Comparing the British experience with that of Norway, Canada, and even France, it would seem that actuarially sound and satisfactory insurance schemes are easier to organize if they are designed to supplement rather than to replace a basic scheme which is providing only a minimal benefit. Any redistribution between different income levels is achieved much more equitably through a basic scheme, particularly if it is organized on a universal rather than a contributory basis, and can be financed out of a more progressive tax than the insurance contribution. This leaves the supplementary schemes free to make the fullest use of insurance techniques; contributions and benefits can be related to the whole wage or to a high ceiling, and allowance made for the diverse conditions of different occupations. There are some interesting lessons to be learnt from France's use of new and unorthodox techniques in this field, particularly in the supplementary retirement pension schemes, set up under agreements between employers and workers, but subject to considerable direction and control from the Social Security Division of the Ministry of Social Affairs.

One of the major problems, perhaps the major problem, facing social security administrators in recent years, has been the greatly increased proportion of old people, often coinciding with higher birth rates which reduce the proportion of active to inactive or dependent members of the population even further. Thus, ways and means of providing economic security for old age tend to predominate in any discussion about social security techniques. Nevertheless, there are some interesting variations in the way in which benefits are provided against loss of income suffered by the younger, normally active, self-supporting members of the population. The

[1] This was not the case in Italy, which makes their experience more interesting for us in Britain.

widows, mothers and orphans allowances under the Norwegian Pension Plan, and the rehabilitation allowances under their National Health Insurance scheme deserve some comment, as do also the diverse and ingenious techniques exploited in the French family allowance system.

Widowhood

In Britain the national insurance scheme has been dominated by the Beveridge principles of comprehensiveness and uniformity, and there has been a great reluctance to complicate the eligibility conditions for any of the benefits by tailoring them to meet need in a more refined way. Widowhood is a case in point. Even though Beveridge himself suggested that widows should be provided for in a more discriminating way, the widow's allowance, the widowed mother's allowance and the widow's pension, are still only for women who are unsupported because of the death of their husband. In the USA and Canada, even before old age and survivors' insurance schemes were introduced, categorical assistances[1] variously provided for a much wider range of unsupported women—mothers whose husbands were physically or mentally disabled and unable to support them, separated wives and unmarried mothers.

Norway has succeeded in introducing this flexible interpretation of a 'widow' into her insurance scheme, and under The Widows' and Mothers' Insurance Act, 1964, and now under the National Pension Plan, not only orthodox widows, but separated and divorced women, unmarried mothers, and an entirely new category of 'family widows',[2] may be entitled to pensions. In all these cases alternative forms of benefits are available to enable the woman to take advantage of any education, training or rehabilitation courses likely to help her to become entirely, or partly, self-supporting. The rehabilitation allowances under the National Health Insurance scheme[3] may, in the same way, be substituted for sickness or invalidity benefit in the case of an employed person paying the N.H.I. premium, or may be given to other dependent members of his family (adults or children) even though they are not entitled to sickness benefits, if some form of rehabilitation seems desirable.

[1] Aid to Dependent Children (ADC), and Mothers' Allowances.

[2] Unmarried women who have been caring for parents or other near relatives. See p. 110.

[3] See p. 122.

Family Allowances

In other countries, family allowances too are usually more flexible than the British standard allowance for the second child with a slightly increased allowance for the third and subsequent children. In Canada, where an allowance is made for *every* child up to 16, and for dependent youths up to 18, differential rates are paid according to the age of the child and may be withdrawn if the child is not attending school. In Norway, where allowances are not normally made for the first child, very flexible arrangements permit this to be paid where there are any special circumstances, e.g. an unmarried mother or a handicapped child.[1] In Germany and the Netherlands, those falling within certain low income groups are entitled to family allowances from the first child. All other residents, with not less than three children, are entitled to the allowances from the third child.

The French system, although unlike the British, Canadian and Norwegian, in that it is mainly financed out of insurance funds (contributions from employers and the self-employed), rather than from general taxation, is by far the most liberal and flexible of all, the most 'tailored' to meet the special needs of families of all kinds. It has, however, been fairly fully described in the case study, and will be discussed again in a later chapter on family policies. The diversity of techniques used in family allowance schemes (and their relation to tax allowances) of these, and many other countries[2] should be of the greatest interest to those concerned with the development of social security policies in this country. Poverty in large families, and indeed in many smaller families where the wage-earning capacity of the father or unsupported mother is very low, or where there are special needs (e.g. high rents), is still to be found in Britain.[3] The increasingly inadequate[4] and rigid system of family allowances has signally failed to prevent this serious breach in the much vaunted

[1] See p. 123.

[2] Much information about family allowance schemes all over the world is collected by the Permanent Committee on Family Allowances of the International Social Security Association. The latest report is published in the *ISSA Bulletin* July, Aug., Sept. 1965.

[3] See The Report of the Ministry of Social Security, 'Circumstances of Families', H.M.S.O. 1967.

[4] Little attempt has been made to keep family allowances in line with the cost of living; the rate was barely doubled while the standard insurance benefit was more than trebled between 1948 and 1966.

'national minimum', in the economic security for all, which was the aim of the Beveridge strategy.

The Relative Importance of the Different Schemes

Both the coverage and level of the different benefits have been indicated in each of the case studies and some comparisons made with their British equivalents. More general comparisons (e.g. of the total economic weight of 'official social security') are not easily made, but some further figures available for the EEC countries show how, even within this group, there is considerable difference in the emphasis given to different schemes. Table 1 shows how expenditure

Table 1

Social Security According to Branch of Insurance in 1964 (as percentage of total expenditure)[1]

Branch of insurance	*Belgium*	*France*	*Germany (F.R.)*	*Italy*	*Luxembourg*	*Netherlands*
Sickness and maternity	28·3	31·6	30·4	29·3	21·1	28·0
Invalidity, old age and survivors	34·8	30·6	51·4	42·6	49·8	47·2
Employment injuries and occupational disease	6·5	8·2	6·1	5·9	11·4	2·9
Unemployment	6·6	0·1	3·1	3·7	0·0	4·5
Family allowances	23·8	29·5	4·0	17·3	17·7	17·4

[1] *Source, Exposé sur l'Evolution Social dans la communauté en* 1967.

on the various branches of social security vary in the six countries. A breakdown of the expenditure of the UK and Norway on approximately the same services (but for different years) is given in Table 2.[2]

[2] A slightly different breakdown of the British figures for the year 1959–60 made by The European Coal and Steel Community, for the purposes of a Report comparing the social security systems of Britain and the Community, indicated differences of much the same order. The proportions were as follows:

To the National Health Service	40 per cent
To the National Insurance (cash benefits)	49 per cent
To the National Insurance (industrial injuries)	4 per cent
To the Family Allowances	7 per cent

Table 2

Branch of insurance	*U.K. (1964)*[1]	*Norway (1964)*[2]
Sickness and maternity	42·6	35·5
Invalidity, old age and survivors	43·7	34·3 1·3 13·1
Employment injuries and occupational disease	2·6	4·0
Unemployment	2·6	3·2
Family allowances	5·0	7·3
War pensions	3·5	1·3

[1] Based on the C.S.O.'s analysis of National Income & Expenditure for 1964.
[2] See table on p. 103.

Some of these variations can be partly explained by differences in what is regarded as 'official social security expenditure' in the different countries. For instance, most of the rehabilitation and resettlement services financed out of social security funds in the continental countries are provided by the Ministry of Labour out of general taxation in Britain. On the other hand, the whole of the national health service expenditure has been included in the British figures in Table 3, while the cost of some of the publicly provided health services (in the fields of mental health, tuberculosis, and maternity and child welfare) are probably not included under 'Sickness and Maternity' social security expenditure in the other countries. Supplementary pension schemes if they are an integral part of the official basic pension plan will be included, others like the French *régime complémentaire* will not.

Differences in the proportions of the dependent groups in the various countries and of the population covered also enter into the picture, but the variable place occupied by family allowances arises more from considerable differences in rates of benefit than from demographic considerations or the extent of their coverage. For example, *for a family with three children*, the monthly amount of allowances (calculated in US dollars) amounted on 30 June, 1962, to the following:

$37.6 in Belgium
$51.8 in France—including the single wage allowance
$10.0 in F.R. Germany ($16.2 in cases where the annual income was below 7200 D.M.)

$23.9 in Italy
$28.8 in Luxembourg
$17.6 in the Netherlands
$10.0 in the UK
$20.0 in Canada
$10.0 in Norway

Financing Social Security

So far, these social security schemes have been discussed from the point of view of the beneficiaries and of the adequacy of the coverage given. But social security policies are determined by resources as well as by needs, and every government must be concerned with the ways, as well as the extent to which economic resources are to be made available for redistribution through the social security system. These resources arise in varying proportions from the contributions of insured persons, of employers, or of the public authorities.

The share of the public authorities in the financing of social security is much smaller in the EEC countries than in Britain, as is shown in the following table taken from a new study by The European Community Statistical Office.[1]

Table 3

Financing Social Welfare 1963
(as percentage of total revenue)

	Contributions			
	Insured persons	*Employers*	*Public Funds*	*Interest*
Belgium	20	44	28	8
France	18	60	21	1
Germany	23	53	22	2
Luxembourg	20	44	26	10
Italy	13	62	19	6
Netherlands	35	42	14	9
U.K. (1964)	22	21	55	2

In Norway the public authorities contribute about 25 per cent of the cost of the National Health and 10 per cent of the cost of the National Pension scheme, while meeting 100 per cent of the cost of family allowances and of assistance given under the Social Care Act.

[1] *Op. cit.* No. 5, in the Social Statistical Series.

In Canada the situation is much more complex, but family allowances and public assistance fall almost exclusively on the tax payer, and old age security benefits on special income and sales taxes. Public expenditure on health services represents an increasing proportion of the public authorities' total contribution to social security services: 22 per cent in 1958–59, 35 per cent in 1964–65.[1]

In Norway the employer's contribution to the National Health Insurance scheme is less than the employee's (75 per cent of his 'premium') but he contributes over three times as much to the National Pension scheme (employer 13·7 per cent, employee 4 per cent of wages and salaries). In Canada employers pay the full cost of Workmen's Compensation and rather more than half of the contributions to the Canadian Pension Plan and Unemployment Insurance scheme. Under many industrial agreements they pay the full cost of insuring their employees for comprehensive medical care and hospitalization.

To describe the extent to which the public authorities, employers or the insured, are contributing to social security schemes does not of course tell the whole story. It is particularly difficult to trace the incidence of social charges paid by employers. They are added to labour costs, and are reflected to varying degrees in different industries, in lower wages, or higher prices reducing the real income of wage-earners and non-earners alike. The shifting of the incidence of social charges to the consumer is not easy to follow; the process is not instantaneous and there are so many other important economic variables. The shifting directly to the employee—reflected in lower wages—is rather easier to investigate statistically, though again it is impossible to show cause and effect. A United Nations bulletin, discussing the relationship between wages and social benefits, noted that the depressing of wages in France, Italy and Belgium was not necessarily due to the existence of high family allowances, but rather to the particular method of financing them (i.e. by social charges on the employer). High social charges may have different economic results but in the long-run proportional social charges (any kind of pay-roll tax) will have little effect on production costs. But even when the shifting process has worked itself out employers paying contributions based on a ceiling will tend to minimize the effect of social charges on labour costs by not employing additional workers if they

[1] 'Health and Welfare Services in Canada'. Dept. of National Health and Welfare. 1967.

can avoid it, which in turn may lead to changes in the structure of the labour force and extensive overtime.[1] The Selective Employment Tax is having much the same effect in Britain.

Social Assistance

Assistance schemes play a secondary though increasingly vital role in the social security systems of most developed countries today. Except in Australia and New Zealand, where there is no statutory insurance scheme, and where the basic provision against all the main 'social risks' takes the form of a means-tested or a universal benefit, the amount spent on assistance is usually small in relation to total social security expenditure. In the UK in 1965 £1912 million was distributed in national insurance benefits (including industrial injuries and family allowances) and £251 million in national assistance and non-contributory old age pensions.

However, although total expenditure on assistance may not be very great, a substantial proportion of the population may still be in receipt of some form of means-tested benefit. Some assistance schemes are providing a *basic allowance* for those not entitled to any insurance or universal benefit (e.g. the Retired Workers Allowance in France or the categorical assistances in Canada); others are providing *supplementary allowances* to those who have no resources other than a basic benefit, insufficient in itself to maintain them at a decent living, or even bare subsistence, standard (e.g. the supplementation of retirement pensioners by the Supplementary Benefits Commission in Britain, and by allowances from the National Solidarity Fund in France). Yet others are designed to give *additional help*, in services as well as cash allowances, to the individual case with special needs.

Techniques will vary according to the role which the particular assistance scheme plays in the whole complex of social security services. Where assistance allowances are being used to maintain the incomes of large numbers—where it provides a basic benefit for a sizeable category of persons or where basic benefits need to be supplemented on a large scale—the means-tested benefit or the Income Guarantee is most likely to be favoured.

[1] These findings are taken from a discussion of supplementary labour costs in Europe and Britain by G. L. Reid in Chapter 4 of *Fringe Benefits, Labour Costs and Social Security*, edited by G. L. Reid and D. J. Robertson. Allen and Unwin, London, 1965.

Income-conditioned Benefits

The means-tested benefit is usually at a flat-rate, although it may vary from one part of the country to another if there are wide variations in the cost of living. The means test is likely to be reasonably generous, 'disregarding' the value of the dwelling-house and personal property and a certain amount of savings and even earnings. The legal liability of relatives is usually restricted to the spouse and dependent children, or in some cases, particularly for non-contributory old age pensions, the means test is an entirely personal one. The formula is kept as simple as possible so that 'entitlement' to the 'pension' is widely understood, 'eligibility' can be fairly easily established, and appeals can be made against a rejection of the 'claim'. Everything is done to make administration of the scheme as automatic and as acceptable as possible.

The British non-contributory pension of 1908 is a classic example of this kind of assistance, although the technique was copied from other countries who had already experimented with old age pensions along these lines. At this time social insurance techniques had only been developed to any extent in Germany, where a contributory old age pension scheme was started as early as 1889. But, in Britain, it was felt, as in many other countries before and later, that contributory pensions would take too long to mature, and that a more immediate remedy had to be found, if economic security was to be given to the large numbers of old people who were known to be in poverty and unwilling to take such relief as was offered by the Poor Law.

When introduced, the British non-contributory pension was 5s. a week and could be claimed by all resident citizens over 70, who had no more than roughly 5s. a week coming in from other sources (in most cases the assumed income from savings). At that time 5s. a week would just about meet the minimum average cost to an old person of food, clothing and fuel, but not rent. It was assumed that the average old person had a few savings, owned his own house or could live with a son or daughter. If he did not have any of these resources, or if he had special needs of any kind, he would have to seek poor law relief or eke out his existence in poverty—in primary poverty as defined by Rowntree in his survey at the turn of the century. In fact, this first British old age pension must have borne much the same relationship to subsistence needs as defined at that time, as the basic retirement pension did later to the minimum standard of living guaranteed by the NAB's scale rate plus rent. The tendency for all basic benefits, whether provided on an insurance, assistance or universal basis, to be set at a level just on, or slightly below, average subsistence needs, has already been noted, and explains why most countries have had to develop supplementary assistance schemes in order to establish an effective national minimum: to guarantee that all basic needs (for food, shelter, fuel, clothing, medical care) are fully met for every individual or family.

The Income Guarantee

This would appear to be what the 'Income Guarantee' is designed to achieve, although as a social security technique it has still to be translated from a political programme into administrative reality. It differs from the old type of income-conditioned benefit just described in that the emphasis is not so much on *means* (in France, in 1965, you were entitled to 700 francs a year from the National Solidarity Fund if your total income including this supplementary assistance did not exceed 3300 francs) as on *needs*. Income is *made up* to whatever level is considered necessary to maintain minimum living standards. The claim is not for a flat-rate benefit or pension, but for whatever sum is needed to bring the individual's income up to the guaranteed level. In determining what the claimant's income is before he is granted this kind of assistance, certain resources may still be disregarded.

The problem remains, however, of determining the level of the guaranteed income. Is it to be the same for all single persons, with appropriate modifications for married couples and dependent children? Is it to be set at a higher rate for certain persons who are regarded as having special needs—old people or the disabled? Differences in the level of income guaranteed for any, or all, of these reasons would not detract from the essence of the Income Guarantee concept, and the actual amount of the assistance granted could be anywhere along the line from the total guaranteed income to the few shillings needed to supplement whatever other resources the claimant already possessed. But if, in individual cases, income is made up to a higher level varying from case to case because of special needs (e.g. a rent above the average allowed for in the calculation of the guaranteed income, or the need to pay for some invalid requirement or help in the house) then the whole basis of the Income Guarantee concept is undermined. The scheme will be no different from any modern form of flexible, assistance administration, from the 'budgeting deficiency' technique in North America, or from the way in which the National Assistance scheme has been operating in Britain since 1948. In the latter case, uniform scale rates may be made more generous from time to time to subsume some of the discretionary additions to meet special needs, when it is found that they are being given in a substantial proportion of cases. This was the basis of the 9s. supplement for all old age pensioners and long-term cases given in 1966. But as long as the essence of the guarantee is to meet not *average* but *individual* needs, by means of a scale-rate plus a rent allowance adjusted to precisely what is needed in each case, and any discretionary addition for exceptional circumstances, the British system can scarcely qualify as an income guarantee scheme. For this has been presented as something different from the role national assistance was designed to play in the Beveridge strategy of establishing a national minimum.

The assistance method presents all sorts of difficulties if used to supplement the incomes of those who are working. Ever since Speenhamland it has been feared—with some justification—that an allowance of any kind given in inverse relation to wages, and cut off as soon as earnings rise above a certain level (even if it is tapered off), is bound to act as a disincentive to both workers to earn more and employers to pay higher wages. In recent years there has been a tendency to decry this argument, to feel that it is time we buried the ghost of Speenhamland and ceased to tremble at the thought of abolishing the wage-stop. Experience of the earnings rule, the only test of 'retirement' that any country has been able to devise, scarcely supports the argument that marginal increases in earnings will be preferred to a social benefit to which no stigma is attached. As long as the rule operates (in Britain for the first five years of retirement) there is no incentive whatsoever to the retirement pensioner to earn more than £6 10s a week, until he can earn over £11, when no more reductions can be made because his £4 10s. pension has disappeared.

There will always be problems in devising social security schemes to supplement the wages of marginal workers, even where the benefit is not means-tested, but dependent on the beneficiary falling within a defined degree of disability or of reduced earning capacity. The industrial injury and disability insurance schemes manage to cope reasonably well with these disincentives to a return to nearer normal working capacity. The Norwegian use of a rehabilitation benefit has already been commented on. But it is much more difficult to devise a formula which will avoid the disincentive inherent in any means-tested benefit given to a family man in full employment, whose wage even with family allowances is not sufficient to maintain minimum living standards. 'Selectivity' and 'negative income tax', like the 'guaranteed income', are not a complete or even an easy answer to these problems. At best they may remove some of the emotional reactions which 'assistance' and 'means tests' always arouse. At worst they encourage superficial thinking about how the ordinary citizen is likely to react to this particular form of social assistance.

DISCRETIONARY ASSISTANCE AND WELFARE SERVICES

Flexibility in assistance administration is not just a question of discretionary powers to depart from a uniform scale rate in order to meet individual needs more adequately. It allows for the provision of services as well as cash benefits; not the 'relief-in-kind' or 'indoor relief' which poor law officials used as a substitute for monetary assistance, in cases where they thought the money would be misspent or the recipients were incapable of looking after themselves; but the provision of services of all kinds in addition to, as well as instead of, cash assistance. The decision as to what services are needed in each case cannot turn on any automatic assessment or administrative formula. Any medical treatment needed will be determined by a medical diagnosis, so any welfare services should be decided on the basis of a social work diagnosis.[1]

Who should *provide* these social work and welfare services, for not only those who happen to be in receipt of assistance will need them? Early poor law systems provided their own infirmaries and schools because it was obvious that even paupers, whose condition should be 'less eligible' than that of the poorest, independent working man, had to receive some medical attention when they were ill, and their children some schooling. In the 1830s Dr Kay argued that the principle of less eligibility should be applied in reverse to poor law children, who needed a better education and training than 'free' children, as they would have to fend for themselves once they passed

[1] In 1938 in New Zealand, a Select Parliamentary Committee which had been asked to look at the proposed discretionary Emergency Benefit, recommended that where necessary individuals applying for this benefit 'should be examined by a board of specialists in psychology, medicine and social welfare' who would decide on the form of assistance to be given.

out of the care of the Poor Law. Gradually, as education and health services were developed by voluntary organizations and public authorities outside the poor law, public assistance was able to relinquish its own services (in England under a fire of criticism for the quality of the services they were providing) and to discharge its duties towards those in receipt of assistance by paying for their medical care, education or training in hospitals, schools or Homes run by voluntary organizations or other local authority departments. After 1948, when all these services came to be provided on a universal basis, the British assistance authority, the NAB, did not even have a residual responsibility in these fields. But medical assistance is still needed in France and Canada, where comprehensive medical care is not yet available to all under health insurance or public health schemes.

Apart from these costly and highly specialized health and education services, there is, however, a whole range of welfare services, which those in receipt of assistance may need, if they are to be helped constructively: help, which will enable those who are young and fit enough, to get back to work and self-support, and which will secure for those who are likely to remain dependent on social benefits more or less permanently, not just an income but a reasonable standard of living. Most of these welfare services are of a kind which provide a substitute for the help and comfort of family and friends, on which the majority are able to draw when they are sick or old, or have problems in caring for their children, in home-making or personal relationships. They comprise a wide range of institutions for day or residential care of children or adults, special housing, help in the home, holidays, clubs, meal services and so forth, all provided within a discriminating social work approach to each individual or family. This approach constantly affirms how dependent all these services are, if they are to be really effective, on securing the co-operation of the client and on strengthening his, perhaps latent, capacity for self-help and self-determination.

Even if this approach is well understood by the assistance authority, the problem still remains as to which administration should provide these welfare services. The answer will clearly be different for each country according to how far any or all of these services are already adequately provided for by voluntary organizations or some other statutory, usually local authority, department. Where there is insufficient provision for all who need the particular service, or where the authority which provides it takes a restrictive view of who *needs* it, or rejects difficult or unco-operative clients however great their need, the assistance authority may well feel it can only fulfil its responsibility to its clients by making direct provision. In this case, the service provided, though primarily for assistance cases, may be offered to others, who would normally be expected to pay what they can afford for it. In France, public assistance has always provided a variety of health and welfare services on this basis, and it is now often difficult to distinguish what a municipality is providing under Social Aid legislation and what under its general powers to provide any service (with the approval of the Prefect) which will promote the welfare of its citizens.

In contrast, in Britain, where welfare services are organized on a more strictly functional basis by different local authority departments (health, welfare, child care, and even housing and education), the prime function of the National Assistance Board (now the Supplementary Benefits Commission) has been to meet financial need, using a fairly flexible combination of standard allowances, discretionary additions and grants for exceptional needs. Its welfare function is in most cases restricted to looking-out for any other needs of its clients which cannot be met in this way, to informing them of where and how they may get an appropriate service, or where necessary to making a more positive referral to a social work agency. Only in the case of homeless persons ('men of an unsettled way of living'), and of men with very poor employment prospects who appear unable to benefit from the Ministry of Labour's services, does the Commission make direct provision of welfare services, in the form of reception, resettlement and re-establishment centres. Should it ever see fit to extend its direct provision of welfare services, it will only be acting in default of the voluntary organizations and local authorities, who have the powers but do not always have the resources (mainly of staff) to provide all the welfare services needed, often urgently, by the Commission's varied clientele.

It is clearly preferable, that this wide range of developing welfare services should be provided and co-ordinated at the local level by voluntary organizations and local authorities working in partnership. Thus all who need them may benefit and not only those who happen to be in receipt of an assistance allowance. Changes in social security legislation may from time to time take considerable numbers of old people off the assistance rolls, and the chequered career of a typical 'problem family' tends to take it on and off assistance, and so on and off the assistance worker's case load. In France, this difficulty does not arise in quite this form, and in Norway the Social Care Act promises to find an effective solution to this problem of integrating the flexible end of assistance administration with local social work and welfare services. In Britain the Seebohm Committee (set up in 1966) is expected to make proposals for a reorganization of the local authority's personal social services, which should take account of the need for closer and more effective co-operation with the Supplementary Benefits Commission (assistance administration) of the new Ministry of Social Security. In Canada the problem is particularly acute and is discussed in relation to services for families and old people in later chapters.

But when everything possible has been done to develop and co-ordinate social welfare—and health and education—services for the benefit of all who need them, the social security administration is still left with a special responsibility for the 'economically weak'; a concept which in modern, affluent societies is replacing that of the indigent. If it is to break the vicious circle of inherited poverty, and to improve the lot of those who are destined to live for long periods at the lowest income levels, it will need every weapon in its armoury. This means not only devising more flexible techniques of assistance administration and closer co-operation with local social welfare agencies, but also means engaging the Government's whole social strategy in this 'War on Poverty'. Services which are universal and generalized may need to be specially adapted to cope with the needs of the poorest. A more concentrated attack may need to be made on the under-staffed, ill equipped down-town schools, on the lack of opportunities for training, on the poor health facilities and the slum dwellings, on the one hand, and a more skilful, perceptive social work approach made to each individual case of persistent poverty, on the other.

The report of the Study Committee on Public Assistance in Quebec (the Boucher Report[1]) is a penetrating analysis of assistance administration in one province of Canada. It is particularly interesting in showing how and why the present, complex system, fails to give effective aid to the small minority in this lowest stratum of poverty—those whose poor conditions persist in even good periods and who appear to be suffering from a kind of congenital or inherited poverty.

[1] See p. 167.

It criticizes the various special categorical assistance schemes in Canada, arguing that the categorization of assistance (for needy mothers, old people, the unemployed, etc.) appears to have been devised for administrative convenience according to the immediate cause of the financial problem, rather than with possible rehabilitation in mind. It shows how unemployment assistance to marginal farmers has encouraged a tendency to dig in on farms unsuitable for cultivation and crystallized the latent dependence of a large section of an under-privileged class. (There are interesting parallels here with agricultural poverty in France—both with the problem, and the way it is being tackled.) It continually reiterates the danger of any form of assistance, if given to such groups on some automatic and administratively convenient formula, becoming a 'reward for indigence', rather than a constructive measure to remove them from poverty.

CHAPTER 3

Co-ordination

Problems of co-ordination inevitably increase as social services are developed, cover more people and attempt to serve them in ever more sophisticated ways. Some co-ordination of the initiatives, and of the on-going administration of the many different agencies involved is essential at both consumer and policy making level, and no study of the social administration of a country is complete which does not attempt some analysis of the policies and techniques designed to achieve these ends. Each country will have its own particular problems in this matter, and the problems like the machinery evolved to deal with them will vary according to the political, constitutional and sociological realities: the power and influence of the various occupational, professional and religious groups within the community; the relative strength and independence of the local authorities and the different departments of the central administration; the density and distribution of the population in urban and rural areas and in large conurbations; the degree of social mobility changing or creating new communities.

Finally, problems of co-ordination are vitally affected by the extent of democratic participation at every level of the administration of the social services. The best systems of social administration are those which respond to social change, are geared to dealing with new problems as they arise and to taking advantage of increasing wealth, of new knowledge and techniques. In the name and process of co-ordination there should not therefore be any suppression, or even discouragement, of those who have ideas, who are prepared to make experiments and to take the initiative in developing an old, or establishing a new, service. Co-ordination for its own sake, or for the peace of mind of the tidy-minded, unimaginative and pedestrian, must be avoided at all costs.

In the case studies frequent reference has been made to the particular problems of co-ordination in social administration in each country, and to some of the ways in which these problems were being tackled. In France, strong sectional feelings which permeate so much of public life probably present the biggest problem. Much of the

French system is designed to exploit this community of interest or group solidarity, but at the same time it creates formidable problems for those who are concerned with any kind of national planning or administration. But, doubtless because they have lived with the problem for so long, French administrators seem to be able to meet the challenge with considerable wisdom and ingenuity.

Norway has the advantage of a small, homogeneous population, with a strong tradition of self-help in its many remote, scattered communities; the problems are largely those of size, of widely separated municipalities not strong enough to provide or even administer the growing range of public and local social services. The situation is exacerbated by a steady internal migration, which demands co-ordinated action so that appropriate services are provided in the few rapidly expanding urban areas, and special economic and social measures are taken to reduce the difficulties of the many small declining communities.

Canada has many of the Norwegian problems but on a larger scale. She has greater resources but additional difficulties presented by a heterogeneous population, and by the immense solidarity within the nation of the French-speaking Roman Catholics of Quebec. Federal government was the only possible means of achieving national identity and national policies in certain areas of economic and social administration. Problems of co-ordination at consumer or local community level are not so different from those experienced in the other countries. But at regional (provincial) or national level, federalism presents its own peculiar problems in the co-ordination of policies and administration.

Before looking at some of the more interesting systems of co-ordination developed in these three countries, it will be helpful to distinguish two dimensions and five different levels at which co-ordination is needed and to illustrate these from examples of social administration in Britain.

Vertical co-ordination between different tiers or levels of administration is obviously essential in every social service organization, since all but the very smallest local voluntary agency has some hierarchy of staff. The art or science of public administration is much concerned with effective forms of vertical co-ordination, which facilitate, if they cannot ensure, good two-way communication from the top to the bottom of any administration. Students of social administration carry their concern even further, because of their particular interest in 'consumer reaction', and in the part which beneficiaries, or potential beneficiaries of the personal social services play in shaping social policy.[1] The voluntary organizations also come within their field of study and the vertical co-ordination of Citizens Advice Bureaux through local, regional and national committees (usually attached to a Council of Social Service), is a good example of an effective technique devised for this kind of service. Besides giving information and advice to the individual citizens, it is an important CAB function to be sensitive to consumer reactions, to see 'where the shoe is pinching', and to be able to pass this information on up the line, to a voluntary organization which can speak with authority to the appropriate local or central government department. The NSPCC, providing a very different kind of service of protection, often involving emergency action, on behalf of children, has developed a very different system of co-ordinating the work of its local 'branches'. It is the technique of a unitary rather than a federal system not often used by national voluntary organizations.

Horizontal co-ordination is used at every level, and every kind of co-ordinating machinery—case conferences, mutual registers, joint committees, liaison committees, regional planning boards—is used to improve co-operation between different administrations. This may be on a functional basis, as for example within the National Health Service (liaison committees between hospital and local authorities) or the education service (regional advisory committees for higher education), or on the basis of a particular clientèle (e.g. Old People's Welfare or Disablement Advisory Committees). Here again the student of social administration will be interested in ways of co-ordinating not only the activities of social welfare agencies, but of a wider range of social and economic activities, in order to plan the development of a whole area at regional or national level, or to secure genuine 'community care' for individuals at the local level.

For the purposes of this analysis of co-ordination the five levels to be distinguished are the consumer level, the local community level which may or may not coincide with the local administrative level for different social services, the regional and the national level. Vertical co-ordination of all or any of these levels of administration

[1] A theme explored in *Social Policy and Administration* by D. V. Donnison, V. Chapman and others. Allen & Unwin, London, 1965.

will be needed for the effective operation of a particular service. Horizontal co-ordination of a range of different services may be needed at any level.

Co-ordination at *consumer level,* in order that the individual or family may derive the utmost benefit from the wide range of social services available to him, is usually achieved through case conferences, sometimes supported by a systematic mutual registration of cases, and through improving the competence of social workers by common or co-ordinated systems of basic training and staff development. In Britain, the Citizens Advice Bureaux, and a few experimental, and many projected, Family Advice Centres, are also directed to securing a better co-ordination of services at the point at which the individual needs and uses them. The physical grouping together of services for a restricted area, the basis of the new Family Advice Centres, should also help to secure that 'continuity of care' (a third dimension?) which is so often lost as social services and social workers become ever more specialized.

At the *local community level* the accent is on helping people to make the best use of their own resources of family, friends and neighbours in conjunction with the more formally structured social services. Many if not all of these services will be administered from a centre outside this 'local community', which is usually smaller and less well defined than the areas of administration of the major social services.

Any formal co-ordination of local community resources of good will and self-help is usually done by voluntary organizations in this country and takes many different forms according to the nature of the 'felt needs' of the community. In newly-developed areas, whether out-of-town estates or flat-redevelopment in slum clearance sites, tenants' committees or community associations may take the initiative. Such organizations are often affiliated to a district federation of community associations, which in turn is a member of the national association which is affiliated to the National Council of Social Service, thus bringing a well-structured national organization to the aid of the smallest local association. In some urban areas, local authorities are themselves employing community workers: a new town often appoints a Social Development Officer, or a housing department may appoint a Community Development Officer. In other areas the local education authority may be paying the salary of the organizer of a district federation of community associations.

Even in the smallest of the older established rural communities there are usually a number of voluntary associations, mostly of a social or recreational nature. Some, like the Women's Institute or the British Legion, with a more clearly defined purpose, are linked up with a county, regional and national (and even international) organization. Formal co-operation of the ongoing activities of these local associations is rarely necessary as there is usually much overlapping membership and plenty of key people in the community who are well aware of everything that is going on. But new ventures, especially those which serve the whole community (a new village hall, playing fields or annual festival), or a part of the community less able to help itself (the old or the handicapped) may need the concerted effort of a number of local associations working in co-operation with some seemingly remote statutory departments, before they can get started. Once a going concern they may carry on as an independent organization. The leadership necessary to launch such ventures may come from one of the natural leaders of the community and from whatever association(s) he or she is associated with—the Parish Council, a local branch of the WRVS, a church or chapel organization, the village hall committee, or the Old People's Club. Ideas and specialist advice and help, may come from outside through such organizations as Rural Community Councils (with their Parish Councils, Village Halls and Rural Industries Committees), from the higher levels of the WRVS, the Women's Institute or the County Old People's Welfare Committee. Different departments (education, health or housing) of the local authorities, whether county or rural district council, may be interested in encouraging with advice and financial aid specific ventures, but it is unlikely that they will see the need for any kind of community development work as such, and will be more interested in grant-aiding special departments of a rural community rather than its general work.

There may be more than one level of *local administration* to consider. This will depend on the structure of local government, and on the extent and kind of deconcentration practised by central government departments in each country. In England, county boroughs and county councils are the principal units responsible for the administration of the personal social services. But a co-ordination which starts with these local authority services, has to be extended to cover these administered over the same area by central government departments, and in county council areas by the second tier local authorities, the county districts. County borough and county council areas rarely coincide precisely with the area offices of the Ministry of Social Security, or with the catchment areas of local hospital management committees. The areas of the county districts, which have important public health and housing functions, do not always coincide with the area of deconcentration of county council services —county health divisions or divisional education executives.

As these statutory services, whether administered by local authorities or the area office of a central government department, are largely or wholly dependent on the allocation of resources from a higher authority, vertical co-ordination of each service is vitally important. Anyone familiar with central government administration and central-local government relationships knows how much these administrative relationships can vary from service to service. The comparisons already made with public administration in France are of particular interest in this connection. But given a certain amount of control over what services a local authority shall or may provide, how it shall administer, and how much it shall spend on them, British local authorities are still left with a fair measure of freedom to determine local policy as regards the administration of these services, and a great deal of freedom to work out their own ways of co-ordinating them.

Administrative functionalism expressed in the local authority's statutory committees and in its use of professional or specialist chief officers, has however, become so deep-rooted in the structure of the British social services that until quite recently little thought was given to ways and means of co-ordinating them. In a county borough the town clerk, the town council itself, and its finance and general purposes committee, and other specially appointed joint or liaison officers or committees ostensibly have this function. However, they often achieve little in the face of the entrenched empires of the different committees and departments, and of a narrow but understandable concentration on the particular service for which they are responsible. In the administration of the personal social welfare services, which may be a subsidiary function of health, education and housing departments as well as the primary function of children and welfare services departments, there is often a total failure to appreciate the impact that a number of distinct though often very personal welfare services are having on individual clients. The confusion which persisted in many local authorities all through the

1950s and into the 1960s, of the different contributions of a co-ordinating committee and of a case conference to the prevention of child neglect and to the rehabilitation of problem families, is typical of this very superficial thinking about the machinery of co-ordination. The case conferences, concerned with co-ordinating field work rather than policies, were frequently held for too large areas, attended by the wrong people and conducted in a manner which showed little understanding of the good social work principles and practice they were designed to encourage.

Much of course depends on the kind and area of service to be co-ordinated. Different kinds of co-ordinating machinery are obviously needed to formulate social policies and to encourage good field work practice. Similarly a different kind of machinery is needed to ensure the smooth running of a basic service which is not entirely the responsibility of one administration (to see that so far as possible there is no overlapping, no waste, no gaps and a reasonably uniform standard of service), from that needed in a field which is less well established. Where there is still much pioneering to be done and where uniformity is less important than new ideas and new approaches, loose, more flexible forms of co-ordination which can involve all concerned are likely to bear the best results. The problem is how to preserve the drive, the cutting edge which comes from a lively concern and a close knowledge of a particular problem, with the more cautious and circumspect approach which comes from broader perspectives and a wider knowledge of social administration.

The Service of Youth and the Welfare of Old People are two areas of service in which since the early 1940s attempts have been made to get more concerted action without stifling initiative. Here the co-ordination, or partnership, of statutory and voluntary is of prime importance; the voluntary organizations ranging from the large, powerful philanthropic society, part of a national organization employing paid staff, to the small, informal, mutual aid association with its roots in the local community. In such cases, any attempts to set up some kind of formal co-ordination probably comes best from the voluntary organizations in the first place. Local authority initiatives may be regarded with suspicion by the many different organizations whose efforts are to be co-ordinated. Some philanthropic and mutual aid societies may well feel that they have a special mandate to provide a certain service, either because they have done so successfully in the past, or because they are particularly close to the community or beneficiaries concerned and can better represent what they need, or feel they need. In these circumstances the pace cannot be forced. Nothing is gained if the mechanics of co-ordination are established when the desire to co-operate is still weak; although the desire may be stimulated by the influence on public opinion of well publicized reports and national discussion of the problems involved, stimulated by some national co-ordinating body such as the National Old People's Welfare Committee of the National Council of Social Service.

At *national* and *regional levels* co-ordination is primarily concerned to facilitate planning: the collection and analysis of vital data, the assessment of problems and decisions about the allocation of resources. Again the distinction must be made between the co-ordination needed for the effective administration of a particular service (e.g. the hospital service with its Hospital Management Committees, Regional Hospital Boards and the Ministry of Health) or of a group of services, and for the more general development of a whole area involving a closer integration of economic and social planning. In the first case the emphasis is on vertical, in the second on horizontal, co-ordination.

In the UK, with its homogeneous and compact population, practically every well-established social service, whether statutory or voluntary, has developed its own local and national structure often, but not always, with an intervening regional administration. The extent to which this local-regional-national organization provides effective machinery for the planned development of a particular service, or of a group or range of services, varies greatly. There are some obvious and serious weaknesses in the co-ordination of the statutory social services at the national and regional as well as at the local level. The almost complete lack of co-ordination of the activitives of central government departments in relation to the recruitment, training and employment of social workers is a case in point.[1] Even special legislation passed in 1959 for the training of social workers for health and welfare departments failed to face up to the situation, and to take the opportunity of co-ordinating departmental policies with respect to social workers.

[1] The Probation Training Board and Central Training Council for Child Care of the Home Office, the Ministry of Health and Council for Social Work Training and the Ministry of Educaton, ultimately responsible for the training institutions and student grants, are all involved.

Local statutory authorities may also form voluntary organizations, so that they can get together for mutual consultation and concerted action. The Association of Hospital Management Committees was formed within a few years of the setting up of the National Health Service. The Association of Municipal Corporations and the other local authority organizations are powerful and influential bodies without wielding any statutory authority. These co-ordinating bodies will inevitably act as pressure groups on occasions, and the interests they set out to protect may be narrow and conservative. But they can equally well be a means of spreading new ideas and good practices through mutual emulation, rather than through the statutory supervision of a higher authority.

Despite the examples already quoted, national voluntary organizations have not always succeeded in co-ordinating a range of specialized but related activities in certain fields. The National Association for Mental Health was set up in 1946, after a Mental Health Emergency Committee and then a Provisional National Council for Mental Health had brought together three of the major national voluntary organizations working in this field to provide various emergency mental health services during the Second World War. A satisfactory system of co-ordinating the three major national voluntary societies to which associations for the physically handicapped may be affiliated has still to be worked out.

Most statutory social service departments have some form of regional organization,[1] although their functions may vary considerably and, despite attempts to standardize government regions, not all their areas of operation coincide. Where voluntary organizations have regional offices they are even more varied in function, and much more varied in the areas they cover. A Scottish or Welsh Association may be a separate or parallel institution rather than a regional office of the National body.

Despite these many examples of regional administration at some level between that of local and central government, none of this amounts to Regionalism. Regionalism implies a far-reaching form of horizontal co-ordination of many different services—economic, social and physical—at the regional level.

In this country a kind of regionalism was developed during the

[1] e.g. Regional Hospital Boards, Regional directorates of the executive services of the Ministry of Social Security and of Labour, and the Regional inspectorates of the Ministry of Health, of Housing & Local Government, of the Home Office and of Education.

Second World War, but for war purposes, and fell into desuetude soon afterwards. The old Defence Regions became the Standard regions for the regional administration of a number of Ministries, but the responsibility for such regional policy and planning as was carried out for the Special Development areas was vested in the Board of Trade. It was only in December 1964, two months after the Labour Government came into office, that the Secretary of State for the new Department of Economic Affairs put before Parliament the Government's blueprint for the new regional machinery. For England, six, and later eight, economic planning Regions were defined and two separate regional economic planning bodies, a Council and a Board, were established in each Region, as well as in Scotland and Wales. The Councils are composed of part-time voluntary members appointed by the Secretary of State for Economic Affairs. The Board consists of senior civil servants from government departments in the Regions meeting with an Under-Secretary from the Department of Economic Affairs as Chairman. The offices of the Board are situated in the 'regional capitals' and the staffs of most regional departments are housed in the same buildings.

The terms of reference given to the Councils were primarily concerned with economic planning: the formulation of regional plans and advising on the regional implications of national economic policies. 1965 saw the gradual manning of this machinery, and 1966 the publication of some regional development plans. The Government has set the regional bodies plenty of tasks but it is still too soon to assess whether or not Regionalism is going to take root in this country. A study made of this first year's experience[1] suggested that its future would not be assured until certain major problems were settled. There were still doubts as to the best size for the Regions, as to whether the Councils should be composed of elected representatives, and whether both regional bodies needed to be given more formal powers. In brief: 'the fate of Regionalism is still in the balance. The danger to it stems not from a party political change—Regionalism in principle is "tripartisan"—but from the resistance of local government and the ambivalence of central government'.[2]

This analysis of the different kinds of co-ordination needed if social services are to be effectively developed and economically

[1] T. E. Chester and I. R. Gough, 'Regionalism in the Balance: Whitehall and Townhall at the Cross Roads'.

[2] *Op. cit. District Bank Review*, March 1966.

administered could be amply illustrated from the three countries studied as well as from Britain. Many examples were in fact given in the case studies; for the purposes of this comparative analysis it will only be necessary to describe some of them in more detail, and to underline their significance and particular interest for us in Britain.

FRANCE

In France, where a longer experience of national economic planning is now demanding more sophisticated forms of social planning, a whole hierarchy of co-ordinating bodies is needed to collect the relevant information about needs and resources and to draw up orders of priority within their own particular field.

At national level bodies such as the *Commission Nationale d'Organisation Hospitalière* (The National Committee for Hospital Services), the *Direction de l'Education Surveillée* (the Central Government Department responsible for Probation and Approved Schools), and the *Conseil Supérieure de l'Aide Sociale* (the Higher Council for Social Aid), and the recently formed *Commission National de la Vieillesse* (National Committee for Old Age) will all be involved in these initial stages of the planning process, and there will be similar interested bodies at regional, departmental and municipal level. In the *Haut Comité de la Population et de la Famille* France has a unique body, particularly well qualified to integrate the separate policies drawn up for particular groups (e.g. for the old people, for families or for immigrants), into a general demographic and family policy. In this task the *Haut Comité* is greatly strengthened by the excellent work of the *Institut National d'Études Demographiques*, whose research provides a scientific basis for decisions which have to be taken and implemented, often in the face of strong pressures from the various interests.

The *Haut Comité* makes good use of the technique of setting up study committees from time to time to collect information, to promote research and to make recommendations about national policy. Recent examples of this approach were the two *Commission d'Études* (Working Parties) set up in 1960 to study problems of the family and problems of old age. The former, which led to the Prigent[1] report, was only the most recent of a series of reports (there

[1] Published in the *Bulletin des Gaisses d'Allocations Familiales*, March 1962, No. 3.

were two in the 1950s) on family policies. The National Union of Family Allowance Funds[1] and the National (and Departmental) Unions of Family Associations are the interested bodies in this field and regard the collecting and dissemination of information, as well as the championing of the interests of families, as their continuing function. The Laroque report was, on the other hand, the first major report on a policy for old age, and the National Committee for Old Age, which should help to co-ordinate action in this field, was one of the important recommendations of the report and was only set up in 1961. Both these reports instigated by the *Haut Comité* show a nice appreciation of the interdependence of all social services and of social needs (better provisions in one field, e.g. home care for the aged, may lead to less demand in another, e.g. *hospices* or *maisons de retraite*), and of the importance of influencing public opinion through effective public education, if sound social policies are to be evolved—and implemented.

All this information and assessment of problems, leading to recommendations as to priorities in the different fields of social service, is fed into the Planning Commission, on whose final report the ultimate political decisions are taken and formulated in the next four-year Plan. However closely the different ministries and national institutions work together in this kind of social planning, however much they may be able to consult and draw information from their counterparts at lower levels of administration, the national plan can only be formulated in the most general terms and is primarily concerned with the allocations of resources for new investment according to agreed priorities. The decisions, which determine the resources allocated to the various services, have then to be reported back to the bodies responsible for their administration, who fill in the picture in more detail and settle certain priorities for the best use of resources allocated to their area. Horizontal co-ordination at regional and departmental level is achieved through the prefectorial system, as described earlier; the regional Prefect being primarily concerned with regional planning, with the elaboration and subsequent implementation of the regional investment programmes of the '*tranches opératoires*'[2] of the national plan, leaving the departmental

[1] *Union Nationale d'Allocations Familiales* (UNCAF), an example of a voluntary organization set up by the statutory Family Allowance Funds.

Similarly, the *Fedération Nationale d'Organisations de Sécurité Sociale* (FNOSS) was set up by the local and regional social security funds.

[2] 'Operational sectors' is perhaps the best translation, but is not very satisfactory.

Prefects with the administrative control and co-ordination of all services within their departments.

The French prefectorial system is particularly well suited to the task of securing the co-ordination of the basic health and welfare services at the major local administrative level—the department. The Prefect has the authority to require that he be kept informed of all decisions and proposals made regarding central or local government services, and various means of exercising a technical control over the ways in which the services provided by the local authorities, social security agencies or voluntary organizations in receipt of public funds are administered. His power of approving the appointment of certain staff, of passing the budgets of communes and towns, of fixing annually the *prix de journée* (the daily charge) of all kinds of residential establishments and of making regulations on a wide range of matters, may be exercised to co-ordinate certain services which are primarily a departmental responsibility (e.g. maternity and child welfare, child protection, the TB or mental health services). They may also be used to strengthen the hands of some co-ordinating body of which he or one of his representatives is an ex-officio member, such as the Liaison Committee for the co-ordination of social work services.

A recent change in the internal structure of the departmental services reflects this growing concern for a closer co-ordination of health and welfare services at the prefecture itself. Until the early 1960s there were separate health and welfare services, the former headed by a *Directeur départmental de la Santé* (a doctor), the latter by a *Directeur départmental de la Population et de l'Action sociale*. Now there is one *Directeur d'Action Sanitaire et Sociale* and the combined service is headed up by a Director (an administrator or a doctor), aided by inspectors. A medical officer in an advisory capacity is responsible for the supervision and control of the purely medical aspects of the services only. He is not subordinate to the Director, but of equal status in relation to the Prefect.

Co-ordination of rather a different kind is needed to improve and develop a wide range of different services concerned with the health, welfare and protection of a particular group, e.g. 'handicapped' children[1] or old people. In such cases prefectoral initiative and prefectoral powers will be less effective and may indeed be regarded

[1] *L'enfance inadapté*, as defined and translated in the case study.

with suspicion by the many different organizations whose efforts are to be co-ordinated.

The initiative for setting up any formal co-ordinating machinery often comes best from outside the prefecture, even if the procedure is eventually generalized and the appropriate officials from the prefecture are *ex-officio* members. This was the way in which the interesting system of co-ordination of social work services developed in Paris before 1948.

Recent moves to get some more co-ordinated action in the field of old people's welfare has been more concerned to develop community services—holidays, home helps, restaurant clubs—than to avoid overlapping. Since many of these services are not very costly in terms of capital equipment, there is no need to wait on an allocation of resources from the central government. Local committees can go ahead if local initiatives and local goodwill are forthcoming. At this local level there are probably fewer, small, active, voluntary organizations than would be found in Britain, and co-operation between them and the local authority tends to be more difficult. There is nothing equivalent to the Women's Royal Voluntary Service or to the numerous old people's clubs found in any town in England, particularly of the kind run mainly by the old people themselves with the help of some younger voluntary workers and a little grant-aid from the local authority. How much does this difference stem from the greater natural 'clubability' of the Anglo-Saxons, whether young or old, and how much from the greater mutual suspicion between municipal employee and voluntary workers which, for many and various reasons, is found in France?

The regional *Associations pour la Sauvegarde de l'Enfance et de l'Adolescence* referred to in the case study are an interesting example of yet another piece of co-ordinating machinery, which seems to have been particularly successful in enabling the very best use to be made of scarce resources of educational, training and treatment establishments for 'handicapped' children. This field has traditionally been the province of the voluntary organizations, although the Ministries of Health and Population, of Education and of Justice (*la direction de l'Education Surveillée*) are today actively concerned, making some provision directly and controlling and grant-aiding most of the rest. But resources of capital equipment and trained staff continue to be in short supply despite extensive plans for the development of new institutions of all kinds. The regional associations have wisely given priority to the setting up of Observation Centres and to developing staff training.

Originally looser, more informal associations of the voluntary organizations concerned, the regional associations are now semi-public bodies, sponsored and financed by the Ministry of Health and Population, with representatives from the other interested ministries and from all the voluntary organizations concerned. These now include organizations such as the Family Associations and the Scouts, who contribute to the preventive aspects of work with children and young people, on which increasing emphasis is being laid. At national level an interdepartmental co-ordinating committee of the three ministries concerned was set up in 1945, before the regional associations were formalized. At a more local level some departmental associations have been formed to increase co-operation among those whose work lies in the department, many of whom would not be represented on the regional association.

Co-ordination at consumer level is greatly facilitated in France by the common training and status of its social workers and by the fact that administrative functionalism has not been carried so far as in Britain. Thus, the range of benefits offered by the social security agencies includes social workers who can help beneficiaries to avail themselves of any services which they or their families may need, whether provided by the Fund itself or by referring them to some other agency. The value of this particular service to the family in receipt of family allowances, or to the sick or disabled person in receipt of an insurance benefit is obvious. For not only is the Fund concerned that any benefit which will help the recipient is made available to him, but that the benefits should be as individual as possible and adapted to the circumstances of each case. By employing its own social workers to follow through any case of serious sickness or injury the Fund can ensure that continuity of care which rarely obtains in this country despite our extensive medical, rehabilitation and resettlement services.

Despite all these advantages, there is still plenty of scope in French social administration for overlapping services and gaps, and perhaps more temptation for social workers to have a proprietary feeling about their clients, if only because the agencies for which they work often offer such an all-embracing service. The system of co-ordinating social work services which is being worked out in order to overcome these problems was described very fully in the case study. Despite differences in the structure of the social services, and in the training and to some extent the functions of social workers, there is much in their experience and their ideas that is relevant to us. The kind of agreement reached between the social workers themselves to avoid overlapping, and to facilitate referrals between general and specialist social workers, are particularly interesting. (There is no muddled thinking about co-ordinating committees—The French Liaison Committee is the nearest parallel —and case conferences in France.) The Co-ordinating Act of 1950 (the same year as the Joint Circular[1] was addressed to the local authorities in the UK) only provided a broad framework within which each department had to work out its own system and procedures.

The Co-ordination Act was primarily concerned with the need to co-ordinate, in the interests of the client, the social workers' services. But in focusing attention on more effective ways of helping clients, it has naturally engendered among the agencies represented on the Liaison Committees, and among the social workers meeting more informally, a greater awareness of other gaps, other needs (for home helps, hostels, recreational facilities, etc.). There are a number of instances where the co-ordinating system has been largely responsible for the municipality, the Department, a social security fund, or a voluntary agency extending its provisions, or developing a new service, to fill such gaps.

CANADA

The constitutional limitations on the federal government's co-ordinating powers, and the political and economic problems involved in framing policy and administering services for which financial responsibility is in varying degrees shared by national, provincial, and local governments, is fully explored in the case study. There is no need for any more detailed description of the administrative devices (advisory and consultative committees, approval of programmes, matching grants, etc.) designed to secure some co-ordination of the policies of the different departments of the federal and provincial governments. It only remains to point out that this formal machinery of inter-governmental co-operation, much of it primarily concerned with audit and treasury control, is not the whole

[1] From the Ministries of Health and Education, and the Home Office.

story. Much is achieved, out of the political limelight, through informal contacts between top officials of the federal government and their opposite numbers in provincial departments. In this situation voluntary organizations also have a powerful influence. They can bring all parties together in conference and consultation, focusing attention on a particular social problem and giving a lead to the search for the most appropriate remedies, without being too concerned, initially at least, about the implications their proposals may have for provincial rights or federal funds.

The Canadian Welfare Council (to French-speaking Canadians *Le Conseil de Bien-être*) has been particularly successful in bringing together not only voluntary organizations and voluntary and statutory bodies, but all the different levels of government, and most importantly, French and English speaking Canadians. It has been described as 'a meeting place of the two Canadian cultures in matters of welfare'. In its submission to the Royal Commission on Bilingualism and Biculturalism (in December 1966) the Council described its experiences—its successes and failures—over the past forty years as a national voluntary organization that had committed itself formally to a policy of full bilingualism and biculturalism. The Council's commitment to such a policy arose out of the conviction that cultural patterns penetrate community approaches to welfare, and its history gives evidence of this concern and its willingness to do something about it. It described the problems—and expense—of running a bilingual organization, but also paid tribute to the diversity in points of view which comes from such a commitment. Without it the Council would lack much of its dynamism.

Canada not only has a federal government and bilingualism and biculturalism to contend with, but a medley of local government arrangements in the different provinces, none of which provide a really satisfactory local unit for welfare administration. Such local units are necessary for certain services which cannot be administered successfully without local knowledge of individual circumstances. They are also necessary as a focal point for the co-ordination at the local community level of all the personal social services, whether provided by central or local government or by voluntary organizations.

In most of the Canadian provinces the search is going on for such an appropriate local unit.[1] It is not to be found in the basic unit of

[1] See, articles by John S. Morgan and Amy Leigh on 'The Contribution of the Municipality to the Administration of Public Welfare' in Canadian Public Administration, June 1964.

local government. Most of the municipalities, like the French communes, are far too small. (In Ontario there are 900 or more, varying in size from a small village to metropolitan Toronto.) A solution of grouping the smaller units into counties has been tried in some provinces, but most provincial governments have taken the line of least resistance and have been taking over more and more responsibility for welfare services; only to find that they still need a local unit of administration onto which they can devolve responsibility for effective decision-making, whether or not political and financial responsibility remains with the provincial government.

In Saskatchewan, where the provincial welfare service spans the province and few tasks are left to the municipalities, the Saskatchewan Local Government Continuing Committee has stated: 'We should be actively concerned with strengthening local democracy to counter the trends towards centralization of traditionally local services. Local government provides the only important means by which political power can be decentralized. . . . It permits the adjustment of programmes and policies to reflect local conditions. Local government can avoid some of the inflexibilities inherent in large-scale organization.'[1] The Quebec Report on Public Assistance is very critical of its centralized administration: 'The employees of the (Social Allowance) Commission work in Quebec. They are far from the areas where the persons assisted live and they have only an imperfect idea of the socio-economic situation. Although the Commission has inspectors in the four corners of the Province, the psychological distance between the applicants and the Quebec Government employees remains the same.'[2]

Provincial administration of welfare services facilitates their vertical co-ordination but makes horizontal co-ordination at the local administrative level much more difficult, and does little to encourage (for it cannot command) the concern and active participation of local citizen groups at the community level. Local government reform, though needed even more urgently in Canada than in Britain, is slow in coming and is opposed by the usual conservative interests in the *status quo*. Moreover, provincial administration remains the only practical solution in many areas where people are too widely scattered over vast territories for effective local government.

[1] Saskatchewan, *Local Government in Saskatchewan* 1961, p. 6.
[2] *Op. cit.* p. 135.

So the problem remains: what form should the devolution of functions to local units of administration take, and what kind of support should the senior government (be it federal or provincial) give to its junior partners? Most social services came into being as *ad hoc* arrangements to deal with special problems, and have been grafted onto a system of public administration which has stressed legal and financial accountability rather than social accountability. Until there is more widespread understanding of the nature of social administration, of the interdependence of all social services and of the importance of the response which they arouse in the client and of the support which they get from the community, appropriate administrative structures will not be found. To quote once again from the Quebec Report: 'Instead of conservatively stated bureaucratic accountability, administration will need to present a clearly stated social purpose.'

NORWAY

As suggested earlier, Norway has many of the same problems as Canada, although in terms of size and population a more appropriate comparison would perhaps be with one of the larger Canadian provinces. Without any of the complications of a federal government, and with a more firmly established tradition of local government and of collectivism, Norway has succeeded in working out many interesting ways of co-ordinating, both vertically and horizontally, the policies and administration of the social services.

She has had to reform her local government. The reforms needed were an amalgamation of many of the smaller municipalities, and a reduction in the number and an increase in the powers of the 'counties'. This two-tier system of local authorities is now able to carry direct responsibility for most of the social assistance, health and welfare services, and at the same time provide an area of administration and a point of access to those other social security services which are the responsibility of the central government. Whereas in Britain the areas serviced by the local offices of the Ministries of Labour and of Social Security rarely coincide with those of county boroughs or county districts, in Norway practically every municipality has its local insurance office. This office is now responsible for paying out all cash benefits and refunds for medical benefits, whether entitlement to them is under the national insurance scheme, or under the health or unemployment schemes, or even under some of the supplementary voluntary insurance schemes. While the National Insurance Institution supervises the work of these local offices, decisions about what benefit should be paid, or the form it should take will be referred to the County Rehabilitation Committees in the case of disability and rehabilitation benefits, and to the Ministry of Labour Directorate and the County or Urban District Labour and Development Boards in the case of unemployment benefit.

It remains to be seen whether the municipal social care offices which are being set up under the Social Care Act will provide as good a point of access, and achieve as satisfactory a co-ordination of the community's health and welfare services for the individual at his point of need. Experience in other countries with advanced modern welfare services suggests that this co-ordination will be much more difficult. Personal problems and the range of social work and welfare services devised 'to help people help themselves' are much more varied and subtle in definition, diagnosis and treatment than the economic problems for which a local insurance office can provide the remedy of a cash benefit. Much will depend on the lead given by the Chief Social Welfare Officers, the County Governors and Medical Officers of Health, whose co-ordinating functions are discussed in the case study. Much also will depend on the extent to which the intraining and refresher courses designed for the untrained social workers-cum-administrators in the municipal social care offices can give them sufficient insight into the aims and methods of what may broadly be termed the social work services. Only so will they see their primary task as one of co-operating with colleagues in the more specialized services rather than of mere administrative co-ordination. Varying degrees of co-ordination must already be achieved; for old people through the health and welfare centres, for families through the family counselling offices or family health centres found in many of the urban municipalities. Clearly nothing would be achieved by imposing on these varied welfare activities the kind of local co-ordination which can be more uniformly applied to the administration of social security benefits.

As in Britain the voluntary organizations are co-ordinated vertically with varying degrees of firmness. Horizontal co-ordination and collaboration with statutory bodies, at all levels, is widespread and most prominent in the health and welfare services. For the reasons given in the case study there is more incentive for local authorities to use voluntary organizations as their agents for the provision of such services as maternity and child welfare centres, children's homes, home nursing or home help services, than in Britain, where acting as an agent of the government would not be regarded as the prime function of most voluntary organizations. In Norway, and in the Scandinavian countries generally, co-ordination of the activities of governmental and non-governmental organizations does not come up against the same kind of political (in the broadest sense) differences, which are particularly evident in France, and to a lesser degree in Canada and Britain. As Mr Greve has pointed out: 'the voluntary organizations are themselves collectivist in inspiration, origin and operation'. If the political complexion of the government were ever to be radically changed, more of the voluntary organizations might lay more emphasis on their independence of government, their freedom to stand outside and criticize, and to make alternative rather than parallel arrangements.

CHAPTER 4

Social Policies and Care for the Old

To compare the social policies and social care provided for the aged in different countries involves, as did the study of family policies, two things. We shall have to try to assess how far the basic services of income-maintenance, housing, health and welfare are specifically designed and effectively directed towards meeting the needs of old people, and how far additional special services have been developed either within a general service (e.g. geriatric clinics within the health service) or separately. Secondly, we have to look at general attitudes to the situation and problems of old people in modern society. What concern is shown nationally and locally about the conditions in which elderly people are living, and, particularly, the very old and infirm, and the isolated? What is known about their situation in general and in individual terms? What attempts are being made to identify those who most urgently need help from the community, and what priority is being given to the development of welfare services, which are rarely wholly adequate and very often grossly inadequate?

What is known is likely to be found in the major reports and surveys about the situation of old people, which most countries have published in recent years. The on-going concern that social services should be developed and more effectively directed to meeting the special needs of old people has in many cases been institutionalized in various kinds of statutory or voluntary bodies, such as Old People's Welfare Committees or Institutes of Gerontology. To identify and provide appropriate and sensitive services (in the right place and at the right time) to each individual old person when and as he needs help of one kind or another, can still remain a teasing problem of social administration locally even when national policies are favourable.

Mention has already been made in the case studies of the Laroque Report, *Politique de la Vieillesse*, published in France in 1962, and of the Report of the Senate Committee on Aging, published in Canada in 1966. In Norway, a national institute for geriatric research was established in 1957, and a permanent official committee studies the problems and care of old people and produces information and reports.

In this country there has been no official report which attempted to look at the whole spectrum of needs and services for the aged, and to define a social policy for old age as did the French and Canadian committees. Nevertheless, attention was focused on this area of social policy in Britain earlier than in most countries. The National Council of Social Service set up a provisional committee to consider the problem of making adequate provision for the aged in 1940. Local Old People's Welfare Committees now cover most of the country. From 1944 to 1946 the Nuffield Foundation conducted a survey into the needs of old people and in 1947 published its Report 'Old People'. The National Corporation for the Care of Old People was set up in 1947, and with the continued financial assistance given by the Trustees of the Nuffield Foundation, has been able to help a considerable number of voluntary organizations to provide a wide variety of services for the aged and to promote many experiments in this developing field of welfare. There have been four major government reports,[1] and a great deal of research has been carried out by universities and research institutes into every aspect of the living conditions and use of social services by old people. But as Norway has recognized, the situation needs to be kept under constant review, and no official body has as yet been given a mandate to stimulate and correlate research over this whole area.

In Canada the Senate Committee underlined the need for much more on-going research and recommended the setting up of a National Institute of Social Research within which specific provision should be made for research in gerontology.

At the instigation of the Social Research Committee of the International Association of Gerontology a cross-national survey of the living conditions and attitudes of elderly people (over 65) was set on foot in 1961, the investigation in the three countries

[1] The National Advisory Committee on the Employment of Older Men and Women (1953).

The Phillips Committee on the Economic and Financial Problems of the Provision for Old Age (1954).

The Boucher (Ministry of Health) Report on Services available to the chronic sick and elderly.

The Ministry of Pensions and National Insurance Report on the Financial and other Circumstances of Retirement Pensioners (1966).

chosen (Denmark, Great Britain and the United States) carried out in the spring and summer of 1962, and the results to be published in 1967.[1] The aim of this cross-national survey was: (1) to provide a factual basis for comparisons between living conditions and attitudes of the elderly in countries with somewhat different economic, social and cultural patterns, including differences with regard to the structure of health services, social security systems and family relations; (2) to identify any similar traits which are connected with aging as such, irrespective of specific national situations; (3) to indicate the extent of groups with particular difficulties and to point to welfare problems among the elderly. To this end the investigations in the three countries covered: (*a*) Health status and utilization of health and welfare services; (*b*) Family and other social relationships; (*c*) Employment and retirement; (*d*) Economic situation; (*e*) Housing.

Our emphasis in this comparative study is rather different. We are more interested in what is being done about the problems than in the problems themselves. We shall be attempting to analyse the policies and the administration of social services to benefit the elderly in Great Britain, France, Norway and Canada. To make this analysis and assessment we shall broadly cover the same areas, as did the British, Danish and American investigators for the cross-national survey. Some of their findings about the living conditions and behaviour patterns of the elderly will, therefore, be very relevant to our considerations.

We shall be looking at social policies and at *some* of the problems of social administration which arise in the different countries as regards:

(1) Employment, retirement and income-maintenance.
(2) Medical care.
(3) Residential care of all kinds and domiciliary social and recreational services.
(4) Problems of co-ordination and of sensitizing public opinion so that all these services may continue to be adapted and developed in response to the changing needs and aspirations of the elderly of today, and, indeed, of the under 65's who will in their turn become the elderly of tomorrow.

[1] E. Shanes, P. Townsend, D. Wedderburn, *Living Conditions of the Aged in Three Industrial Societies*. New York and London, 1967.

EMPLOYMENT, RETIREMENT AND INCOME-MAINTENANCE

The percentage of the total population over sixty-five in each of our four countries was shown in a table in an earlier section.[1] But these figures need to be supplemented by those for the expectation of life (of men and women) and related to the retirement ages (for purposes of drawing the statutory pension) and to any additional information about the numbers of old people who continue in employment after sixty-five.

The following table brings together all this information for the four countries and for the two others included in the cross-national survey.

Table 1

	% of population of 65	*Expectation of life* *m.*	*w.*	*Normal statutory pension age*	*Approximate % over 65 working (men only)*
UK	12·0 (1965)	67·9	73·9 (1961–3)	m. 65 [70][1] w. 60 [65]	28[3]
FRANCE	11·8 (1962)	68·0	75·1 (1964)	60	38·8 (agricultural workers only) (1954)
NORWAY	12·0 (1965)	71·3	75·6 (1959–60)	[67][2] 70	
CANADA	7·6 (1964)	68·3	74·2 (1960–62)	68 in 1967 (65 by 1970)	25[4]
DENMARK	10·9 (1962)	70·3	74·4 (1962–63)	m. 67 w. 62	38[3]
USA	9·3 (1964)	66·9	73·7 (1964)	[62][2] 65 [72][1]	32[3]

Figures in columns 1 and 2 are taken from the Demographic Year Book

Notes: [1] Dependent on retirement until higher age in brackets.
[2] Reduced pension can be drawn at lower age in brackets.
[3] Figures from cross-national survey, they are for men only and refer to 1962.
[4] Report of Senate Committee on Aging (p. 20).

---

[1] See p. 226.

Employment

The cross-national survey showed that the main explanations of why the old people worked longer in Denmark than in Great Britain or the USA were the difference in pensionable age and the fact that fewer are employed in large-scale industry and more in agriculture. (This finding would seem to be borne out by the one figure available for France.) But ill-health or strain or heaviness of work was the main reason for retirement in all three countries, and the proportion of retired indicating interest in work was only 10 per cent in Denmark, 20 per cent in Britain, and 26 per cent in America.

Whatever the normal retiring age, all countries are concerned that the minority of old people who wish to continue working beyond these ages should not be prevented from doing so. The Ministry of Labour or National Employment Service of many Western countries is concerned with the employment of older workers as a part of their man-power problem. Where there is full employment, married women and older workers (with the exception of immigrant workers) offer the only elasticity in available manpower. In both cases more opportunities have to be made for part-time employment, and more flexible arrangements for training and retraining, if more married women and more older people are to be effectively employed.

The situation as regards the employment of older persons is explored in the Ministry of Labour's Advisory Committee's Report,[1] the Laroque Report and in the Report of the Senate Committee on Aging. It is difficult to assess what progress the national employment services of these countries have made in encouraging employers, and those responsible for training, to adapt their employment practices and training schemes to take advantage of what the older worker can offer. No country appears to have tackled this problem with any great energy and enthusiasm, although a few employers are blazing the trail. Some employment services (in Canada and more recently in the UK) have begun to offer a counselling service to the older man seeking work, and there is no reason why this should not be developed as a special placement service like those already established for young people and the disabled. But it is probably true to say that as a matter of national policy, employment services are still more concerned with the older man and woman who are thrown out of work, often the victims of technological progress,

[1] See p. 284, (footnote).

before retirement age. These men may have the greatest difficulty in finding a suitable job to see them through the last five or ten years of their working life.[1] A long spell of unemployment in these crucial years has serious implications for a man's pension and is the worst possible kind of 'Preparation for Retirement'.

These problems are much more serious for those in the industrial, technical and executive jobs than for those employed in agriculture, in service jobs and in the liberal professions. If government action is to make any real impact on them, any special placement service for the older worker will need to be backed up by a radical rethinking and extension of training facilities. All four countries have now well-established rehabilitation and training services for the disabled, it only remains to extend and adapt them to tackle this problem. In Great Britain, Norway and Canada there is evidence that a tentative start has been made in giving some places in these rehabilitation and training centres to the older, unemployed non-disabled.

Income-maintenance

The way in which the social security services for old people are organized in each country is described in the case studies. Some of the more interesting features and techniques of the income-maintenance schemes are analysed in the earlier chapter on social security. Within the context of a discussion of policies for old age we only need to add an assessment of how far each country has gone towards achieving: (*a*) a satisfactory long-term pension plan and (*b*) a reasonable standard of living for all those already retired.

The Long Term Problem

Norway and Canada have their national pension plans. Both have established them too recently—1965 and 1966—to allow of any final judgement as to whether they are going to provide satisfactory pensions for all those retiring in the future. But both countries have drawn on all the experience they have gained from their own previous pension systems (of the assistance and universal type), and on that of others, such as France and the USA, who had had more experience

[1] In Canada, where the average rate of unemployment rose to 6·7 per cent in 1958–62, this problem is particularly acute. In its submission to the Senate Committee the National Employment Service wrote, 'A person is an older worker when he encounters, or may expect to encounter, difficulty in obtaining or keeping a job primarily due to his age . . . . the problem is most likely to arise after a person reaches the age of 45'.

than they of dynamic, wage-related insurance schemes. The financing of their two-tier pensions (a universal, basic flat-rate pension with a wage-related supplement) is a mixture of contributions from employers and employees and the state; with employers contributing most, and with local as well as central government making a small contribution to the basic pension in Norway.

The aim of the Norwegian scheme is to provide a full pension (basic plus supplementary) normally equivalent to about two-thirds of pre-retirement income for the average income-earner. This will work out at more than two-thirds for the below-average earner and at less than two-thirds for the above-average. Occupational insurance schemes are only important in Norway's three basic industries—the merchant marine, fisheries and forestry—where full pensions may be drawn at 60 or 65 instead of at 70. But these too are statutory schemes. The National Pension Plan will eventually require forty years' contributions for a full pension, but as usual special concessions are made to those who are older at the start of the scheme, although it will be 10–15 years before the supplementary pension will have a substantial effect.

The Canadian plan is basically the same, providing a pension with flat-rate and wage-related components, the latter to be 25 per cent of average wages at the maturity of the scheme in 1967. The full flat-rate, and a reduced wage-related component (on a test of retirement between the ages of 65 and 70), will by 1970 be available at 65. Supplementary occupational pensions, controlled by provincial Acts in some provinces, obviously figure more largely in the total picture of the resources of old people in Canada than in Norway.

France's present solution to the long-term pension problem is also a two-tier one, but both tiers are wage-related insurance benefits, administered by two quite distinct bodies—the Social Security Funds providing the basic wage-related pension, and occupational schemes, regulated by statute and affiliated to federal institutions, providing the 'complementary' pension, related to a wage whose ceiling is set three times higher than that for the statutory schemes. The techniques used are ingenious and many workers in industry and commerce have already been able to retire on good pensions. But too many important groups among the active population are not included in any such complementary schemes (mostly agricultural workers and the small self-employed artisan), and they are the same people whose basic pension scheme already provides, or will provide them, with a very inadequate insurance pension or assistance allowance. In the General Scheme the pension is only 20 per cent of the actual wage to a relatively low ceiling, and this goes only to those who have contributed for thirty years. Admittedly it rises by 4 per cent for each year the pension is deferred: 40 per cent at 65, 60 per cent at 70, and some of the special schemes pay a pension as high as 75 per cent of the wage. But others, like the agricultural scheme, have a much lower ceiling of wages for contributions, and so for benefits. The Laroque Committee recommended a more automatic system of raising the ceiling for contributions and benefits and a basic pension representing 60 per cent rather than 40 per cent of the wage at 65. But the Report makes a more fundamental criticism of the whole of the French social security system for the aged. It argues that too much reliance is put on the insurance method, on benefits closely related to previous contribution records, on occupational rather than national solidarity, on the concept of the capitalization of savings rather than on the solidarity between generations. All these criticisms are of course even more relevant to the short-term problem of guaranteeing a national minimum income for every old person, which France so signally fails to do.

The Standard of Living of those Already Retired

There are several ways of assessing the situation. One can try to compare the absolute living standards of elderly people in the different countries, but this is likely to be closely related to the *per capita* income per head of the population. In the cross-national survey where this was attempted, the conclusion reached was: 'The various comparisons between the countries, based on the survey data, indicate that the absolute living standards of elderly people in the USA are, on the average, higher than in the two European countries, which reflects the higher levels of living generally of the United States population.'[1]

Income inequalities between retired persons and the rest of the population, on the other hand, reflect more clearly the adequacy of the overall social security arrangements. The cross-national survey found that: 'income inequalities as between elderly retired persons and the rest of the population are smaller in Denmark than in the two other countries'.[2] There have been no surveys which would

[1] *Living Conditions of the Aged in Three Industrial Societies*. An article on the survey published in ISSA bulletin July–August 1966.
[2] *Op. cit.* p. 283.

enable us to make a comparable assessment of our four countries, though it would seem likely that those inequalities would be smaller in Norway than in Canada, France or Britain.

Income inequalities among the elderly population themselves reflect most clearly the extent to which each country is succeeding in establishing (in practice as well as in theory) a minimum standard of living for all retired persons, and at what level that minimum is set. In the cross-national survey the estimate made of how many old people were living in poverty, and the measure of subsistence income taken as the criteria of poverty, is necessarily somewhat crude, and of course refers to the position in 1962. However, their findings were that 'income inequalities among the elderly population tend to be greater in USA than in Denmark and Great Britain'. In all countries the elderly women, whether single or widowed, were relatively least well off, though their position was markedly better in Denmark than in the other two countries.

Most of the national reports on the living conditions of old people have attempted this sort of estimate and related it to their current policies with regard to a national minimum—to the minimum benefits which all old people can claim as of right.

In Great Britain the comparatively recent survey carried out by the Ministry of Pensions and National Insurance into the Financial and other Circumstances of Retirement Pensioners revealed how many of the 6½ million retirement pensioners had not at that time claimed the supplementary national assistance allowance (making their income up to a scale-rate plus rent with certain disregarded capital and income) to which they were entitled. Some 700,000 pension householders had not done so (17 per cent of retirement pensioner households). Because of the full and detailed information collected about each of the 10,000 cases in the sample, it was possible to assess how many of the near three-quarters of a million had not applied because they were only a few shillings short of their entitlement, had disregarded income, or were living with relatives, so that although entitled to claim a supplementary grant to their national insurance pension (at that time 80s. per week), they were not, by failing to do so, necessarily in actual need. It was the 250,000, about whom none of these qualifications could be made, who were the cause for greatest concern, and the object of the survey was to find out not merely how many had not claimed a supplementary grant and the extent of their consequent 'poverty', but *why* they had not claimed. On this point it was found that the most important reasons for not applying to the Board appeared to be that they did not think they would be entitled to anything, or that if they were, the amount would be very small. About a quarter said that their pride would not let them ask for 'charity'.

In the light of this information the Ministry of Social Security Act, 1966, brought the Ministry of Pensions and National Insurance and the National Assistance Board under one Ministry, made some changes in nomenclature and in administration, which it was hoped would make the new supplementary pension more easily understood and more acceptable to old people, and raised the guaranteed income (the scale rate plus rent) to which retirement pensioners and others on long-term benefits would be entitled. Combined with a vigorous campaign to reach out to those ignorant, or diffident about their entitlement, this manoeuvre succeeded in the six months after the passing of the Act, in attracting a further 400,000 successful applications for the supplementary pension. Little is known about the diminishing but still substantial number (425,000) of old people over 65 who are not entitled to a retirement pension, but at the beginning of 1967, 185,000 of this group had already applied and were in receipt of a supplementary pension making their income up to the guaranteed income.

The complexity of the French social security arrangements—in this respect more than in any other a complete contrast with the British situation—makes it much more difficult to assess what sort of standard of living is obtained for the poorest old people and how many there are of them. However, the Laroque Report attempted to do this using the material available from a survey of family budgets (1956) and of housing (1961).

The Report, published in 1962, argued for a guaranteed minimum income of 2400 NF per annum for a single old person (roughly £4 per week). This included enough for an average rent; any exceptional housing costs could have been met by a rent allowance from Social Aid. The 1961 Survey findings had shown that 36 per cent of households whose head was 65 or more had declared incomes of less than 2000 NF per annum and 52 per cent less than 3000 NF per annum. (Therefore probably about 40 per cent had less than 2400 NF.) As is usually the case in such surveys the declared income was probably about 20 per cent lower than the old people's actual income from all sources, including their drawings on capital.

At this time (1961) the minimum income to which the very poorest old person was entitled was 972 NF per annum (30s a week).[1] This was made up from three sources: the special allowance (for those old people not in any occupational group which entitled them to a retired workers' allowance), Social Aid and the National Solidarity Fund. Those over 75 were entitled to a slightly higher allowance, and all would be able to claim from Social Aid a rent allowance, free medical assistance and the other benefits in kind given to those holding the Social Card. However, there were not more than about 50,000 old people in this lowest category. Far greater numbers are in receipt of the retired workers' allowance which by 1966 was set at 1900 NF (£146 per annum), which could be supplemented by 700 NF (£46 per annum) from the National Solidarity Fund, so long as the total income including the two allowances did not exceed 3300 NF (£246 per annum). But even this (the RWA plus NSF supplement) provides a bare £3 per week, and although it can be used to make an income up to 3300 NF (£5 per week), this only indicates how much other income may be disregarded and is *not* the national minimum, in the sense that incomes are automatically made up to this amount.

In the same year (1965), nearly 2½ million old people were in receipt of this final 'topping up' by the National Solidarity Fund, and this included half of those receiving insurance pensions or a retired workers' allowance under the General Scheme. There are clearly a larger proportion of poor old people in France than in Great Britain and a substantial number who are very poor indeed.

In Norway and Canada the basic pension, which is provided on a universal basis and so presumably taken up by every person reaching 70 (or 68), provides a minimum income guaranteed in principle and practice to all old people at this higher retirement age. For those not able to work so long, Norway has special occupational pension schemes, unemployment, sickness, disability and widows' benefit, and a fall back on to the municipal pensions or assistance available under the new Social Care programme. It is in fact left to the local authority to provide any discretionary assistance, which may be needed over and above, and in the interstices, of the fairly generous and flexible benefits provided under the national pension plan. So long as other national schemes ensure that medical care and adequate housing are also brought within the means of all

[1] In each case these are approximate equivalents on the basis of 13 NF = £1.

retired persons, the economic situation of old people is probably as well protected in Norway as in any Western country.

In Canada, the $75 a month, which by 1967 is being paid without any conditions (except of residence in Canada) to all persons of 68 years and over, would not be regarded as an adequate income for most old people living independently, unless they have some other resources. Provincial old age assistance allowances have had to supplement and bridge the age gap of 65 to 70 up-to-date. They have, of course, varied from province to province, but have on the whole probably been a less adequate and less acceptable form of public assistance to old people than the supplementary grants of the old NAB in Great Britain. Nevertheless, on past experience some 20 per cent have benefited. The new federal supplementation of old age security benefits to provide a 'guaranteed income' to current recipients, introduced at the end of 1966, is likely to be more acceptable if not more generous. But whatever level of income is guaranteed, allowances will have to be made for high rents or for any other variable or exceptional expenditure. It is difficult to say what additional assistance will be needed from provincial schemes to secure a reasonable standard of living, and not just a guaranteed (means-tested but not needs-tested) income for all old people. With the relatively undeveloped programmes of public medical care and public housing in Canada, social assistance is likely to continue to play a significant role for those without any or few private resources.

MEDICAL CARE

The social security aspects of medical care, the extent to which health services are available to retired persons on a universal, insurance or assistance basis was described in the case studies. Our concern here is with how far each country's general medical and nursing, and the more specialized, geriatric services, are adequately meeting the needs of old people, and more particularly of the older and more infirm. Have we any measure of these needs for medical services? What is the state of health of elderly people? Another stereotyped opinion refuted by the findings of the cross-national survey was that most elderly people are in a bad state of health. The survey was confined to persons living in private households, so that some of those who are particularly incapacitated would not be included. In fact, 5·3 per cent of the elderly population in Denmark were residents in institutions of one kind and another (hospitals, mental hospitals, nursing or residential homes), as against 3·6 per cent and 3·7 per cent in Great Britain and the USA.[1] However, in all three countries far more old people are bedridden and housebound at home than in institutions. Even so, the number of bedridden and housebound persons living at home did not amount to more than 10 per cent in all three countries, whereas 90 per cent were ambulant, about 80 per cent could go out of doors without difficulty, and about one-half of the elderly in Denmark and Great Britain and two-thirds of the elderly in the USA reported no functional incapacity.

There have been no similar recent investigations into the state of health of the elderly in France, Norway and Canada, but it is reasonable to assume that the incidence of obvious need (because the old person is bedridden or housebound), and of felt need for medical services is probably much the same as in Denmark, Great Britain and the USA. The major national surveys and reports which have been made, however, do give us a fairly clear picture (although at different dates) of the services available to meet these needs. The number of beds in the country's general, chronic or mental hospitals occupied by old people, their adequacy in quantity and quality, and the development of any hospital-based geriatric services (clinics, rehabilitation and convalescent services, day centres, etc.) are usually noted. Similarly, they review the extent and quality of the domiciliary medical services, which are of particular importance, and may indeed be specially run for old people: home nursing and health visiting, chiropody and physiotherapy, along with such essential supporting services as home helps, meals services and social workers.

In comparing the health and welfare services available to old people we shall be drawing on the findings of these reports, in order to fill out the necessarily brief references to them in the case studies. Comprehensive and detailed comparisons of each and every service would be tedious. It will be enough to indicate some of the more significant similarities and differences in the problems, achievements and avowed policies of the four countries with respect to certain of them.

[1] For Canada, The Department of National Health and Welfare estimate was 6·4 per cent in 1964.

The Laroque Report underlines some interesting differences in the French and British[1] approach to geriatric services. There have, of course, been developments in both countries since this report was made, but nothing to indicate that the approaches have been changed. While both countries distinguish between the active treatment which old people should receive in general hospitals and the care of the chronic sick in special wards or hospitals, the British are developing geriatrics as a specialism in the general hospitals whereas the Laroque Committee would restrict geriatric departments to the Regional University and Hospital Centres. However, none had been established at this time, although there were already ninety-five geriatric departments in British hospitals. The French argument against this specialization by age in ordinary hospitals was that it could lead to the segregation of old people and to their receiving a second-rate service. They felt that geriatric centres were only needed in the teaching hospitals for research, and for the training of doctors, nurses, physiotherapists, social workers, etc., who would be specializing in the care of old people at home, in day centres or ordinary hospitals. More understanding of the psychiatric aspects of aging would also be gained in these centres.

Every country has problems—administrative and social rather than medical—in providing, at the right time and in the right place, the appropriate medical and nursing care for the elderly as they grow older and more infirm. Most are anxious to improve their domiciliary medical services so that more old people now in hospital could be treated at home, and so that the much greater number of bedfast or housebound old people, now being cared for at home, usually by relatives, should receive more skilled professional help from doctors, home nurses, chiropodists and others. Although these home care services tend to be badly distributed and generally inadequate in most countries, there are more of them within the reach of the poor and middle income groups in Great Britain and Norway than in France and Canada. This could be inferred from the case studies, where the basis on which such services as general practitioners and drugs, home nurses and home helps, chiropodists and occupational therapists are provided, is described.

Again this can be illustrated most clearly by comparing the development of the home nursing service (the most important item)

[1] The Report draws a number of comparisons with the services for old people in Great Britain and Sweden.

in Britain, in Canada, and in France. In Britain home nursing for the poor, and later for the working-classes, was originally provided by voluntary nursing associations, which by the Second World War had practically a national coverage. The National Health Service Act made home nursing a duty of the local health authorities, who not only had to take financial responsibility for the existing nursing services, but had to expand them as they became part of the universal national health service. In 1959 over 10,000 nurses paid some fifteen out of twenty-four million visits to old people over 65.

In Canada there are well-established and widespread home nursing services of the Victorian Order of Nurses in many urban areas (half the people cared for being in the age group 65 and over). The Senate Committee recommended that home nursing services be extended to urban areas now without them, and increasingly to rural areas, and that the services be provided by or closely integrated with local health departments, as they already are in British Columbia.

In France, the Departmental health service has very limited powers to provide a home nursing service. It can be provided as part of medical assistance (in Paris in 1959, 1300 sick people benefited from it), and the Laroque Report recommended a considerable expansion of this service by Social Aid Bureaux. The Red Cross and religious bodies are probably the biggest providers of home nurses, who usually work, like many of those employed by Social Aid, from a district dispensary or centre attached to some other institution, such as a social centre or nursing home. Those who are not entitled to free medical assistance are expected to pay for these services, with the possibility rather than certainty of getting part of the fee refunded from their social insurance. A home nurse was also provided in the hospitalization-at-home experiment in Paris, referred to in the case study. This service was directed and financed by the hospitals, which reckoned that in 1958 during a four-month period, they freed on average twenty-four beds by extending this hospital-at-home service to 117 sick people. The home nurse, working under the direction of the patient's doctor, is the mainstay of any such domiciliary medical service. If it is to be developed in France, should the Department or the hospital service take the final responsibility for seeing that home nursing is available wherever and whenever it is preferable to hospital treatment? Until one or other is given the responsibility the old people, who potentially are in greatest need of this service, will suffer.

RESIDENTIAL CARE AND DOMICILIARY WELFARE SERVICES

Official British policy with regard to these non-medical services can be traced in annual reports, in circulars sent by the Ministry of Health to the local authorities with respect to their powers and duties under the National Assistance and National Health Service Acts, and in the plans for the development of their health and welfare services which they have been required to submit from time to time.[1]

Broadly speaking, since 1948 when the final break with the Poor Law was made, official policy has gradually moved from a pre-occupation with improved standards of residential accommodation ('Hotels for Old People' was the slogan in 1948) to an increasing encouragement of a policy of maintaining old people in their own homes by provision of more domiciliary care services.[2] This broader concept of welfare, moving from institutionally based minority provision to a community oriented, positive, universal care has tended to confuse the boundaries of responsibility by involving a wide range of departments and bodies in its scope. The implications of this policy have not yet been fully grasped. There has been an increasing emphasis on the necessity of co-operation and co-ordination between authorities (the different departments—housing, health, welfare—of local authorities and the hospital service) and between statutory and voluntary bodies; and the Ministry's role is gradually being revised from the negative one of keeping local authorities within the statutory limits to the more positive one of insisting on the provision of a uniformly high standard of community care.

But achievement still falls far short of these aspirations. To judge the quality of these community care services and how far they are meeting the felt needs of old people as opposed to the official assessment of them, is not easy. Various surveys, for the most part by non-official bodies, provide us with a certain amount of information. One of the most recent and comprehensive was carried out in conjunction with the cross-national survey and relates to the situation in 1962.[3] On the whole the findings confirm what a number of local

[1] 'Health and Welfare—The Development of Community Care. 1963.' 1964–66 H.M.S.O.

[2] Peter Townsend and Dorothy Wedderburn: 'The Aged in the Welfare State'. *Occasional Papers on Social Administration*, No. 14. London, 1965.

[3] This developing situation is well described in Kathleen Slack's 'Councils Committees and Concern for the Old' *Occasional Papers on Social Administration*, No. 2, and is reflected in the annual reports of the Ministry of Health.

and regional surveys had already implied: that substantially more old people than are receiving different services feel a need and otherwise seem to qualify for them; that many of those receiving certain services—particularly the hearing aid, home help and meals services—are not getting all the help they might from them; that the services are not properly co-ordinated and many people receiving only one service seem to need at least two or three services.

This pattern of official policy, moving slowly from a pre-occupation with institutional provisions to an encouragement of all those domiciliary services which will enable old people to go on living in the community as long as possible, is found in most countries and can be seen reflected in the ministerial statements and in the recommendations of the national reports of France and Canada. While moving in the same direction they have, however, moved at different paces, and the official encouragement given to community care has not in many instances gone much beyond exhortation. There has as yet been little systematic financial aid given to develop those domiciliary services (comparable with that given to hospitals) and no mandatory powers laid on local authorities to make certain minimum provisions. In Norway the position is rather different. The smaller communities have on the whole been able to care for their old people up to the time of their needing a bed in the nursing home or geriatric ward. Official policy has never therefore been much preoccupied with institutional provisions, but has tended to concentrate on improving the domiciliary services available to old people.

Although no longer the major pre-occupation the problem of assessing and meeting in appropriate ways the need for special care in residential establishments for those old people, unable and unwilling to go on living independently, remains. In all four countries the ultimate duty of the local authorities (or of the provincial governments in Canada) to provide residential care for any old or infirm person who cannot look after himself, and who has not sufficient resources to arrange privately for the care he needs, stems from old public assistance legislation, now embodied in new Social Aid, Social Care or General Assistance Acts. Only in Great Britain is the duty to provide for those 'in need of care and attention' completely divorced from the financial status of the old person, in the sense that the *first* duty of the local authority is to decide whether or not the old person is in need of care and attention, and only after he has been offered a place in a local authority or approved voluntary home, to decide whether he can pay the full cost, or will need to be subsidized. He can always pay part of the cost out of his pension; whether or not he can pay more must be determined by the same personal means test as that applied by the Ministry of Social Security. The significance of this order of approach can perhaps only be fully appreciated by those who knew what it meant to receive *indoor* rather than *outdoor relief*, and to become an *inmate* of the *institution* under the pre-1948 public assistance regime. However, where these old institutions are still in use, despite the new names, the new regulations and the better amenities, the old people see little change, and none but the most desperate will seek this service from the local authority.

The official encouragement, backed by grant-aid to local authorities and voluntary organizations, to provide a new, more informal type of Home for Old People, which started in 1948 in this country, came later, towards the end of the 1950s, in France. The special Assistance Act of 1905, which required the local authorities to provide *hospices* for the aged, the infirm and the incurables, was only modified by an ordinance of December 1958, which allowed for the setting up of *maisons de retraite* (homes for retired persons), reserved for old people only, alongside the *hospices*. Such small Homes had previously only been established by some voluntary organizations; and those in receipt of old age assistance could only be helped to meet the costs of residence in a voluntary Home if there was no place available in the public *hospice*. Although this change in social aid legislation has enabled many Departments and communes to set up small Homes of their own, and to assist more old people in the voluntary Homes, there remain more old people in larger institutions in France than in Britain, both in the public and private sector. A number of these points are illustrated in the following comparative figures for 1960 given in the Laroque Report.

In France:

	152,505	old people in	1,879	public hospices or homes
plus	65,947	old people in	1,100	private hospices or homes
	218,452	old people in	2,979	homes of all kinds

In Britain:

	75,000	old people in 1,100 L.A. institutions or homes
plus	10,000	old people in 1,900 voluntary or privately run homes
	85,500	old people in 3,000 homes of all kinds

To make these figures comparable there should be added to the British figures about 50,000 old people in the chronic wards of general hospitals, since the *hospice* cares for more infirm old people than 'Part III Accommodation' in Britain.

In Norway and in most of the Canadian provinces (Quebec would be an exception), there is not the same legacy of large institutions caring for old people as in the older, industrial towns of Great Britain and France. Thus, by and large, the local authorities have had a less formidable problem in adapting existing or building new establishments, in keeping with modern ideas. But whatever the legacy of old-type institutions, and whatever headway has been made in replacing them with smaller, pleasanter homes for old people, each country has to face, to a greater or lesser degree, certain problems, inherent in making this kind of provision for old people. For every country is facing an absolute increase in the numbers of the very old and infirm, who have outlived or are removed from the relatives and friends who would otherwise care for them.

The first problem is associated with the old institutions and will therefore be felt more acutely by Britain and France. There is the heavy capital cost of replacing large, outdated institutions with a number of much better equipped small Homes and with some increase in more hospital-type provision for the very infirm. (The equipment and standards of medical and nursing care in many of the French *hospices* is much criticized in the Laroque Report.) The physical replacement of the larger institutions by a number of smaller establishments must be accompanied by a better quality of care to the old people. This will only be achieved by substantial increases in the number of staff, and in their better selection, training and management. This means a substantial increase in running costs, and even if the community is prepared to meet these, shortages of appropriately trained personnel will almost always present problems.

Few countries have faced up to the staffing implications of their new policies of residential care for the aged. In this country training courses for the staff of old people's Homes were pioneered by the National Old People's Welfare Committee and the National Corporation for the Care of Old People in the late 1940s, and the Ministry of Health emphasized the importance of training in a circular to the local authorities as early as 1949. In subsequent annual reports it regularly mentions the various courses and praises the local authorities using them, or, latterly, running them themselves. The Ministry's interest, however, is limited to one of advice and exhortation. The Government has not seen fit to help the local authorities by a more active policy of promoting the recruitment and training of appropriate workers. This was done for local authority children's departments when the Home Office set up the Central Training Council for Child Care in 1947, since when a good deal of public money and thought has gone into training and refresher courses of all kinds for child care officers and residential workers.[1]

There is no evidence that Governments in other countries have committed themselves to anything more than this.[2] Yet all emphasize the vital importance of having trained staff, if the right attitudes and some insight into the needs of old people are to prevail in these Homes. The Laroque Report lays down some general principles for the running of old people's Homes and recognizes the need for trained staff, but makes no specific recommendation about their recruitment and training.

The second problem is even more intractable: how to provide for each individual old person who may be relatively fit when he enters a Home, the increasing amount of personal and nursing care he will need if he falls ill, or in the natural course of events becomes older and more infirm. The temptation is to run each establishment for a particular type of resident or patient, and to ignore the anxiety of the old people at being liable to be moved on if their condition deteriorates, and their helplessness and humiliation at being treated as categories rather than as individuals. Either they remain too long in Home or hospital getting inadequate or inappropriate treatment, or are pushed from one to another, or 'swopped', with a total disregard for their feelings. A future of 'staging posts' is no substitute

[1] It remains to be seen whether the Government will take note of the recommendations of the latest Committee of Enquiry into staffing residential Homes. *Caring for People*. Allen & Unwin, 1967.

[2] With one exception: Sweden has been training administrators of Homes since 1908 and the course lasts three years.

for the home which an old person has reluctantly had to give up, even if the first stage is a small 'homely Home'.

In the initial excitement of setting up the new small Homes and of reducing in some measure, the indiscriminate mixture and numbers being cared for in the big institutions, these problems inherent in caring for those whose physical and mental capacities are declining, tend to be ignored. The Ministry of Health's increasing awareness of these problems is reflected in its annual reports, while the problem of the gap between Home and hospital was considered in the Boucher report, published in 1957[1] on a survey made in 1954–55 of the services available for the chronic sick and elderly. An absolute shortage of both kinds of accommodation was revealed, the respective roles of Home and hospital redefined, and the solution sought in an increase of places or beds, and greater flexibility on both sides. Flexibility, particularly with respect to those who have already made a particular establishment their home, is obviously the only way round this problem. But shortages, particularly of staffing, are always the worst enemy of flexibility, and in this country old people are still suffering from abrupt transitions from one establishment to another, or even worse, from failing to find a place in either.

In France the Regional Social Security Funds are now using a lot of their free money to make capital grants (normally 40 per cent of capital costs) to any local or approved voluntary organization setting up a *maison de retraite*. They are rather rigidly insisting that only modern homes for not more than eighty active, old people should receive grants. The Funds recognize the need for more and better provision for the aged sick but are firmly leaving this to the hospital and Social Aid authorities, which they argue, should be given more State aid.

It is perhaps significant of the shorter experience of providing smaller Old People's Homes in France that the Laroque Report does not really seem seized of this second problem. All its criticisms are directed against the inadequacies of the out-moded *hospice* concept, and it insists on the importance of making the new *maison de retraite* a quite distinct provision, appropriate for active old people. In reporting on British experience and British policies, the Laroque Report never mentions the problems we have encountered and the second thoughts we have had about the contribution of the small

[1] Ministry of Health. *Reports on Public Health and Medical Subjects* No. 98. HMSO, London 1957.

Home and how it should relate to better domiciliary provisions on the one hand (supporting them by taking some short-stay cases), and to the skilled nursing care more appropriately provided in the hospital on the other. In reporting on the residential care for old people in Sweden and Denmark, however, a note of doubt seems to creep in. While admitting the excellence of the varied (and graded) care available for old people in the Old People's Town in Copenhagen and in the Stahagsharden in Stockholm, where every kind of accommodation from 'sheltered housing' to hospital ward is concentrated in one vast institution, it questions whether this Scandinavian solution would be acceptable in France. One suspects that whatever official policy may be, French sensitivity and respect for the individual will mean that the old people will stay on in their *maisons de retraite* long after they have ceased to be the active, alert old people for whom they were originally designed, just as many of their small *hospices* were in the past less bound by rules and regulations than our public assistance institutions. (In the 1930s a small *hospice* in *Haute Savoie*, the local 'workhouse', used to let all its old people out for the day on *Quatorze Juillet*, and in the evening send a donkey and cart round the village to pick up the residents, who after their day's celebrations were in no state to get home unaided.)

A third problem is concerned with the encouragement and supervision of residential establishments in the private sector. This sector includes the Homes run by the voluntary philanthropic or non-profit-making organizations as well as by private enterprise. As is to be expected, the voluntary organizations have done much pioneering of smaller Homes, and of Homes which are able to provide more nursing facilities to keep their residents longer than the small Homes (as opposed to the *hospices* or institutions) in the public sector. This is particularly the case in Britain, Norway and Canada, where they have also made some useful experiments in different types of 'sheltered' but independent accommodation—the old alms-house concept but today more often provided through Housing Associations.

It is probably true to say that most but not all of the residential care provided by the private sector is for the slightly better off. Unlike the local authorities, voluntary organizations can be more selective, and many of their small Homes are run for a particular occupational or social group. Homes run by religious bodies, particularly the Roman Catholics, are less likely to discriminate in this way. Most of the old people's Homes of the Little Sisters of the

Poor, however, are still and will doubtless remain of the *hospice* type. However, they too have been undergoing modernization, the infirmary wing becoming a more distinct, while remaining an integral part, of the whole set-up.

In Britain, the National Assistance Act of 1948 encouraged voluntary organizations in two ways. Assuming their Homes were satisfactory, and their fees comparable to those charged by the local authorities, welfare departments could help old people who were deemed to be 'in need of care and attention', by making up the difference between what they could afford and the charge made by the voluntary organization. Voluntary organizations wanting to set up a new Home could get the same exchequer subsidy (an annual contribution to loan charges) as the local authority.

Under the same Act any one running a voluntary or private Home for old people had to register it with the local authority. Such Homes could be inspected by the Ministry or the local authority, but it has been found that registration and inspection are ineffective in guaranteeing uniform standards, particularly in the case of the private profit-making Homes. Inspections, and a number of recent surveys,[1] have revealed wide variations even though the Ministry made the conditions for registration more stringent in 1961. These conditions are concerned with the numbers which may be accommodated, the equipment and conduct of the Home; the latter is extremely difficult to inspect and even more difficult to enforce, owing to the chronic shortage of staff and to the lack of any specific qualifications for this work. The private Homes are of course faced with the same problem as the public ones. The residents get older and more infirm, and the Homes are not staffed and equipped to care for old people who need a great deal of nursing. But where can they go? Nursing Homes must be registered and inspected by the local health department, but can be more easily kept up to recognized standards in terms of training and ratio of staff to patients. But private nursing homes are very expensive and their patients are not entitled to any assistance with their fees as are the residents in old people's Homes run by voluntary organizations.

In Canada most provincial welfare departments licence, regulate and share in the costs of maintenance of 'indigent' residents in either Homes or Nursing Homes. In Ontario in 1965 there were 558 Homes

[1] The latest: 'Private Homes for Old People' was published by The National Corporation for the Care of Old People in 1967.

for Special Care (long-term) with a total capacity of 24,126 beds. Over 60 per cent of these beds were classified as *domiciliary*, the balance as *nursing* beds. The local health authority also inspects these Homes. It is estimated that about one-third of the residents in Homes for the aged are bed or wheel-chair cases receiving nursing services. For a nursing bed a higher charge is allowed than for a domiciliary one. In Saskatchewan, with a much smaller population, the Housing and Nursing Homes Branch of the Department of Welfare licences accommodation for elderly persons in housing units, hostels, homes for the aged and nursing homes. Construction and maintenance grants are paid to licensed, non-profit organizations. In Quebec in 1965 it was estimated that there were over 14,500 beds in some 339 Homes or units for special care. Two provincial departments, the Public Assistance Services of the Department of Health, and the Division on Services for the Aged and Other Adults of the Department of Family and Social Welfare, are concerned with licensing, setting standards and paying costs of (indigent) patient care in nursing or domiciliary beds in hospitals or Homes run by local authorities, religious or approved private non-profit organizations.

As in France, payment of maintenance charges by provincial or local authorities is only made on behalf of those old people who have applied and been found eligible for assistance. However, the encouragement and extensive use (for assistance cases) of the 'special care' provided in a wide range of private (religious, philanthropic and non-profit making) establishments means that old people in receipt of assistance are barely distinguishable from those who are meeting the charges themselves; charges which may of course be subsidized to some extent by the voluntary organizations running the Homes. The licensing and standard-setting (or registration and inspection) can always be more firmly applied to Homes receiving public funds in one way or another. As in Britain and Canada, the problem lies in exercising any kind of control and supervision over private Homes, usually those run on a profit-making basis which are in receipt of no public money. The problem will remain so long as there is an overall shortage of places for old people in well-run establishments, well distributed and reasonably priced.[1]

[1] In Canada the situation, according to the Senate Committee, is so desperate that even nursing homes of such poor quality that authorities feel they should not be in operation, have long waiting lists. *Op. cit.* p. 110.

THE LOCAL CO-ORDINATION OF SERVICES

We started this review of social policies and care for the old by considering what fact finding, policy making and co-ordination of the efforts of all concerned was going on in each country at national level. It is appropriate that we should complete it by seeing what is being done to co-ordinate all these services at the point at which they are to benefit the individual old person—the retail rather than the wholesale distribution. It is obvious that every country is going to have difficulties in 'retailing' its social services for old people. As we have seen, difficulties are encountered even in the administration of what looks like one kind of service—the special care provided in residential establishments. How much more difficult to co-ordinate such different services as housing and hospitals, domiciliary care and monetary assistance, which are very often the responsibility of different administrations. Local co-ordination must aim to ensure that there are enough of all these different services, and that the changing individual needs of all old people living in a particular area are identified and appropriate services offered in a sensitive and acceptable way.

In a modern welfare state it is the sheer numbers of those who can expect to benefit from its services, and the more ambitious concept of welfare, that makes co-ordination of services at every level such a formidable problem. At the beginning of the century France's Old Age Assistance Act, 1905, which guaranteed to every old person in need, as of right, a pension, a bed in a hospital or a place in a Home, all provided by the local public assistance authority, represented an adequate policy for the welfare of the aged, or at least for the aged poor, which is as far as statutory concern went in those days. Today all old people whatever their income benefit from certain universal services, and for the rest, it is not only those eligible for assistance (in cash or in service) who are receiving some subsidy from public funds. Many other old people are benefiting from the concealed subsidies which have gone into the special housing, Homes, cheap fares, clubs or restaurants provided by public authorities or voluntary organizations, for all old people quite irrespective of means.

Greater wealth and greater sensitivity means that many more old people are benefiting in many more ways from the social services than the old people of fifty or even twenty years ago. Both needs and expectations have changed, too, but how aware are we of these general changes? How can we ensure that all old people, and especially those most in need of help, are having their needs met adequately and in a fitting way? Is the best possible use being made of the greatly increased resources directed to the many different services for the elderly? How far can the specialist, in field work or in administration, exercise his skills and concern to see that a particular need is met, while remaining sensitive to the total situation of the individual old person; for it is essential that he appreciates that in many cases, and in most cases of serious need, his service will only be effective if it is complementary to, and complemented by, others.

All four countries have to face these problems, and are beginning to ask themselves questions, and experimenting in ways of meeting them.

In Great Britain local old people's welfare committees are primarily designed to be sensitive to the needs of old people in their area, to detect gaps in existing provisions and to see that these gaps are filled by one of their constituent members, or by the old people's welfare committee itself. They all too often fail to carry out their co-ordinating function; either because they are not strong enough to break down the departmentalism of local authorities, their local authority representatives paying no more than lip service to the co-ordinated policies and action which the old people's welfare committee is supposed to promote; or because the voluntary organizations are financially too weak to expand, or to provide services of a more uniform quality over the whole area; or because the committee itself gets so involved in executive action that it loses sight of its primary co-ordinating function and becomes just another voluntary agency providing specific services—a club, chiropody, or a meals service—for old people.

In smaller, less populous areas some local old people's welfare committees have worked out fairly satisfactory ways of getting to know of any old people in their areas who are in difficulty and of ensuring that they are put in touch with the appropriate statutory or voluntary services, not forgetting the less formal neighbourly services which each local community is encouraged to promote. But in the large towns this is rarely achieved and is never likely to be unless and until the local authority takes the initiative in basing its health and welfare services in district offices, which can provide a rallying point for voluntary community effort, and a known point of access to all services for the old people living in that area. This is recommended in the Laroque and Senate Committee reports, but has received scant attention from the Ministry of Health or local authorities in this country up to now, although the Report of the Seebohm Committee can be expected to deal with this issue.

Attempts to establish and keep up-to-date registers of all old people, who are or might at some future time be in need of help, have been made in some towns. But they usually run up against the problem of who is to make all the routine visits such a register demands, if it is to have any practical value. Local housing, health and welfare departments and the local hospitals have in many areas been more successful in co-ordinating their policies, with regard to the provision of services for which they are each responsible. Some particularly interesting arrangements have been made between housing and welfare departments over the provision of sheltered housing, and between local health departments and the hospitals over joint appointments of geriatricians and social workers.

In France, despite the Laroque Report, there is no widespread concern about the co-ordination of local services, but much more about the undeveloped state of many basic domiciliary and other desirable social and recreational services for old people. The inventory of such local services made by the Laroque Committee certainly suggested that a big effort was needed to develop among other things the home nursing, home help, chiropody, recreational and meals services, and various forms of 'sheltered' housing for old people. Co-ordination of the policies of the Regional Funds, of the Department and voluntary organizations is likely to be reasonably well secured through the *Comités Techniques* and the prefectoral system. Co-ordination at field work level should in theory be achieved through the general purpose social workers and the relationships they have worked out with their specialist colleagues. It is more likely that old people suffer from the little time which the district social workers, whose health visiting functions tend to focus their attention on families with children, can spare for them. The Laroque report recognized this and recommended that some special workers with additional training should be employed as specialist social workers for old people by the Funds, the municipalities or the Departments, who should also ensure that old people have one point of contact which will lead them to all the social services they need. This should be at the level of the *quartier* or group of small villages. In practice, some towns, or certain districts of towns, have the rudiments of such a service-centre for old people. It may take the form of a dispensary and social centre run by the Red Cross, or of a municipal old people's club and restaurant, where the Social Aid Investigator and district social worker have an office and a nurse calls to give minor treatments and to which some small serviced apartments for old people (*foyer-logements*), set up by the Social Aid, are attached.

In Norway the closer co-ordination of local assistance and welfare services envisaged under the Social Care Act should encourage a less departmentalized and piecemeal approach to the welfare of individual old people and lead to the development of appropriate services. In some Norwegian cities the Health and Welfare Centres get the names of all people in their area when they begin to receive the pension (at 70) and they are all routinely contacted by letter or visit. But, as has been pointed out,[1] many people do not grasp the size and complexity of the problem of the care of the elderly. Pensioners are not a homogenous group. Needs differ. Pension incomes differ; lone women are in Norway, as elsewhere, heavily over-represented among the elderly, and are financially worse off than men. Housing needs differ. Moreover it is not only a matter of material needs, but opportunities for achieving general well being. It is essential that local communities be aware of their responsibilities and that at national level the official committee studying the problems and care of old people is as concerned that the needs of the exceptional case are identified and met by the local social care department, as that the needs of the average case are met by adequate universal services. It is also clear that despite financial aid from the State, the initiative for developing the essential home nursing and home help services lies with these same local communities whose responsible members will only act if they are aware of the actual conditions and needs of individual old people in their district. It is always pertinent to ask whether the local statutory and voluntary institutions are fostering this local sensitivity and local sense of responsibility.

In Canada, a number of factors make the local co-ordination of services for the aged peculiarly difficult. Firstly, there is the weakness and declining efficiency of local government, which is discussed in the chapter on co-ordination. Although some provincial governments are realizing the importance of achieving a genuine devolution

[1] Viktor Gaustad De Eldere in *Kontrast* No. 1. 1967.

of responsibility for personal social services on to municipalities, or on to their own regional or district offices, in many parts of Canada there are as yet no suitable local units, which could be made responsible for the administration and planned development of all the relevant services for old people in relation to actual local needs. Secondly, while under the provincial Social Assistance Acts public welfare departments are now able to provide most of the services which old people need (medical care, Homes and home-making services, etc.), they can only be offered to those old people who qualify for assistance under the Act. Thirdly, voluntary organizations, which in the case of child care have often through Children's Aid Societies acted on behalf of local or provincial authorities to provide a comprehensive service for the protection of children and their families, have found it more difficult to provide an integrated local welfare service for old people. Such a service inevitably involves most of the basic health and welfare services which the provincial government or municipality normally provides directly, or indirectly through buying services for its clients from private institutions.

Despite these difficulties one example can be given of a comparatively recent experiment in the local co-ordination of services for old people: co-ordination at policy level in the development of the appropriate local health, welfare, housing and hospital services and at consumer level, at the point of assessing and meeting the needs of individual old people. The Care Services[1] Office of the departments of Health and Welfare of Manitoba in Winnipeg was opened in 1964 to provide an integrated health and welfare service for old people and to facilitate co-operation with the Manitoba Hospital Commission and the Director of Elderly Persons Housing. More elderly people in the population, more people unable to meet the costs of caring for themselves had produced a tremendous pressure on facilities. More care services for the elderly were obviously needed; there was more knowledge and understanding of the desirability of care in the community; and finally, in 1959 The Social Allowances Act allowed the province and the municipalities to provide a wide range of services as well as financial aid for those old people in need of such assistance.

The Care Services office represents a joint venture of the two departments and comprises two main sections. Under the welfare

[1] The Care Services in Manitoba are described in greater detail in an article in *Canadian Welfare*, November–December 1965.

director, who is responsible for administering the Social Allowances Act, is an assistant director who supervises a staff of three supervisors and nineteen workers (a mixed team of trained social workers and welfare workers). An intake section receives all referrals, develops the psycho-social and financial aspects of the case, presents it at a conference and carries out any recommended placement or arranges for the various services required for home care, such as home help and invalid aids, and authorizes financial assistance as necessary. On-going support or counselling is provided as necessary by the other workers, while one full-time and part-time worker are assigned to a foster-home finding service.

The health director is responsible for issuing licences, for the supervision of Homes and medical services to Care Services clients placed in Homes and institutions. Under him a clinical director (a specialist in internal medicine employed on a part-time basis) supervises the physicians, paid on an honorarium basis, who are providing medical services to welfare clients in Homes and institutions. He is usually the medical representative at the case conference. The health section also includes a nursing supervisor, three nurses, a nutritionist and a public health inspector, who provide direct services to clients in the community as well as supervising the nursing and health standards in the Homes. The nursing supervisor contributes her assessment of the health aspects of the clients' situation at the case conference. The plan made at the conference is offered to the client, and alternative plans considered if it is not acceptable, or if the resources needed for its implementation are not immediately available. The Director of Elderly and Infirm Persons Housing occupies an office in the Care Services building and works closely with Care Services staff. The provisions of the Elderly and Infirm Persons Housing Act provide for building and maintaining housing, hostels and personal care Homes throughout Manitoba.

The major limitation on the Care Services programme arises not from its structure but from its origins in the Social Allowance Act. While private patients do benefit from the overall planning, the office can only extend a minimum of counselling services or information to the elderly and their families who are faced with care problems but who are not eligible for financial aid under the Act. More and more demands for services are received; there is a clear need here and sometime, and in some way, Canada will have to find a new legislative formula to meet it.

CHAPTER 5

Family Policies

What constitutes a family policy? Since all social services are designed to promote individual welfare, and since most individuals live a substantial part, if not all, of their lives as members of families, it can be argued that every social service will have its repercussions on families and family life. If, as was suggested in the introduction, we follow Donnison in defining the policies of a social service as 'its functions—what it does—which may or may not coincide with its official aims', then to evaluate a country's family policies we must assess, as best we can, in what ways its existing social services are in fact affecting family life. As most countries (including Britain) have become much more aware of the relevance of the family to welfare policies in recent years, they have themselves been making this kind of assessment, which makes our tasks so much the easier.

This sensitivity to the repercussions which the social services may be having on family life is evident in all four countries; all would subscribe to the importance of the family as the basic social unit. On the other hand, what is actually attempted and achieved through the social services to strengthen and support the family, generally reflects assumptions about the family and ways of family living which prevail in a particular country, and, equally importantly, the assumptions which underlie all social action about ways in which the State can, or should, intervene to promote the welfare of its citizens. Taking each country in turn we shall therefore examine each country's social policies under the following headings:

(1) *The political significance* of the family—the assumptions about the family and family life which stem largely from a country's demographic situation and social structure.

(2) *The economic situation* of the family—particularly the extent to which the social security services effect a redistribution in its favour.

(3) *Family welfare*—its psycho-social aspects in relation to:

(*a*) *preventive service*, which many families will use and which are often provided on a universal basis;

(*b*) *remedial services* for families with special problems: broken families, families with maladjusted or delinquent children, etc.

FRANCE

Political Significance

We will take France first, because of the four countries under consideration she is undoubtedly the most articulate about her family policies, appears to be most conscious of the need for *a politique familiale*, and most explicit in its formulation. In France a family is defined in law by the presence of children of French nationality, and family policies are specifically concerned with this legal entity. The Family Code lays down its rights and duties and the statutory benefits to which it is entitled. France's demographic concern and consequent natalist policies are well known and of long standing. This concern has been institutionalized, at central government level in the President's *Haut Comité Consultatif de la Population et de la Famille*, and at national and local level in the Family Allowance Funds, and in the voluntary Family Associations.[1]

Since the Second World War there have been three major government reports on the family; the last, the Prigent Report on *La Politique Familiale* was published in 1962. Its terms of reference were typically broad: 'To study family problems, and to suggest to the Government how they should be solved within the framework of an overall family policy, taking account of general demographic trends.' Its findings give a fairly up-to-date picture of current issues, and its conclusions and recommendations are as much concerned with the general climate of ideas, which the Committee regarded as fundamental to France's family policy, as with specific measures. Thus, on the demographic front it argues that the increase in the birthrate since the war did not, as some people in France seemed to think, amount to a demographic revolution; the trend could easily be reversed. There should therefore be no going back on the policies which had been introduced to help families, and a particular effort should be made to see that the increased number of young people about to leave school received appropriate vocational and professional training, and that the necessary additional housing was available when they come up to the age of marriage. The political significance of the fact that 60 per cent of households have no dependent children, and that 60 per cent of the children are in one-eighth of the families is underlined. Some very specific and

[1] Since 1951 the National and Departmental Unions of Family Associations have received a grant of 0·03 per cent of all contributions to the family allowance Funds.

practical recommendations are made about strengthening the consultative, administrative and representative bodies concerned with family welfare, in order that a family policy may be kept politically viable.

Economic Situation

As we have seen, the French system of family allowances represents an extensive redistribution of wages and salaries in favour of those with dependent children. A recent report on the Conditions of Families[1] (or more precisely on families with two to six children living in towns with a population of more than 10,000 and drawing allowances from the General or Miners' Family Allowance Funds) evaluates the total resources, and the relative significance of family allowances to families of different size, different income groups and living in different regions of France. While an average family receives 70 per cent of its income from regular earnings and just under 20 per cent from family allowances (of all kinds), the proportions for the lowest (of three) income groups are 65·5 per cent from earnings and 25 per cent from family allowances, and for those with two children 74 per cent and 10 per cent as against 62 per cent and 27 per cent for those with six.

Nevertheless both this Report and another submitted to the OECD Seminar on 'Low Income Groups and Ways of Treating their Problems', by Professor Maurice Parodi, shows that the standard of living of large families has suffered a relative decrease in recent years and that such families can still be at a considerable disadvantage if not actually in poverty. Professor Parodi quotes figures to illustrate the extent to which family allowances have not kept up with the cost of living:

From 1956–1962 family allowances increased 20 per cent for father with two children
From 1956–1962 family allowances increased 28 per cent for father with five children
From 1956–1962 SMIG[2] increased 33·8 per cent
From 1956–1962 earnings increased 60 per cent
From 1956–1962 retail prices increased 40 per cent

[1] *Les Conditions de Vie des Familles*, a study carried out jointly by the National Association of Family Allowances Funds (UNCAF) and the Centre for Research and Information on Consumption (CREDOC), 1967.

[2] *Salaire Minimum Industrial Gratuit*—Guaranteed Minimum Industrial Wage.

The UNCAF/CREDOC Report was particularly interested in social mobility and showed that although among the urban families studied there was a general movement upwards (agricultural and immigrant workers moving in to take up the least well paid, unskilled jobs), a child's chance of achieving a higher social status than his parents was still much influenced by his father's job and education which largely determined the social and cultural context of the family, and by the number of children in the family. The Report also describes in some detail the ways in which families managed their budgets, and showed that the allowances because of their regularity, were a source of security; they made it possible to buy goods on hire purchase. Even families with relatively low incomes bought sound radio and television sets and household equipment. Above a certain standard of living, expenditure turned more to leisure and cultural activities, travel and household improvements.

Family Welfare

(*a*) *Preventive services*. The local Family Allowance Funds not only pay out the statutory cash benefits (in whatever way their families prefer, and most choose to have them delivered monthly by the postman), but also make housing allowances (after a complicated investigation repeated annually) and provide a wide range of social welfare services. Despite a great increase in the number of housing allowances which has accompanied the post-1958 housing drive, there is concern that the poorest, largest and worst housed families are the least likely to benefit from them. According to the Parodi and UNCAF/CREDOC Reports this is partly because not enough HLM dwellings have been provided for large families, and because the poorest families are the least well informed, and the least likely to know how to set about acquiring a dwelling of a standard which will entitle them to benefit from a housing allowance.

Medical expenses are refunded in part by the social insurance Funds, and for those families without an insured head there is medical assistance; but the Parodi Report quotes a survey (by INSEE) of medical consumption, to show how low income groups and large families are making least use of medical facilities. For every 100 persons of each category the consumption of medical services in 1962 varied from 11·7 per cent for agricultural employees to 23·6 per cent for salaried workers, and from 27 per cent for one person households to 15·7 per cent for six person households.

The Prigent report recommended that more money be allocated to the social welfare services of the family allowance Funds, and that the vocational and marriage guidance services in particular should be considerably developed. It also laid great stress (reminiscent of the recommendations of the Plowden Committee[1] on Primary Education) on improving communication between parents and teachers, and between parents and those concerned with vocational guidance and training. Nevertheless the family allowance Funds are already making extensive provision of such services as mother's helps, nurseries, holidays, social and domestic training centres, and (in rural areas) co-operatives. The Boards of Management of the Funds and their social workers are continually concerned to find new and better ways of helping not just children or mothers, but families, *their* member families. This focus is of immense importance if the felt needs of families living in such widely different milieux—in a rural area, a small provincial town, or in Paris—are to be met. The Prigent report was most concerned to encourage these local initiatives, particularly those of the young married people acting through their local family associations. It even suggested that opportunities for study leave should be given to the officers of these associations, as they are to trade union leaders.

(*b*) *Remedial services.* It would seem that the more specialized social work services for deprived, delinquent and handicapped children provided by the Department or voluntary organizations are by and large well co-ordinated with each other and with the preventive family welfare services. It is only in certain depressed areas in the *bidonvilles* and twilight areas of some of the large towns, where there is a concentration of poor immigrant and 'problem families' that this normal social service structure is proving inadequate. The Parodi report describes in the graphic words of l'Abbé Wresinski, who has worked in the *bidonville* of *Noisy-le-Grand* outside Paris, the concentrated misery and hopelessness in which these 'disinherited families' are living. In this vicious circle of poverty there is no principal cause, but the all-pervading influence of appalling housing conditions, poor health and education services, practically no facilities for vocational, social or domestic training of any kind, and a generally low level of employability. But above all Wresinski is at pains to emphasize the isolation of these families and the

[1] 'Children and their Primary Schools', 1967 HMSO, London.

hostility which they invariably arouse. The passage is worth quoting in full, for it describes a phenomenon well known to those concerned about the 'pockets of poverty' which persist in most large modern industrial societies.

'*Que de fonctionnaires, petits et grands, a travers les capitales de l'Europe, nous l'ont affirmé: ces gens ne sont pas des pauvres, ce sont des vicieux, des alcooliques, des malades mentaux, des inadaptés. Ils se regroupent sans cesse, mais ce voisinage est néfaste et nous les dispersons. Que de familles avons-nous visitées, a travers ces capitales, isoleés, tapies dans leur logement, encourées d'un voisinage hostile, où l'assistante sociale devait leur apporter* l'ersatz *des relations humaines, fraternelles, qu'aurait pu leur offrir un voisinage familier qu'aurait partagé son sort. Est-il necessaire d'ajouter que cette ségrégation voulue on inconsciente ne repose sur aucune donnée sociologique ou psychologique objective?*'[1]

The report argues that such a concentration of problems demands a concerted attack by the welfare services of the family allowance Funds, by the school, health and child protection services of the Department, by the social aid bureaux and by any voluntary organizations active in these areas. These last two, perhaps because of their wide, discretionary powers to supplement any of the statutory benefits with every form of help in cash or kind, have shown the greatest awareness of the nature of this kind of poverty. In some of these areas they are endeavouring to make a more effective impact by improving the physical amenities: by setting up social centres, dispensaries, nurseries, more facilities for education and training, youth clubs, etc. But they lack money. In the Parodi report, however, there is no suggestion that they should receive any financial support from the government, that there should be any kind of positive discrimination in favour of 'priority areas' such as was advocated in the Plowden Report.[2]

[1] 'How many officials high and low throughout the capitals of Europe have assured us that these people are not poor so much as vicious, alcoholics, mentally ill, anti-social; they are continually getting together in certain areas, but this is an evil kind of neighbourhood which we shall break up. How many families have we visited throughout the capitals of Europe, isolated, cowering in their dwellings, surrounded by a hostile community. The social worker brings them a substitute for human relations and brotherliness that should be offered to them by friendly neighbours who share their lot. Is it necessary to add that this conscious or unconscious segregation does not derive from any objective sociological or psychological facts?'

[2] *Op. cit.*

BRITAIN

Political Significance

In Britain there has never been sufficiently widespread concern about a declining birth rate to promote natalist policies. Indeed, there has always been a strong school of thought ready to argue that there are already too many people in this small country. There has been little pressure to develop services to protect and help the family as such. The maternity and child welfare service which arose out of a concern at the high infant mortality rate at the end of the nineteenth century, and the voluntary (philanthropic) family welfare associations inheriting the Charity Organization Society's tradition of encouraging family responsibility, have come nearest to fulfilling this role. But from the Webb's Framework of Prevention to Beveridge's Five Grants, collective action for social welfare in Britain has been primarily directed towards meeting individual needs. This has resulted in an extreme administrative functionalism, which created a built-in resistance to treating the family as a unit.

In the post-war years a growing conviction that much individual unhappiness and social maladjustment is caused by family poverty or by faulty family relationships, has led to an increasing number of social work services becoming more family-centred or family-oriented. In this context, however, the term family is used more loosely, and the care and mutual support provided by extended, or even foster families, is valued and encouraged. Only in the assistance services where the legal liability of relatives is in question, is the nuclear family of parents and dependent children clearly defined as the legal 'client'.

These early developments, and the more positive steps taken in recent years towards more family-centred services, can all be traced to the political pressures of philanthropic, voluntary action and to professional associations. There has never been any trace of a family movement, of the kind of mutual aid and pressure group activities of family associations, or of unions of family organizations, which have such a long history in France and other continental countries. How much family movements are an expression of the greater importance attached to the family as an institution, and so of a readiness to support a redistribution of resources in favour of families, and how much they are in fact educating public opinion to treat a minority group favourably, it would be difficult to say. But the political significance of these democratic family associations, and the recognition and encouragement given to them by the government, is obvious.

Economic Situation

The important differences in the history, in the approach and in the financing of family allowances in France (and in a number of other continental countries) and in Britain are rarely appreciated. As a consequence of this lack of understanding superficial comparisons are constantly being made of the relative benefits to families of the two systems. In France, where family allowances are almost entirely financed by employers (14·25 per cent of wages up to a ceiling of 12,960 F per annum), they are a part of labour costs. Trade unionists as well as employers are well aware of the origins of the family allowance funds, and of the redistribution of wages which is involved in the employers' financing of them. It is a horizontal redistribution of wages between those with, and those without, dependent children, and has little to do with any transfer of income between rich and poor.

It has never been seriously suggested that we in this country should accept this kind of redistribution of wages and salaries, although a horizontal redistribution at every level of *taxable income* is accepted and incorporated into our fiscal policies. But family allowances proper in Britain, as in Canada and in the Scandinavian countries, although a universal provision paid to rich and poor alike, are financed out of general revenues, thus involving a measure of vertical as well as horizontal redistribution of income.

When, in the early 1940s, Beveridge proposed and the Government accepted the need for family allowances, it was generally understood that this had something to do with abolishing want—Rowntree in the 1930s had shown that one-sixth of the poverty was to be found in large families of low wage-earners. But even Beveridge's carefully spelt-out argument as to *why* family allowances were an essential part of his social security scheme, and *how* they should be administered (a universal benefit at near subsistence level), has been largely forgotten by governments and electorate alike. Family allowances have not, like all the insurance and assistance benefits, been kept up with the rising cost of living, and consequently have ceased to do the job for which they were introduced. In the mid-1960s, a country which prided itself on having abolished want by establishing a national minimum, finds that in spite of family allowances a substantial number of families are living in poverty.[1] It is hardly surprising that the demand that 'something be done about family allowances' still concentrates on the theme of abolishing want—'child poverty'—rather than on that of maintaining the standard of living of *all families* with dependent children relative to those without.

Family Welfare

(*a*) *Preventive services.* In Britain the universal method of distributing social benefits has been applied much more boldly and successfully to the education and health services than to family allowances. One rather crude but nevertheless significant measure of the relative use of social services by ordinary families, is to be found in the PEP survey of Family Needs and the Social Services carried out in 1957 and published in 1961.[2] This was an analysis of the use made of the social services by a representative sample of 734 households with children under 16 in the Greater London Area.

Eighty-six per cent of the sample had used between eight and fourteen of the twenty-two different services. The number of services used depended rather more on the number of dependent children than on social class, varying from an average number of 9·10 services where there was one child to an average of 14·27 where there were four or more. Whereas the variation by social class ranged from an average of 8·82 services used by families of the managerial and professional group to 11·19 by those of the unskilled operative. From this factual analysis of the number and kind of services used, the survey passed on to what the consumers thought about them: did they find them 'a real help', or were they inadequate or defective in some way. The overwhelming impression gained is that the generally enthusiastic attitude of mothers (and it is primarily their opinion which is covered by this inquiry) towards the social services is governed by their enthusiasm for the national health service.

[1] The latest survey by the Ministry of Social Security, 'Circumstances of Families' (HMSO 1967) showed that out of 160,000 families whose resources were below the national assistance scale, 70,000 had fathers in full-time work, 15,000 did not receive full allowances because of the operation of the wage-stop, and 75,000 who appeared to be eligible for national assistance had not applied (most were families of men who had been sick or unemployed for a short time only).

[2] PEP *Family Needs and the Social Services.* Allen & Unwin, London, 1961.

Ninety-nine per cent of them had used it and 82 per cent regarded it as the service which had helped their family most.

Much of the interest of this survey lies of course in the mother's opinions, whether appreciative or critical of particular services (the health service group, for instance, was broken down into twelve different services ranging from the doctor used by 99 per cent to the home help by 7 per cent. But this rather crude consumer survey, carried out ten years ago, referred to the families' experience of the social services in the previous decade, and is only useful to us now for its assessment of the extent to which social services provided by the community as a whole are benefiting and felt to be benefiting families—defined in this case as households with at least one child under 16, and representing about 40 per cent of the population.

Various British studies[1] bear out the findings of the French Report on the Living Conditions of Families; that even where services are provided on a universal basis the social and cultural context of the family are an important factor determining how much benefit is actually derived from them. In Britain, this is particularly true for all kinds of education and vocational training services; less true perhaps for those services provided by the local authority on a discretionary basis and depending on a social diagnosis of need, e.g. the home help, day nursery or child care services. Slum clearance programmes have been pursued by the local authorities for longer and more energetically in this country than in France. If a sample of urban families, similar to that in the French study,[2] were taken in this country, it is unlikely that as high a proportion as 27 per cent would be found to be 'badly housed', since this meant accommodation with no sanitary conveniences at all, or a WC or a sink and stove only. (Practically all in this category were also grossly overcrowded—less than one person per room.)

(*b*) *Remedial services*. Dissatisfaction with the over-specialization in social work encouraged by the functional structure of British social services (each employing its own social workers, whether probation or child care, education or housing welfare officers, etc.) was first aroused by the 'discovery' of the 'problem family' in the 1940s.[3] Throughout the 1950s the remedial work with problem families,

[1] e.g. J. W. B. Douglas, *Home and the School*, London, 1963, and of course the Plowden Report: 'Children and their Primary Schools,' HMSO, London, 1967.

[2] See p. 315.

[3] Tom Stephens, *Problem Families*, London, 1944.

the rehabilitation of broken families and some tentative efforts to prevent families breaking up, were mainly undertaken by the voluntary Family Service Units and by 'problem family caseworkers' employed by local authority departments. It was significant that any of four local authority departments: health, education, welfare, or children's, might appoint such workers. But the FSU and local authority family caseworkers together numbered little more than a hundred, and the families who could receive the benefits of their intensive casework service (case loads were usually kept down to under twenty) were necessarily limited. Co-ordination of the efforts of all the existing specialist social workers was seen as the best way of giving more effective help to larger numbers of these families. This implied, though it was not always recognized, some co-ordination of the policies of the different departments and voluntary organizations which employed them.

The additional powers given to local authorities under Section I of the Children and Young Persons' Act, 1963,[1] and the very title of the White Paper put out soon after the Labour Government took over from the Conservatives: 'The Child, the Family and the Young Offender',[2] underline the nature and the reason for this concern for a more effective family service. The proposals for re-organizing local authority services in Scotland contained in 'Social Work and the Community'[3] reflect further thinking that co-ordination of the activities of so many different departments (and empires) is not enough, and that a more fundamental reorganization of the local administration of the personal social services is now needed. It is not difficult to show how irrational and inefficient is the present fragmentation of these social work services, particularly when so few of the social workers share a common training, or indeed have any professional training at all. It is more difficult to see just how much will be achieved by the reorganization of local services, by the appointment of more family caseworkers, and by the setting up of Family Advice Centres. Such action should certainly improve the remedial services for families with serious problems. But there

[1] Part I Section I—(1) reads: 'it shall be the duty of every local authority to make available such advice, guidance and assistance as may promote the welfare of children by diminishing the need to receive children into or keep them in care . . . or to bring them before a juvenile court; and any provisions made by a local authority under this subsection may, if the local authority think fit, include provisions for giving assistance in kind, or, in exceptional circumstances, in cash.'

[2] CMD 2742.

[3] 'Social Work and the Community', October 1966, CMD 3065.

is a tendency to confuse two related but still different goals: the provision (from above) of a more effective professional social work service for the minority of families in real difficulty, and the development of *all* social services, voluntary as well as statutory, in a way which will involve more participation by the community, and encourage more self-help and mutual aid among ordinary families.

NORWAY

Political Significance

In Norway family life has not been undermined by an industrial revolution spreading over some 150 years, which broke up communities as well as families, and led to the large towns and vast industrial conurbations with their many 'non-communities' of modern Britain. On the other hand, family life was undermined by emigration on a very large scale between 1830 to 1920. The diffuseness of Norway's population and the loneliness of the village communities have strengthened family ties. In recent years the substantial movement out of the old occupations of fishing and forestry, and the internal migration into the towns and relatively densely populated places (inhabited by under 50 per cent in 1945, 57 per cent by 1960 and likely to rise to 75 per cent by 1980) has, as has been shown, created social problems, but nothing to compare in size and complexity with those of Britain and France.

The towns, with the admittedly important exception of Oslo, are still few and comparatively small; the country is easily reached and the opportunities for healthy family life are not seriously threatened. All the problems which beset families in modern Western society—except those of absorbing large immigrant populations—may be there, but they are on a smaller scale. For this reason it is easier to involve local communities and indeed the families themselves in their solution. Even national services can be related to local problems and local administration in a more flexible way. What may be lost in the thin-spread of specialist and professional workers is more than gained in the more widespread understanding of local problems, and the greater readiness to accept responsibility for the welfare of individuals and families in the local communities. It is not surprising that the Scandinavian countries have led the way in community care.

The demographic position can be regarded as fairly healthy with

33·5 per cent (1962) of the population under 20 and a steadily increasing population (twice as fast as in Britain) in a large country with an expanding economy.

The basic structure of the comprehensive and universalist services of the Norwegian Welfare State is closer to the British than to the French model. It is within the framework of these basic social services that special welfare services are provided for vulnerable groups. However, an appraisal of Norway's economic security and welfare services suggests a more sensitive awareness of the needs of the family—of ways of helping ordinary families as well as 'families at risk'—than is the case so far in Britain.

Economic Situation

Family allowances in Norway as in Britain were a part of the reconstruction of social security services. Financed by the State and the commune they are a universal benefit. The great income adjustment between the various occupational groups, which has taken place since the Second World War, and the generally speaking successful efforts to maintain full employment, have probably done more to increase the economic security enjoyed by families generally in Norway today than any redistribution of income through social benefits. Fiscal policies have also played their part. The financial advantage derived from income tax allowances in respect of family commitments is considerably greater even for the average wage earner, than that from family allowances (about three times as much for a family with three children). These family allowances are no higher than their British counterparts, but they are not taxable. More liberal regulations, however, allow benefit to be paid in respect of the first child, where there are special circumstances. This is not seen as detracting the universalism of the scheme.

As we have seen, financial assistance to owner-occupiers and tenants, and special housing provided by the local authorities and voluntary agencies, are all designed to favour those with family commitments, and the normal system of helping families to meet the cost of a reasonable and improving standard of housing, is less haphazard in Norway than in Britain.

Despite the undoubted benefit to all families of the general increase in prosperity, and despite all these financial easements to families with children, their standard of living has not risen to the same extent as that of childless couples and single persons. A paper on the subject of 'The Economic Position of the Family', published in 1956, aroused considerable interest, and showed that yet further measures were needed to improve the economic position of the family.

Family Welfare

(*a*) *Preventive services.* The establishment in 1956 of a special Ministry of Family and Consumer Affairs gave institutional expression at national level to the Government's concern to help local authorities and voluntary organizations to develop services designed to improve the conditions of family life and to help ordinary families. It leaves to the established health and education authorities the responsibility for providing these specialized services to all families, and to the social care and child welfare Boards the task of supporting and giving skilled help to families with special problems. The activities which came under the aegis of this new Ministry included home helps, day care for children, holidays for children and housewives, advice to consumers, information and training in household management. The Ministry also has consultant and co-ordinating duties in matters which touch on family and consumers' affairs but are the responsibility of other departments.

Most of these preventive family welfare services had already started before 1956. They are essentially local services and locally financed. Their provision under the auspices mainly of local health and social care offices and voluntary organizations, have been described in the case study, where they are seen as part of the total framework of social security, health and welfare services 'which', to quote John Greve, 'all contribute to some degree to the maintenance of conditions which enable satisfactory family life to develop'.[1]

It is not easy to draw comparisons, to say that these particular services have been developed with more energy and efficiency (in meeting the needs of families) in Norway, since they were taken over by the new Ministry,[2] or in Norway than in other countries. The Ministry of Family and Consumer Affairs has certainly shown that it can be very flexible in the kinds of service it can encourage and grant aid. There is no restriction to assistance cases as in

[1] See p. 135.

[2] It is a very small department and its responsibilities are significant compared with those of the Ministry of Social Affairs.

Canada, and the family is not so narrowly defined as in France. Elderly housewives may benefit from the free holidays. The home help service is not available only in cases of sickness and infirmity, or confinements, as in Britain.

British experience suggests that almost inevitably limitations will be put on the development of these services if they are left entirely to the health and education authorities. They are after all peripheral to their main job of providing highly specialized—and expensive—medical and education services. Children's holidays, for example, have been left almost entirely to voluntary bodies to organize and finance with limited chances of getting any substantial help from local education authorities. There is no government sponsorship of holidays for housewives, although some maternity and child welfare departments may use their permissive powers to help pay for a recuperative holiday for mothers who are run down and have children under five. In Norway, the Holiday Act of 1947, which gave to every worker with few exceptions the right to three weeks' holiday with pay, led to the setting up of a holiday fund for housewives. The moneys from this fund are applied to equipping inexpensive holiday centres, and to enabling housewives to enjoy holidays, who for domestic or economic reasons would otherwise be unable to do so. (In 1958 some 10,000 housewives, in some cases accompanied by their children, enjoyed two weeks' free holiday.) Preference is given to housewives with small children and to elderly housewives, who as a rule need a holiday most.

Similarly, local authorities and voluntary organizations have been encouraged to experiment with many different forms of day-care for children (including the 'Park-aunts' who look after children of pre-school age). Due to the initiative of local bodies and supervised by local child welfare committees, they are financed out of a mixture of money raised by voluntary organizations and generous grants from the State and municipality, and by parents' fees. The Plowden Report suggested a great extension and a much more flexible system of day-care for the pre-school child in this country, but had to leave it to the doubtful interest and enthusiasm of the education authorities to provide.

(*b*) *Remedial services*. The welfare services for incomplete or broken families, for families with special problems or with handicapped or delinquent children, were described in the case study. They are provided by the child welfare committees and by a multitude of other national and local bodies, statutory and voluntary, which it is the function of the new social care offices to co-ordinate and to supplement. It is they which administer the discretionary assistance which is available from local funds for those, particularly the unsupported mothers, who may not be adequately provided for by the national pension and health insurance schemes, flexible though they have been shown to be.

The child welfare committees, on the other hand, as in France, continue to provide a specialist welfare service for the care and protection of children. Well established on the usual Scandinavian pattern, there is much less recourse to the courts and to the probation service than in Britain. The social workers of the child welfare committees naturally do a certain amount of family counselling and family casework as part of their rehabilitation or preventive work. But the local health authorities and voluntary organizations are also involved in providing marriage guidance and family health centres. It remains to be seen if the implementation of the Social Care Act will mean that every municipality will have a family counselling or family care office, providing a first point of reference for any family in need of help and advice.

CANADA

Political Significance

In Canada as in Norway the problems facing families today are increasingly those of an urban, industrialized, highly mobile society, and are, to quote John Morgan, 'less and less amenable to the simple local solutions of self-help, family inter-dependence and action by local government, characteristic of static rural populations'. In both countries there has been the same sort of movement from isolated rural communities and occupations into rapidly expanding towns and industries, demanding a new structure of social services with more professionalism and more central control. But in Canada it is all on a much larger scale and has involved much immigration as well as internal migration.

Moreover, the Canadian nation was founded on a federal union of two distinct peoples and cultures, and even the individual provinces have for the most part less homogeneous populations than Norway. Family law, social legislation and the relative importance of voluntary organizations, local authorities and the provincial government in the administration of the education, health and welfare services, which are primarily a provincial responsibility, all differ greatly from province to province. In Quebec, where Roman law prevails, great emphasis is laid on the family as an essential unit in the social order, and the church has traditionally played a major role in social welfare, in particular in institutional provisions. But even in the English-speaking provinces the traditional administrative structures vary greatly. It is not without significance, however, that mothers' allowances were among the earliest special assistance schemes to be introduced by the provinces, and that the family allowance was the first universal benefit provided by the federal government.

Economic Situation

It is probably because family allowances had the whole-hearted approval of the Roman Catholic Church and French-speaking Canada that the constitutional validity of the Family Allowance Act was never challenged, and that the Federal Government was able to introduce such a substantial scheme. The allowance for the first child means that the value of the benefits for a family with three children is twice that for Norway and the UK.[1] When the Youth allowances (for dependent youths from 16 to 18) were added in 1964 Quebec had already anticipated them with its *allocations Scolaires* under a provincial Act of 1961. However, the real significance of the Canadian family allowance scheme lies in comparisons with the USA rather than with European countries. Although the American Social Security Act of 1935 laid the foundations for a much wider involvement of the federal government in social security programmes than the Canadian Employment and Social Insurance Act of 1935, family allowances were not then, and have not since, been included or even seriously advocated in the USA.

On the other hand, the mothers' allowances (known as Aid to Families with Dependent Children in the USA), which in Canada, until the Canadian Assistance Plan of 1966, received no federal aid, has been a federal-state programme in the USA since 1935. But in both countries this form of special assistance for fatherless families was introduced early on (the first Mothers' Pension Act was passed in 1911), soon after the first White House Conference on Child Welfare in 1909 wrote into its first Charter of Children's Rights

[1] See p. 251.

that no child should be deprived of family life for purely financial reasons. The emphasis in this movement was admittedly on children's rights (to a family as opposed to an institutional up-bringing among other things), rather than the expression of a thoroughgoing family policy. It was only concerned with *needy*, fatherless families, but it did at least provide for any kind of unsupported mother and not only for the legal widow, which was all the British social insurance scheme offered, and that not until 1925. The welfare services offered in connection with this special assistance scheme, and now under the Canada Assistance Plan, will be considered below.

While the family allowances and the tax exemptions for dependent children make for a relatively favourable redistribution of income in favour of families, there is no national health insurance (sickness benefit) and little universalism in the provision of health services in Canada. The public medical care services are still very limited, and all but the poorest families entitled to medical assistance can find their standard of living seriously threatened if any member of the family has a prolonged and serious illness, or if the principal wage-earner is not entitled to any sick pay.

In so far as the provinces are taking up the federal lead and federal grants offered in the Technical Vocational Training and Assistance and the Vocational Rehabilitation of Disabled Persons Acts, rehabilitation and training services should now be more universally available throughout the country. The Canadian Mortgage and Housing Corporation will have helped, directly or indirectly, many families to acquire their own home. But the lack of large-scale public housing programmes, even though the cost may be shared by municipality, province and federal government, has meant that the loans and subsidies offered by the CMHC go begging for lack of users, when hundreds of thousands of low-rent units are needed by poorer families.[1]

Canada in the 1960s is as conscious as other countries of the presence of poverty in the midst of affluence. It too has its war on poverty, although it has not attracted the publicity and the funds of its American counterpart. Some new agencies have been set up (such as the Company of Young Canadians), but for the most part the

[1] Since the Second World War the total of units built with public assistance for the use of low-income families and single persons amounts to only 2·3 per cent of all residential constructions in that period. (From Canadian Welfare, January–February 1967—an issue devoted to articles on Housing.)

war is being waged through the traditional executive structure with a Special Planning Secretariat to the Privy Council to stimulate and co-ordinate the efforts of the relevant departments. Broadly speaking federal plans can be put in three categories, which are directed towards:

(1) basic economic development for the strengthening of the national economy, and for the provision of jobs as the means both for the creation of wealth and the distribution of income;
(2) improvement of the general level of skill, and the mobility and physical and social ability of individuals to work;
(3) improvement of the levels and organization of health and welfare aid and services for those who cannot work.

The last objective, with its emphasis on aid and services for those who cannot work is significant of the limited view which the North Americans have always taken, and are apparently still taking, of those who should benefit from the public health and welfare services—the 'unemployables', to whom Canada added with the Unemployment Assistance Act of 1956, the unemployed. In the context of a war on poverty or of the British concern to establish a national minimum, this is acceptable enough, but it distracts and detracts from any broader and more imaginative approach to a family policy. The implications will be seen more clearly when we look at the lines upon which Canada is developing her welfare services.

Family Welfare

Family pathology rather than family welfare is, if we omit family allowances, the only concern of comprehensive welfare legislation in Canada. For this reason it is not useful to keep to the distinction between preventive and remedial family welfare services. Every province has its Child Welfare or Protection Act, its Adoption, and its legitimacy or Unmarried Parents Acts. The provincial public welfare department is usually responsible for the administration of the protection and welfare services for deprived and delinquent children and for unmarried mothers, although municipalities or the semi-public Children's Aid Societies (CAS) are still providing the actual service in some areas. The scope of these child welfare departments or of the CAS is nearer to that of the Scandinavian child welfare boards than to the post-1948 British children's departments, which still leave much of the protection work to the NSPCC, and much of the adoption work and work with unmarried mothers to the voluntary societies and local health authorities. Although it varies from province to province, the magistrates, the juvenile and family courts and the probation officers play a more independent role in neglect and delinquency cases in Canada than in Norway, thought it is obviously not so uniform or so clear-cut as in Britain.

The Canadian approach to family breakdown and to family problems is essentially a social work one. The Children's Aid Societies have a long tradition of social work and were using trained social workers long before the local children's committees, only set up in 1948, started to use them in Britain. In fact, the child care service was the main field of operation for the first trained social workers in Canada. In many small towns and rural areas the child care worker was, and in many parts still is, the only professional social worker in a vast, thinly populated parish. In these circumstances he (or she) naturally (and in some provinces statutorily) fell into the role of a general social worker, the core of whose work was with families. This, combined with the weakness, if not the complete absence, of local government in many provinces of Canada, has meant a much greater professionalization of the child care service than in Norway.

In Britain, on the other hand, the statutory maternity and child welfare and education welfare services, which were built up between the wars, had their health visitors and school welfare officers all over the country, and it fell to their lot to carry out the infant life protection, the supervision of adoptions, the boarding out of children and young people committed to the local education authorities on fit person orders under the 1933 Act, the truancy cases, and, in many areas, much of the straightforward child care work delegated by the public assistance to the local health or education committee. Health visitors and school welfare officers were not trained in family casework, or indeed in social work at all. They had the advantage of providing a service which brought them in touch with most families with children, but their efforts were directed by doctors and educationists, and they had no independent social work training, which would help them to look beyond the families' needs for these specialist services to a more fundamental concern for family welfare, achieved with and through the families themselves.

Canada's provincial public welfare departments have also been involved in family welfare through their categorical assistance schemes for mothers' allowances. They were much less likely to use professional social workers in this branch of their work, particularly before the Second World War. Social workers in a public assistance department are, moreover, limited to helping those who are on the assistance roles, and their efforts tend to be directed towards getting them off the relief roles as soon as possible. In North America, even today, the receipt of an assistance grant would still seem to be equated, in public sentiment and in much official talk, with social failure; and rehabilitation is advanced as the main reason for associating welfare services or social work with assistance administration. Success in rehabilitation is measured in reduced relief loads.

The different functions of an assistance authority were discussed in an earlier section,[1] but at this point it is as well to remember the distinction drawn there between the automatic income-tested, or income-guarantee type of non-contributory benefit, and the much more flexible, discretionary service-related benefit, given on a social work rather than on a financial diagnosis of need. In Canada, where there are still many gaps in the income-maintenance services provided on a universal or insurance basis, assistance allowances are still going to be needed to provide a basic benefit for sizeable categories of persons and families. The provincial legislators and administrators, who are establishing new schemes of general assistance under the Canada Assistance Plan, will have to hold fast to this distinction, if, on the one hand, basic assistance allowances are really to be had as-of-right and not at the discretion of some social worker; and if, on the other, important family welfare services (home-makers, day care, voluntary placements, family counselling and family casework) are not to be restricted to families in financial need, even if the standard of need, to be determined provincially, is to be a more liberal one than it has been in the past. Will it be the same standard which determines an applicant's eligibility for a cash benefit as for a welfare service?

The danger of these family welfare services being restricted to families in need, and to some programme of rehabilitation, is much greater in Canada than in Britain, just because most of them are being provided at present by public welfare departments, or by voluntary agencies. Both, for different reasons, tend to regard it as their function to provide them for a limited clientele as part of a social work service. Day care is a good example. The Children's

[1] See p. 253.

Bureau's (USA) *Guide to State Welfare Agencies for the Development of Day Care Services* reads:

'The child who needs day care has a family problem which makes it impossible for his parents to fulfil their parental responsibilities without supplementary help . . . day care should be used only when some family situation exists which makes it impossible for parents to maintain a home without help.'

In other words, a day centre is not something chosen or preferred by independent responsible parents. It is something prescribed by a social worker as a remedy for parental failure or inadequacy.[1]

Compare this with the attitude towards day care of the Norwegian Ministry of Family and Consumer Affairs; and of the Plowden Report; or of the French family allowance Funds towards nurseries, mothers' helps, children's holidays, etc., for their member families. In Britain, the health and education authorities may at the present time, in their ordering of priorities, take a more limited view of how extensively these services should be provided than would a family welfare service. But basically, local health and education are at least universal services, designed to meet the needs of the whole population. They are not, like the supplementary benefits Commission of the Ministry of Social Security, restricted to helping those in financial need.

In France, the old public assistance authorities, and now the social aid bureaux, have traditionally provided some of their services for a wider clientele than those in receipt of cash allowances. Nevertheless their contribution to family welfare has been insignificant in comparison with that of the family allowance Funds.

The Canada Assistance Plan, seen by the federal government as a logical corollary of the Canada Pension Plan, will enable the provinces to rationalize their separate assistance programmes, and to meet basic needs more effectively. But one wonders whether the formula relating income-maintenance and social services will not hinder rather than help the development of effective family welfare services, in any or all of the ten provinces. The Vanier Institute on the Family, recently established by the Governor-General, might well direct some of its early research and study into the social needs and problems of the family in modern society, to this rather nice problem of social administration.

[1] J. A. Messner, 'Day Care—Right or Remedy?' *Canadian Welfare*, March–April, 1966.

Conclusions

This book claims to be no more than an introduction to comparative studies in social administration. It should be regarded by the student as a first exercise in the comparative method, from which it is hoped he will go on to study other countries, and to submit other areas of social administration to the same kind of comparative analysis. In concluding, therefore, it would be as well to remind ourselves of the problems of any comparative study, and more particularly of those peculiar to this field.

The first problem is, how to find and how to use source material; how is the student to build up his picture of another country's social services, and having got it, how keep it up-to-date? It is obvious that many of the facts given in this book will be out-of-date before it reaches the publisher, never mind the student. The student of social administration should be sufficiently familiar with this problem from his study of British social services to know how to deal with it. Once he has been given a base from which to start and has been directed to the sources of on-going information, keeping up-to-date on broad developments, if not on detail, is not so difficult. This assumes of course that his initial studies have shown him how and why the social services of a particular country have developed in a certain way up to a certain point in time.

The second problem is again one of methodology, of how practical it is to make a number of these national studies and at the same time avoid the superficiality which would vitiate any comparisons he might go on to draw. How much background information is necessary to explain what is specific and characteristic about a country's social policies and administration? Obviously, the more we know about the cultural, social, political and economic background the better. All that was possible within the compass of this book was to give what was felt to be essential to any understanding of the characteristic features of social administration in each of the countries studied. Again the student should be encouraged to broaden and deepen his understanding in these matters, wherever possible by field study as well as by further reading. This problem (of the need to familiarize oneself with all the social institutions of another country) explains why no study of social administration in a developing country was included in this introductory exercise.

The third problem is not concerned with how we make national studies, but with the validity and value of cross-national surveys of particular problems and social services. As John Morgan remarked, one cannot compare like with like because there are no 'likes', only 'likenesses'. But confining our study as we did to modern Western societies, there are many 'likenesses' sufficiently significant and relevant to warrant straightforward descriptive comparisons of certain problems and services. Social security problems and measures are an obvious example. Vladimir Rys, Head of the Documentation Service of the ISSA, discusses their comparability in an important article on 'Comparative Studies of Social Security: Problems and Perspectives'.[1]

He points out that while the universal growth of social security is evidence of a common need to be met by institutional measures '. . . this undeniable common need, however, is universal but not uniform. It is universal to the extent that the problems of subsistence for the individual are in a certain sense identical; the differentiation begins when these problems are seen from the point of view of a particular society, whose needs are by no means identical with the sum total of the needs of the individuals who form the society. Social legislation by definition can conceive of the basic universal needs of the individual only in the form of the specific needs of the society of which he is part, with the result that a national social security scheme becomes a specific instrument catering for specific needs of a particular society and reflecting its socio-economic situation'. The student of social administration will want to know not only how, but why, this differentiation is made. He will be seeking an explanation of causal links and relationships, and in trying to trace these links in other countries will probably come to see hidden causal links in the system in his own country, a system with which he has perhaps become over familiar.

Vladimir Rys has some equally wise and useful things to say about the last problem, or set of problems, which arise when one moves on to any comparative *evaluation* of social policies and administration. He writes:

'In considering a social institution of this importance (social security), with so highly charged a political content, care must be taken, from the beginning, to make a distinction between a straightforward

[1] This article appears in Bulletin of the ISSA, No. 7–8 1966.

descriptive comparison seeking explanation of causal links and relationships, and an evaluative comparison aiming at the establishment of classification scales by which to judge the respective merits or shortcomings of individual members of the universe observed.'

Clearly any evaluation of social policies, of the effectiveness of particular social services is only meaningful in the light of what the beneficiaries, as well as the policy-makers and administrators, anticipate of them. These wider aims and values, which lie behind the specific objectives of particular measures are often revealed in what a country is, or is not, prepared to sacrifice to achieve them. In other words one is thrown back on to an assessment of a country's priorities—the very stuff of social policy-making. For when Vladimir Rys pointed out that (a society's) 'needs are by no means identical with the sum total of the needs of the individuals who form the society', he is underlining that we are not concerned with a Utopia but with a real society, whose government must make realistic decisions, and order its priorities in relation to the social values which hold in that society at that time, and to its resources, which are in an economic sense always scarce. Finally, if it is so difficult to evaluate the social policies and achievements of a particular country, what of comparative evaluations? Clearly any kind of League Table, except in relation to some very clear cut and quantifiable facts (e.g. the proportion of old people in each country living below a certain income level) is to be avoided, although one is always tempted to draw comparisons in these terms.

These then are the problems and difficulties, which beset any student of comparative social administration. What are the advantages? In view of all these difficulties is it all worth while?

Many years' experience of teaching comparative social administration to students has shown that after such a study students are in fact better able to analyse social problems, and to make a more objective appraisal of the social services with which they were already familiar. The very effort made to understand why other countries have sought rather different solutions to very similar problems, helps them to look at the social services of their own country more dispassionately. But the student will not rest here, he will want to go on to evaluate the effectiveness of particular services, or to judge how far alternative techniques used with effect in other countries are 'exportable'. If his powers of objective analysis have been sharpened by his comparative studies he will be better equipped to do this. But when all is said and done he can never forget the nature of his subject—collective action for the improvement of individual welfare, and the value judgements inherent in it. They are inescapable, and he must remain constantly aware of them, particularly if he is concerned, as most students of social administration are, to contribute what he can to making that collective action as effective as possible.

Index

Index of Persons